The Tourist Region

Tourism and Mobility Systems Set

coordinated by
Philippe Violier

Volume 1

The Tourist Region

A Co-Construction of Tourism Stakeholders

Jérôme Piriou

WILEY

First published 2019 in Great Britain and the United States by ISTE Ltd and John Wiley & Sons, Inc.

ISTE Ltd
27-37 St George's Road
London SW19 4EU
UK

www.iste.co.uk

John Wiley & Sons, Inc.
111 River Street
Hoboken, NJ 07030
USA

www.wiley.com

Library of Congress Control Number: 2019933966

British Library Cataloguing-in-Publication Data
A CIP record for this book is available from the British Library
ISBN 978-1-78630-416-2

Contents

Foreword

In the first book published by the MIT "Mobilités itinéraires territoires" team, a group of researchers, we proposed a typology of tourist places based on the distinction between those created (complexes and tourist resorts) by tourism and those invested in (cities and sites) [EQU 02]. From this first reflection, it appeared to us that research should be continued in order to consider the question of the extent, i.e. to address the regional scale. Jérôme Piriou set about this task in his thesis defended on November 30, 2012.

He has taken up his analysis again to offer us this book. After a scientific review on the question of the region in geography, from which he deduced that this area is made up of a network of interconnected places, he showed that in the scientific approach to tourism, these networks are co-constructed by the actors who interact to build these links. Tourists, through their second mobility (the first to connect places of residence to destinations), initiate or confirm these links, while public actors (legitimate and technical) try to impose their territories and professional actors develop their own strategies to mobilize the qualities of the space for their benefit. The author thus demonstrates that geographical science provides tools and analyses relevant to the professional world.

Geographers will be challenged by the expression *tourist region* because, even though mentioning natural, agricultural or industrial regions has never been a problem, the concept of tourist region must prove its worth. For how could such a futile social practice contribute to the organization of space? However, the analysis shows that there are regions whose dynamics are mainly based on tourism, others to which activity contributes strongly and others for which the effects are marginal or even non-existent, reversing the discourse of those who see tourism everywhere.

Philippe VIOLIER
Professor of Geography at the University of Angers (France)

Preface

This book is the revised version of a doctoral thesis in geography defended at the University of Angers, in France, on November 30, 2012. This doctoral work consisted of better understanding the concept of a tourist region by questioning the spatial practices of tourism stakeholders, particularly tourists. This subject has been developed through academic and professional experiences in tourism institutions confronted with questions relating to the territories of action and competence. On the scientific level, the quotation by Rémy Knafou, taken from the symposium of the Geography, Tourism, and Leisure Commission of the French National Geography Committee on Diffuse Tourism held in Clermont-Ferrand in 1994, was particularly interesting:

> "Rural cottages, vacation villages, a sausage festival and a Penitents Museum – all honorable initiatives – are not enough to make a given region a tourist region, any more than three factories and four workshops make an industrial region" [KNA 95, p. 15].

These comments have contributed to making our research more difficult. Indeed, the presence of facilities or elements that could suggest that there would be a given place, a tourist region, is not enough. However, we know that tourism is the subject of a system of actors involving tourism professionals, elected officials, investors, developers, etc., as well as tourists! Under these conditions, what does the tourist region mean for all these actors in their practices?

To answer this question, during these five years of doctoral studies, field work was carried out in three study areas: the Côte d'Émeraude in Brittany, the Loire Valley with its towns, castles and gardens, and finally the "Lake Geneva region" of the Lemanic Arc, comprising both the French and Swiss shores. These lands were chosen for several reasons. First of all, these three areas are highly popular with tourists. For example, there are popular tourist areas that receive approximately one million visitors per year, such as the intramural city of Saint-Malo, the castle of Chenonceau in the Loire Valley and the castle of Chillon located near Montreux on the upper part of Lake Geneva. Each of them receives international tourists. These three laboratory spaces benefit from diversified tourist areas: sites, villages, cities. In addition to a sometimes-overriding theme, for example castles, these regions do not operate via a single activity. Finally, these three laboratory areas are difficult to define. There is no tourist border; there are only administrative borders between departments, regions and nations. The flows are continuous and blur the contours of these spaces. Between 2007 and 2009, we collected data (archives, documentation, interviews with tourists, etc.). Field practice, by observation, allowed us to realize tourist situations that would have been difficult to understand at a distance. For example, only the tourists interviewed within a tourist place could report to us on a trip involving multiple visited places throughout Europe.

In this book, we have chosen to mainly present the results of tourist interviews from the Lake Geneva region. Indeed, after analysis, this laboratory area gathers the main observed facts related to the organization of the actors, as well as to their spatial practices.

I would like to thank Professor Philippe Violier, thesis director, as well as the members of the jury, Professors Cécile Clergeau, Jean-Christophe Gay, Christian Pihet, Laurent Tissot and Jean Varlet, for their support and encouragement, without forgetting my family members, including Laurent, for their patience and presence.

Jérôme PIRIOU
February 2019

Introduction

The research theme addressed in this book is tourism. It is studied from the angle of human and social geography, which leads us to question the scale of the phenomenon's localization: the tourist region. By using the term "region" (a controversial and obscure subject of geography), we seek to understand the meaning of the tourism phenomenon beyond the elementary places, i.e. characterized by a distance. In light of the scientific literature, since the 1970s, many geographers, particularly French, who have taken an interest in tourism have adopted the institutional definition of the World Tourism Organization without questioning it[1]. Indeed, it seduces researchers with its ease of use. We can recall two specific points about our subject. First, in the overall definition of tourism, this institution classifies individuals according to their travel time away from home and according to the one and only *sine qua non* condition of an economic nature, which is "unpaid" in another place of temporary residence. Then, depending on the distance of perception and the scale adopted, the World Tourism Organization divides the world into large regions to statistically analyze the flows between sending households and receiving basins. However, concerning our subject on the tourist region, a question emerges: how can we understand what motivates the tourist to make a daily excursion during their vacation?

According to the World Tourism Organization, a tourist cannot be an excursionist[2] since they are already a tourist. So, can we say that they would

---

1 We can, for example, refer to the work of Georges Cazes [CAZ 73], Jean-Michel Dewailly [DEW 84] and Jean-Pierre Lozato-Giotart [LOZ 85].
2 An individual who travels from his or her usual place of residence within 24 hours is called an "excursionist" and beyond one day is a "tourist".

be a "tourist-excursionist" or an "excursionist-tourist"? In addition, what criteria defines the area that the tourists are looking for (according to the World Tourism Organization)? These same geographers argue that the regional approach to tourism must be approached by generalization according to a principle of homogeneity. According to them, a homogeneous space is observed either by an environment integrating places or by places that by their similarity or proximity create a whole. Other questions also arise: would the tourist region be a set of places, the homogeneity of which would define the perimeter? Would proximity and juxtaposition be criteria for homogenization?

Since the 2000s, a new geographical approach to tourism has emerged on the basis of pioneering work in anthropology and sociology [JAF 88, ELI 94], which has focused on individuals and their choices for recreation through tourism that broke with everyday routines[3]. This approach has guided the subsequent research around two fundamental elements, namely the construction of individuals' identities and their societal functioning, as well as their movement and residence. On this principle, they observe the spatial role of tourism through the creation or subversion of places. Tourists travel to places that are adapted to their expectations. Two spatial forms emerge from this work: the elementary place and the complex place[4]. But this approach poses a twofold problem. First, tourists would be exposed to two forms of stay depending on their type of mobility: sedentary and nomadic. However, these studies show that the elementary place with sufficient accommodation capacity would encourage tourists to remain sedentary, while the complex place with heterogeneous accommodation capacity would justify nomadism via roaming. But we can wonder: what if all tourist places did not receive tourists with differentiated mobility? Second, it is questionable whether, once mobility is engaged, the form of the tourist's stay is immutable throughout the time spent outside his or her home. Don't tourists use several types of mobility during their tourist stays? Don't they sequence their stays through multiple trips?

---

3 We can refer to the work of Rémy Knafou et al. [KNA 97b] and Mathis Stock [STO 01] and then the *Mobilités itinéraires territoires* (MIT) research team [EQU 02, EQU 05, EQU 11].
4 According to the MIT team, the elementary places are the site, the community, the tourist resort, the resort complex, the city or the village, and the complex places are the district and the tourist conurbation and the tourist metropolis [EQU 02].

I.1. The place as a starting point

The place is a spatial unit that reflects the ecumene, i.e. the terrestrial spaces inhabited by humankind and in a particularly visible way. The place is "where something is and/or is happening" [BER 03, p. 555]. But if the phenomenon is there, it means that it is not elsewhere. According to Denise Pumain and Thérèse Saint-Julien, "the place is a continuous portion of the earth's surface, defined by geographical coordinates and its extent" [PUM 97, p. 156]. In addition, the characteristic of the place is specific because there is something going on and/or something is happening. The Greek *topos* defined by Aristotle reflects an intrinsic relationship between geographical position and what happens and/or is found there: "on the one hand, the thing and the place are inseparable: If the thing moves, its place becomes another place; on the other hand, the being or identity of the thing does not go beyond its place: If it exceeded this limit, it would be another thing, because it would have another form, the form gives the being to the thing" [BER 03, p. 559]. The concept of place is used in geography to mean a spatial approach in the sense that it is not a population or community that is targeted, but a specific geographical referent [STO 17a]. This approach is inherited from a Vidalian geography developed at the beginning of the 20th Century that strives to take into account places, "geography is a science of places, not of men" [VID 13, p. 298]. Yet, humankind is appropriating places, to make them their territories. This territory is built; it is a "contiguous portion of the land surface appropriate by a group" [PUM 97, p. 156]. The ecumene shows an impregnation between the place and the people, the things that have a common history; it is the *concretus* [BER 00]. Establishing a relationship of intimacy is the result of living in a place [HEI 58].

The individual is at the center of geographical reality, of the world around them; they are an actor in its construction as well as in its realization and meaning. For example, before the 18th Century, the coastal environment crystallized fears, a repulsion based on representations, imagination and beliefs, and it was coveted from the middle of the 18th Century onwards for climatic and therapeutic purposes and would finally become the most anthropized environment in the world [COR 88, DUH 09]. Individuals perceive an interest in living in the places, since they bring resources and attribute an identity and values to them [URR 05]. Naming a place by a toponym gives us a geographical referent on a spatial unit. The toponym shows how to fix and naturalize a reality that has not always existed and that is changing [RET 03]. Also, the place becomes a concrete and appropriate space, "places are distinguished from the most abstract space, by their personalization generally identified by a name" [GEO 06, p. 247]. It is understood here that this spatial unit cannot cover a significant portion of the ecumene; the site is "the smallest complex spatial unit". This complexity is explained because it is a space in which the concept of distance is not relevant [LEV 94]. The definition of distance shows us that the place concerns only one and the same reality and therefore cannot be the subject of a distance "attribute of the relationship between two or more realities, characterizing their degree of separation, by difference with the state of contact" [LEV 03a, p. 267]. However, there is the question of living in/out of the place. This is difficult to explain in Vidalian geography since it seeks to identify portions of homogeneous areas without taking into account the articulation between the units [GAY 95]. The discontinuities allow a better understanding of the distinction between places. They reflect "a more or less sudden change in the characteristics of the places" [CIA 07, p. 23]. The threshold is an idea that makes it possible to express a change of state, thus juxtaposing two spaces with different social, political and economic systems [DIM 02]. This is materialized by the boundary, i.e. "which makes it possible to circumscribe a given spatial unit" [REN 02, p. 40]. The living space, i.e. the places frequented on a daily basis, would be built according to a dialectic of "continuity/discontinuity"; this being verified by spatial practices: "it is the area of spatial practices, a space frequented and traversed by everyone with a minimum of regularity" [DIM 98, p. 30]. The space used is therefore composed of places, not only as a place to live but also as a place of leisure. What distinctions can we make between these places? Do they all engage in the same activities? Moreover, what scale are we talking about?

I.2. Tourism practices and choice of destination

To see the presence of tourism within a place, it is necessary to define what is meant by tourism. From a statistical point of view, this would require knowing the number of individuals present for tourism purposes in relation to the annual resident population, which is the location quotient [STO 17a]. Again, we must be in agreement with what we call individuals present for tourism purposes. The World Tourism Organization provides us with little insight by generalizing these individuals to visitors with multiple activities. The World Tourism Organization considers tourism to be:

"A notion of activity [that] embraces everything that visitors do for or during a trip. It is not restricted to activities considered to be characteristic tourist activities, such as sunbathing and visits, including sites, etc. Travel for business, education and training, etc., can also be part of tourism, once the conditions established to define tourism have been met" [OMT 10, p. 11].

Tourism therefore generates a movement from one place to another, but the reason for the movement is particularly unclear. This confusion is reflected in the work of many scientists who consider any travel as tourism, including business, health, religion, etc. [MIC 83, BRU 93], and rely on the use of so-called tourist facilities and infrastructures [HOE 08, BOT 13]. But can we fully trust a reading of the use of facilities and infrastructures to understand how individuals live in a place for tourism purposes? If we look at the measurement of the tourist function rate of the places, we base ourselves on the number of tourist beds per inhabitant. However, can we consider a place without tourist accommodation as weakly tourist? There are many examples of places where tourists visit without *in situ* accommodation (beaches, mountain peaks, monuments, etc.). It is therefore necessary to understand the reason for moving to some places rather than others. In France, the National Institute of Statistics and Economic Studies defines tourism as:

"Activities carried out by persons during their journeys and stays in places outside their usual environment for a consecutive period not exceeding one year, for leisure, business and other purposes, not related to the exercise of a remunerated activity in a place visited"[5].

The duration would certainly contribute to characterize this traveler. Nevertheless, not every traveler is a tourist. Moreover, tourism is not always the same. The word *tourist* appeared in English in 1800, then in French in 1803 and in German in 1875. It refers to a person who travels for pleasure, away from work, business or any other reason that restricts their freedom of action [STO 17a]. The tourist is therefore not just any traveler. Their journey is different from that made by obligation, as some writers have done. For

---

5 *Institut national de la statistique et des études économiques* [The French Institution of Statistic and Economics Analysis], "tourism" definition, INSEE.fr, available at: https://insee.fr/fr/metadonnees/definition/c1094, accessed on June 1, 2018.

example, as historian Marc Boyer points out, "Madame de Sévigné's correspondence is exemplary of the behavior of the greats of the 17th Century; when they travel, it is more by obligation than by pleasure and think above all of what they lack [...]" [BOY 05, p. 34]. Then, relying on infrastructure and equipment statistics (e.g. accommodation, catering, site) amounts to considering any individual who travels as a tourist. Moreover, the World Tourism Organization encourages this approach to the reading of a tourist mobility. It defines two main categories of travel: personal travel for those who are on business and professional grounds [OMT 10]. Personal trips include visits to relatives and friends, medical treatment, religion and pilgrimage. However, medical treatment is indeed a constraint, since it is only possible on medical prescription. As for parental relationships, they are part of a limited and often routine field of possibilities [DUH 13]. Also, can we consider that an individual who goes to and stays in a city for a funeral lives there for tourist purposes? To answer favorably would ask us to accept an attitude of opportunism, which could challenge morality in a context of mourning. To answer negatively would show us that any night occasioned cannot be considered as the work of an individual who travels for tourism purposes. But the answer cannot be so obvious. And for good reason, an individual can go and stay in a place in a professional context, therefore paid for business activities, and take advantage of the time available for leisure activities. In this case, we will speak of tourist "moments" that are part of a business trip, such as extending a stay with a vacation [COE 10]. Finally, seeking to understand an individual's reasons for staying in a place for tourism purposes is like questioning the spatial practices of individuals. By practice, we mean "human actions that are part of a constituted environment, in particular other practices, and thus transform it, they are contextualized, in a situation" [RUB 03, p. 740]. Thus, according to a geographical code of practices, tourists' spatial practices are identifiable since they are a chosen mobility towards one or more places of the off-day world. Some places are therefore conducive to the practices of individuals seeking recreation. But tourism itself also creates places. Tourist places are located and localized for several reasons such as their geographical location, physical and landscape setting, infrastructure, and inherent activities. We can wonder what justifies the investigation of the places by tourists and why these chosen places are concentrated in the same space. But what can we observe at the regional level? Are regional tourist areas easily identifiable? And what exactly does the concept of "region" correspond to?

I.3. From the practice of tourist places to the practice of a tourist region

Tourists invest in a recreational area. They differentiate and categorize places according to their interest and experience. This space of places would constitute a region. It appears that defining the notion of "region" is complex and ambiguous despite several studies conducted by geographers over the past three centuries. Thus, although geography is a discipline that enables the understanding and representation of spatial patterns of phenomena, whether natural, physical, biological or human factors [LAC 86], the region remains among geographers as a word, which, although much studied, discussed and contested, is still far from being circumscribed. In this sense, the region would be the "most obscure and controversial word in geography" [BRU 90, p. 166]. As such, the region can be defined in a rather vague way, but it can also have a very specific acceptance [BEA 71]. Taking up such a subject may seem ambitious; however, far from the idea of redefining the word "region", we seek, above all and modestly, to enlighten ourselves, through a geographical approach to tourism, on the meaning to be given and to take into account the "region" applied to the tourism phenomenon. What is the region? How to approach it? How to define it? Should natural physical factors be taken into account? What place should be given to human activities in the definition of the region? It is questionable whether the tourist region should have a specific boundary. In addition, among the stakeholders involved, who decides on the perimeter of the tourist region?

We will see that determining what a "region" is would depend on the field of analysis in which it would be tested. We will also see that beyond a delimitation by naturalistic criteria, regional analysis requires considering the environment, as well as the intention of human actions, which delimits or "regionalizes" the space. The other fields of application in geography also demonstrate that the appropriation of the term "region" now also requires a systemic approach. It is in this sense that we wish to contribute our reflection in a geographical approach to tourism. We will present the interest of considering the tourist region as a network of places according to the spatial practices of actors. We will apply the graph and matrix models of the networks to tourist mobility. We will see that there can be several meanings depending on the object of analysis, whether it is organizational relationships, flows of individuals or the location of elementary places. Finally, in this research, we have employed a scientific geography project that is based on questions posed in various ways, whose space is constituted and mobilized by human societies. We adopt the post-structuralist posture defended by Mathis Stock on how to understand geography, proposing a background of questioning and understanding rather than a simple descriptive and argued reading [STO 06]. Also, to answer the question: "what is a tourist region?" This book, which is organized into three parts, will shed light on this topic.

In the first part, we will describe the known spatial approaches to tourism. Work on the elementary places of tourism is a first key to spatial analysis of the phenomenon. But we will also be interested in proposals for analyzing the regional scale of tourism. We will also present the areas considered as tourist areas in order to discern what could be qualified as a tourist region. In the second part, we will present the logic of the actors identified in the practices of a tourist destination with a regional dimension. For tourism, the destination constitutes both a promoted and a perceived territory, whose implementation through tourist mobility makes it possible to determine a elementary place or a tourist region. However, we will see that this transformation from a tourist destination to a tourist place or region requires the intervention of multiple actors. In our opinion, this is a territorial co-construction. Finally, our third and last part deals with the analysis of multi-level regional networks of tourists places built according to tourist mobility. But we will see that the various actors are taking action to ensure that tourists places are integrated into these networks.

The Region, a Complex Concept Applied to Tourism

Introduction to Part 1

To understand the region, it is useful to use the modes of reading geography. This science, which has as its object space in order to analyze society, has several concepts with imprecise outlines. The word "region" is one of the essential concepts of geography, but it remains polysemic and even vague. This is explained by its Latin etymology *regio*, which means country, region, zone, territory, extending around a city or place [DIM 03]. Also, two meanings are attributed to it, *regionis* (direction, line, limit) and *regere* (to govern, to direct), conferring on it a role of power, control and management. However, geographers do not resign themselves to abandoning the term and attribute multiple epithets: agricultural, industrial and tourist regions. However, according to our research, the latter has not been the subject of an in-depth study on the notion of "region" applied to tourism.

This first part reports on regional employment in the analysis of the tourism phenomenon. Also, to understand what the "tourist region" is, we must start from the foundation of these spaces, i.e. the presence of places inhabited by individuals. The presence of suitable places for tourism has been the subject of multiple analyses since the 1970s using multiple criteria (economy, physical environment, etc.), but we will keep for our purposes the practices of the individuals who operate there as well as the spatial dimension of elementary places of tourism. We will see that a regional scale clearly appears in a typology of elementary places of tourism, but this remains little exploited (see Chapter 1). Then, the word "region" connotes a specific meaning to a space which, by appropriation, delimits a territory. But we will see that the ambiguity of the notion of region disturbs the geographical analysis of tourism, perhaps referred to as a region, a part of the world, a continent, a nation or a sub-national region. In addition, actors acting in a country can invent and build a region from the creation of *ex nihilo* places. However, several observations can be highlighted for the purpose of understanding the tourism phenomenon. We will answer the following questions: how can we define a "region" characterized by tourism? Where are the tourist places that would organize a tourist region located? How should this organization, which would constitute a tourist region, be interpreted (see Chapter 2)? Finally, we will deepen the analytical frameworks of the tourist region proposed by different geographical approaches. From pioneering work based on a classical geography, using naturalistic criteria, to a functional reading based on economic models, the definition and particularly the attempts to explain the functioning of the tourist region have undergone a correlative evolution to that of geography in general. The cumulative proposals over time were the subject of numerous discussions, including breakdowns, modeling and perception, on the scientific method used to explain a concept that some authors have transformed into a concept (see Chapter 3).

Tourist Places, with their Foundations in the Tourist Region

The place in geography excludes any distance; therefore, it constitutes the finest spatial unit, with the sub-place (districts, streets, neighborhoods), to study societal phenomena. Living in the area is an "art of doing" according to Michel de Certeau's formula [CER 80], which reveals the ability of individuals to mobilize their resources and skills. Living in it is in this sense the typical spatiality of the actors [LÉV 03c]. Temporarily living in the area is a choice of individuals whose tourism is a reason for it. Tourism transforms places, and this change is observed by individuals' practices within these tourist places. We will see that this results in differentiations in the ways in which tourism appropriates space and whose tourism is observed and analyzed on a local and regional scale.

1.1. The tourist place, a locality chosen in spatial tourism practices

A place used for tourism purposes is a place that is subject to specific mobility. Mobility means that the individual exercises physical movements in temporal data and is a "form of movement that is expressed by changing position" [BRU 93, p. 333]. Tourism mobility is one of the main ways in which mobility is accepted to describe movements in geographical space: among residential mobility, daily mobility and migration mobility [CRE 04]. But mobility is much more than a movement; it is a social relationship with the change of place [LÉV 00] and contributes to the construction of oneself independently of society [CÉR 08]. The change of place, the change of living in tourism, is to temporarily leave one's place of life for one or more places located outside the sphere of one's daily life [KNA 97b]. According to Mathis Stock, the temporary tourist inhabitation of places must be understood by the otherness, familiarity and strangeness of the geographical places practiced [STO 01]. A break with a place of daily life is necessary in tourist mobilities, when leisure in this same place of daily life is no longer effective enough. Leisure time is part of free time, a time of one's own, in which "a person finalizes themself in themself, by the meaning they must give to a time that begins to belong to themself alone" [VIA 00, p. 47]. Joffre Dumazedier defines leisure as the compensation of the demands of society that must make it possible to free oneself from boredom, fatigue due to institutions, stereotypes of work organization and family life, leading to surpassing oneself [DUM 72]. Leisure is finally a release that allows you to free yourself from a certain self-control of emotions, allowing you to experience pleasure. The notion of recreation makes it possible to distinguish moments of "relaxation of constraints" beyond the sphere of work and the sphere of everyday life, which are characterized by routine activities [ELI 76, ELI 94]. The temporary distance from a place of daily life by moving to one or more places where one stays, in a quest for recreation, explains the use of a place by an individual for tourism purposes. It is an essential geographical dimension to explain the practice of certain geographical places through travel, particularly through tourist mobilities [STO 17a]. Also, places are invented by tourism, insofar as the social phenomenon of tourism has transformed the uses and representations of these places [KNA 92]. For Denis Retaillé, tourism is a powerful operator of topogenesis, i.e. the social construction of a geographical place [RET 03]. Tourism, being a practice dedicated to the intentionality of recreation, generates the use of one or more premises, for a "way of living" oriented towards leisure that takes many forms (discovery, rest, play, sociability and/or shopping) [STO 17a]. The tourist situation of a place indicates that the tourist practice is informed at the same time as it informs the context of the action by and in which it takes place [COË 10]. If tourism is happening or is happening in one place, it does not necessarily happen elsewhere, at least not in the same way. The tourist place is a social construction in the sense that tourist places are mythical places, i.e. "made up of a set of mental representations born of texts, iconographies, photographs, flying words,[...] an aggregate of messages composing an entire communication system" [CHA 88, p. 18]. Thus, geographical sites attract the curiosity of walkers. The Pointe du Raz, located in the far west of Brittany, is for walkers a part of the world because of its geographical characteristics, a rocky promontory that fascinates onlookers and experienced walkers, whose increased popularity at the end of the 19th Century is the subject of a picturesque enhancement by writers and local transport or promotional operators [VOU 99] (see Figure 1.1).

Figure 1.1. *The Pointe du Raz tourist site (France) (source: J. Piriou, March 2015). For a color version of the figures in this chapter, see www.iste.co.uk/piriou/tourism.zip*

COMMENT ON FIGURE 1.1.– *A picturesque place praised by writers since the 19th Century, then a place of excursion promoted by the French western railway company and the Finistère Tourism Committee, the reputation of the Pointe du Raz has increased over the past century [CHA 50, GIN 72], and tourist flows have become regular and intense [BAR 96]. Despite a classification of the natural site in 1958 on a surface of 72 hectares, the human degradation linked to the frequent passage of people and vehicles, as well as wild camping contributes to the reduction of the site's vegetation cover. Operations were envisaged as early as 1976 to limit these degradations. The end of the 1980s also marked the desire of players to enhance and preserve the Pointe du Raz site. By escaping the realization of a nuclear power plant project, the Pointe du Raz was developed for its physical and natural characteristics. A major site operation was carried out in 1993. The aim was to demolish car parks and existing buildings near the tip and relocate these facilities. In addition, before reopening to the public in 1996, experiments were also carried out to study the capacity of the natural environment to regenerate itself [LEF 13, PIR 17].*

Mediatization through artistic and literary dissemination also contributes to this mythical construction. For example, as early as the 18th Century, Jean-Jacques Rousseau, author of *La Nouvelle Héloïse*, associated the mountains on the Valais side of Switzerland as a social allegory that suggested a natural character of the site that permeated the mentalities and lifestyles of the populations [DEB 95]. This construction leads, by exaggeration, to the creation of stereotypes, aimed at facilitating the interpretation of the context that is unfamiliar to the tourist, "by speaking of 'stereotyped spaces', we hypothesize that the tourist space taken in its material or immaterial acceptance represents the projection in space and time of the ideals, myths of the global society" [CHA 88, p. 19]. Exoticism translates this quest for otherness constructed as a distraction, an amusement or an enchantment that presents itself "as a point of view, a discourse, a set of values and representations about something, somewhere, or someone" [STA 08, p. 9]. Nanjing, the former capital of China, located between Beijing and Shanghai, is a tourist destination mainly for Chinese people with a very limited international presence (see Figure 1.2). The Chinese are looking for its architectural heritage and the staging of the canals of the Yangtze River, on the one hand, and its memorial to the city's massacre following a Japanese invasion in 1937, on the other hand.

The alchemy of social construction is therefore not an obvious one according to the tourist places. The notion of a tourist perspective explains the interest that tourists have in practicing living in a particular place. This goes beyond the simple visual function, since the perspective establishes the way in which individuals organize the reading of place in the world [URR 90]. On the subject of Rémy Knafou, researchers use the concept of invention to understand the meaning of a geographical place for a specific practice. The shift from an ordinary place to a tourist place can be explained by the practices that are part of it: "The place promoted as a tourist destination thus moves from a mainly utilitarian function to a tourist function, i.e. mainly 'ideal', reflecting the shift from a society of actors to a society where some of the actors temporarily transform themselves into spectators: tourist consumption is above all an aesthetic consumption based on a vision of a territory" [KNA 92, pp. 854–855]. The invention of tourist places is a diversion from the traditional use of the place, which can be seen in place names of tourist places [STO 17a]. Toponyms also show that a place can be defined by a canceled distance. In Brittany in the 1930s, the ingenuity of the resort of Sables-d'Or-les-Pins in the Côtes-d'Armor department revealed this invention of the tourist place. The prime contractor Roland

Brouard, a merchant, relied on political and economic support and benefited from significant media coverage, as well as the presence of famous personalities to accompany the construction of the myth, of this coastal fringe straddling the communes of Fréhel and Plurien [VID 00]. The quality of the places is therefore part of the explanation for the development of tourism in a place. Quality makes it possible to know to what extent the place is a stakeholder or a constituent of tourist practices [ÉQU 05]. Also, although the assessment of the quality of places is subjective since it depends on cultural and personal factors, specific to tourism education [ÉQU 05], it also depends on overall factors such as the layout of the places, the geographical location and justifying the tourist practice of the places.

Figure 1.2. *Sun Yat-Sen Mausoleum in Nanjing (China) (source: J. Piriou, December 2017)*

COMMENT ON FIGURE 1.2.– *The mausoleum dedicated to Sun Yat-Sen, the precursor of the Chinese revolution, stands at the foot of the purple and gold hills to the east of the city of Nanjing. The place is almost exclusively visited by Chinese tourists who cross the access steps and take advantage of the opportunity to have their picture taken to capture the moment. This site is one of the most important places in Chinese popular culture. Each individual takes advantage of the site to commemorate the country's history and enjoy the view of the surrounding hills.*

1.2. Diversity of tourist places according to practices

Tourists have very specific reasons, for recreational purposes, to move from one place of daily life to one or more other places of non-daily life. For Michel Chadefaud, the representations highlight a place, desires, the tourist perspective and contribute to the emergence of places [CHA 88]. Georges Cazes considered that the type of environment or large geographical area is associated with tourism [CAZ 92]. Jean-Michel Dewailly and Émile Flament list several elements that aim to satisfy tourists: "natural sites, climatic conditions, tourist attractions and facilities, accommodation, information, transportation, marketing, various professionals, disposable income and customer choice, socio-political situations in the areas visited, the state of the environment [...]" [DEW 00, p. 9]. However, the deterministic approach, as a fundamental condition for the integration of a tourist situation, is not appropriate. On the one hand, the phytome, i.e. the vegetation, and the hydrome, any body of water, are not enough to explain the development of tourism in an area [ÉQU 02].

On the other hand, the World Tourism Organization's definition remains unclear and creates confusion as to the purpose of travel, integrating any unpaid motive, i.e. ultimately everything that is done outside the workplace and requires an overnight stay away from home. Hence, the need to place the individual at the center of the reflection whose practices explain the development of tourist attractions. Tourists will distinguish between all the spatial offers, the places that suit them. This will be established according to the knowledge acquired by tourists and their habit of frequenting certain areas, bringing a look at a particular area to deploy their activities there [DUH 18]. Moreover, if the tourist acts in tourism development, they do not act alone. Indeed, Rémy Knafou specified that there is no possible tourism development without the tacit or real agreement of the local society or part of it [KNA 92]. Some places have become tourist places either by subversion or by creation *ex nihilo*. But in all cases, they have been invented in the sense that they have been "diverted from the traditional use of the territory, the meaning of which is changing at the same time" [KNA 92, pp. 16–17]. Moreover, while the "discoverers" of tourist places remain unknown, some celebrities have made it possible to popularize places, such as the Duke of Morny in Deauville, in Normandy (France) [CLA 77], Baroness de Rothschild in Megève, in the Northern French Alps [ARV 99] or Brigitte Bardot in Saint-Tropez, in the Cote d'Azur (France) [KNA 97b].

Differentiating tourist places by their functionality avoids obvious biases according to geographical areas, cultural context and/or type of clientele[1] [STO 17a]. The MIT team classifies the places according to three first criteria: the absence or presence of accommodation, permanent resident population, and the density and diversity of urban services. Then, specific elements are added to each type of place according to the logic of tourism development, spatial characteristics, dominant or coexisting tourist practices, and its functioning as the current place of tourism in the functioning of the place [KNA 97b, STO 03].

1.3. Basic tourist places at the local level

Based on the typology of tourist places proposed by the MIT team, by grading the presence of local populations, accommodation facilities, and diversified tourist and urban functions [ÉQU 02, ÉQU 05, ÉQU 11], we will present the elementary tourist attractions from which the presence of tourism is structured.

1.3.1. *Places dominated by tourism*

Among the places dominated by tourism, i.e. places where tourism is the main activity of the place, some are invented by tourism, such as the tourist attraction, the tourist closed complex and the tourist resort.

The *tourist site* is characterized by a function of passage; it does not have a host population. It has only minimal facilities and the fact that it does not offer in situ accommodation capacity does not encourage tourists to stay there [DEW 00]. The site can be considered as an identified landscape that is worthy of tourist interest, as it is a place of quality for the society that identifies it as such [DUH 18]. Quality can be part of the aesthetic and heritage values of remarkable objects [LAZ 11] that deserve a "tourist perspective" [STO 17a]. The site is a place, which arouses the entices the traveler to stop, seeking to contemplate a landscape, a monument, a road and whose viewing quality is a touristic interest [DEW 00]. The practices are based on visiting, discovering and wandering within a time limit not exceeding one day. This is due to access to the location which may be

1 We will not dwell on presenting the conditions for the development of tourism, in particular tourist places; instead, we will focus on presenting the characteristics of each type of elementary tourist place.

restricted, concerning time slots or pricing conditions, as well as because of the functionality of the location which may be multiple. A beach can be a place of rest for residents and tourists alike, but it can also be a place of work for seaweed harvesters who harvest algae in order to market them to cosmetics or agri-food processing companies. But the tourist place can also be staged for its state of nature or its historical monumentality [STO 17a]. Some tourist places that have a high imaginary load and can be a model for other tourist places are high places [ÉQU 05]. Being "high" reveals an evaluation of a value that differentiates it from other places [PIR 11a]. Tourist site therefore do not all have the same tourist position in the world, depending on their reputation, which can be local, national or international. Philippe Duhamel distinguishes between universal sites known to all (e.g. the Great Wall of China), sites of reduced visibility but known internationally (e.g. *Château de Brissac* in the Loire Valley) and sites known by nationals, whether they are inhabitants or tourists (e.g. *la cheminée aux fées* in Saint-Gervais-les-Bains in the French Alps) [DUH 18, p. 189].

Another place invented and dominated by tourism, the *resort complex*, does not have a local population, nor a diversified tourist and urban function. On the other hand, it has a capacity to accommodate tourists. The only people present, apart from tourists, are the more seasonal workers. It is an enclosed place with clear limits and a desire to create a break with the immediate environment that would seem too exotic or too imbued with otherness [DUH 18]. Unlike the site, the resort complex created ex nihilo aims to temporarily sedentarize tourists: "It often provides itself with accommodation in a hotel as a first step, to keep tourists passing through for a few days or weeks" [DEW 00]. The resort complex has its own rules (codes, rites, etc.) that are sometimes at odds with local operations [GAY 16]. Residence practices depend on the resort complex. The care is favorable to thermal or thalassotherapy establishments; rest and sociability will be found in marinas, village clubs, hotel clubs and even island hotels, sometimes even the sport that can be found in indoor structures and finally the game that can be either by simulacrum in a theme park or in a physical and sporting way in a holiday club. This tourist place is built around the project of an investor partnering with a developer who is sometimes the same and only actor [DUH 06]. Finally, the tourist resort complex is a place whose practices are evolving and are jointly bringing new places to the fore, as shown by the development of the Val d'Europe with a shopping center and multiple leisure and business activities around the Disneyland Paris theme park [STO 17a].

The *tourist resort* has no diversified tourist and urban function but has a local population as well as tourist reception capacities. It is a place created *ex nihilo* for tourism. It is defined "by the primacy of tourist activity in this place: It is the creator of the place and always dominant" [BRU 97, p. 200]. Unlike the resort complex, the resort emerges from a village, which could be fishermen or farmers[2] and whose urban development has allowed the settlement of a local population that lives there more or less permanently [DEW 00]. Resorts as places to stay have several tourist infrastructures as defined by Vincent Vlès: "The tourist resort is an organized spatial unit of accommodation and facilities offering a generally differentiated set of services, it is managed like a city, but also as a sales center for services grouping together various companies" (VLE 96, p. 5). The degree of urbanity of the resorts is verified by the level of equipment from their design, so the resort of Saint-Gervais-les-Bains in the French Alps had telephone and electricity before the city of Nîmes [DUH 06]. In addition, specific equipment structures the resorts according to their geographical environment, such as the presence of ski lifts since 1950 in the mountains or marinas on the coasts [DUH 18]. Some authors distinguish the resorts according to the spaces where they are inserted [DEW 00]. To this approach, Jean-Pierre Lozato-Giotart makes a distinction according to their form of openness and specialization in multi-purpose or open tourist spaces and in specialized tourist spaces that are more or less open. It distinguishes traditional resorts built from a site, such as a beach, and whose urban structure is linear, semi-concentrical or checkered in mononuclear or polynuclear form, which can give way to several activities: specialized resorts where the space is structured solely by tourism, sometimes in place of other activities [LOZ 08]. As for city resorts, they are places invested and even subverted by tourism. This means that a place is not originally a tourist place; it is invested to the point of being largely or totally dependent on it [STO 03]. Tourism has invested a place structured by other activities, other practices, other values. This is the case of the resort of Les Sables-d'Olonne on the French Atlantic coast, whose old center has been "enlarged" in its urban functions by the construction of buildings for tourism. We can also mention the case of Agadir in Morocco, whose configuration of the place is arranged like a tourist resort but has a double polarity since there is a

---

2 One example is the creation of the resort of Saint-Trojan-les-Bains on the French island of Oléron in Charente-Maritime, a small village organized around its port intended in the 19th Century for the supply of fish, to export local products such as salt [PIC 02].

discontinuity with the ancient city, however, in the immediate vicinity connected by a promenade [DUH 06, p. 66]. Other places have been occupied by a population of secondary residents, referred to as vacant communities, which are differentiated from those benefiting from a co-presence with tourism, the tourist communities [DUH 08].

Other places, which existed before tourism, are also invested or even subverted by tourism; these are the *touristified villages and cities*. The village or city differs in size in terms of population. Tourist villages are often isolated tourist places, benefiting from an ancient architectural heritage, sometimes dating back to the Middle Ages, and with few contemporary buildings [DUH 18]. The touristified villages have acquired a reputation for their picturesque character, both in terms of the landscape and the silhouette of the village in terms of buildings. One example is the case of the perched village of Gordes in the French regional national park of Luberon, whose painters and other artists have shown the landscape interest of the place, attracting the curiosity of tourists [HEL 04]. The touristified city corresponds to a place where the economy revolves exclusively around tourism and where tourism has spread throughout the city center [STO 17a]. In Belgium, the city of Bruges is frequented by tourists for its heritage qualities. It can be visited by boat and crossing the canals [ASH 00] (see Figure 1.3).

Figure 1.3. *Canals of the city of Bruges (Belgium) (source: J. Piriou, April 2010)*

COMMENT ON FIGURE 1.3.– *The city of Bruges in Belgium is frequented for its monuments, architectural ensembles and canals, allowing an in situ visit of the historic district, the old city [ASH 00]. The city is heavily frequented around certain hubs, particularly around Notre-Dame Church, while other places are less frequented. The city of Bruges has developed a flow management plan since 1995 to encourage the spread of tourism in different parts of the city and limit the excessive concentration [JAN 98]. In addition, this regulation comes at the request of the inhabitants, also in order to better organize parking in the "golden triangle"*[3].

1.3.2. Places not dominated by tourism

Places that are not dominated by tourism are places that have activities other than tourism and for which the tourism economy is only one part of the operation of the place. By definition, "the tourist city welcomes people from elsewhere" [DUH 18, p. 196]. Also, unlike the tourist place, the tourist resort complex and the tourist resort, the disappearance of tourist activity does not mean the disappearance of the city. A distinction is made according to the importance of tourism in the city: the city with a tourist function, the tourist city and the stopover city.

First of all, the *city with a tourist function* or the *tourist city* are places where tourism is integrated into the city; there is a tourist regionalization of certain sectors. There is tourist activity in the city centers near monuments and department stores and commercial spaces. For Jean-Michel Dewailly and Émile Flament, the tourist city would have its own type of tourism, an urban tourism, which would be visible since "the tourist city is characterized by various forms of urban tourism (heritage, cultural, sports, shopping, events, business, etc.) that strongly influence its economy and the functioning of its space"[DEW 00, pp. 56–57]. But, *a priori*, the practice of discovery is the most widespread. It takes the form of a walk and visit. Shopping has also become almost as important an element as discovery in the past [DUH 18]. Nevertheless, characterized by urban tourism, cities orient their tourist offer towards cultural services, either by the existing art reflected in the architecture of buildings, museums, religious buildings, green spaces [TOB 17] or in the creation of new works; such is the case of

---

3 Blogie É., "Pour éviter la masse, le tourisme change de cap", *Le Soir.be*, available at: http://plus.lesoir.be/102577/article/2017-07-02/pour-eviter-la-masse-le-tourisme-change-de-cap, online on 07/02/2017, accessed on June 1, 2018.

the French city of Nantes with the conversion of the industrial and naval wasteland of the island of Nantes into a highly successful leisure and tourism area, particularly through its machines, including the great elephant [GRA 10a]. Rémy Knafou also points out that the city has two motives justifying tourist attendance: one corresponding to the enhancement of a heritage and the other corresponding to urban entertainment and leisure [KNA 09]. However, a distinction between cities is necessary. Some authors observe differences according to the forms of presence and diffusion of tourism. For Jean-Pierre Lozato-Giotart, there are several polyvalent and open urban tourist spaces. It also differentiates a multipolar polynuclear type, namely the large Western historical capitals, from a mononuclear and unipolar type corresponding more to small- and medium-sized cities [LOZ 08]. For Jean-Michel Dewailly and Émile Flament, in small- and medium-sized cities, the practices would be more visible than in large cities with more diffuse tourism [DEW 00]. This is also underlined by Philippe Duhamel and Rémy Knafou, who identify districts in the metropolis with higher concentrations than others [DUH 07].

Second, the *stopover city* refers to a partial tourist activity limited to the accommodation function to receive tourists for a relatively short period of time. These places are located on very busy routes, especially during holiday periods. It should be noted that the location of accommodation has evolved since the 1970s from the city centers to the outskirts, mainly near the main roads, railways and airport sites [DUH 18]. The city of Tours, located in the center of the tourist destination of the "Loire Castles", benefits from an accommodation park that complements that of other cities in the Loire Valley such as Amboise and Blois, benefiting from a reception and accommodation function [AMÉ 07].

1.4. Tourist places on a regional scale

In the typology of elementary places that are at an elementary scale, the MIT team recognizes the need to identify places at a regional scale, "the constitution of places built at a regional scale as a more or less coherent set of links and flows" [ÉQU 02, p. 230]. A dense continuous linear form, the tourist conurbation, is dissociated from more or less diffuse forms of poles with a variable density, the tourist metropolis and the tourist district.

The *tourist conurbation* corresponds to a high urban and population density since the coastline is completely developed, even exceeding the immediate hinterland [KNA 97a]. The tourist conurbation is a system of places "that brings together in physical continuity, including sites and therefore visited but not built, and sometimes organizational, a large number of elementary places of different types" [ÉQU 02, p. 230]. Tourism has contributed to the urban development of large regional areas by building extensive linear conurbations [DUH 09] whose urban continuity ensures quality in terms of proximity of services, employment and real estate. Each integrated place, whether resorts, cities-resorts, to which sites and resort complex are added, constitutes a whole that takes advantage of the whole [ÉQU 11]. The tourist conurbation corresponds to a landscape densely built, crossed and frequented by a significant population and which is based on agglomerations, metropolises and large resorts [DUH 18]. The Côte d'Azur on the French Mediterranean coast is an example. It is a real metropolitan area that stretches over 60 kilometers with up to 1 million inhabitants if we include the urban area of Nice, Menton, Monaco and the Riviera from Ponant to San Remo [GAY 17a].

Figure 1.4. *Promenade des Anglais in Nice (France) (source: J. Piriou, April 2008)*

COMMENT ON FIGURE 1.4.– *The Promenade des Anglais is an emblematic image of the Côte d'Azur. The city of Nice is part of a group of other coastal areas (cities, resorts and sites) aggregated from small towns and villages in the Provencal hinterland. The term "Côte d'Azur" comes from the writer Stephen Liégeard (1887) who made it possible to build representations around the coast and the blue sky and also reflects the organization of urban space [HEY 92]. The Côte d'Azur is the result of a series of resorts such as Cannes, Juan-les-Pins and Saint-Jean-Cap-Ferrat [BOY 02], occupying sunny slopes and occupied by aristocratic winter tourism dating from the early 19th Century and allowing a significant influx of people and capital. Also, the linear occupation of the coastline by an interurban area did not occur until 1945–1950 with the appearance of mass tourism [BAR 70]. Gradually, the gaps between the resorts born in the 19th Century were filled in the 20th Century by urbanization: "this rapid urbanization, which filled the coastal areas between tourist resorts and spread inland, reveals a strong differentiation of space" [STO 03, p. 85] since hotels and accommodations are found primarily on the coastal edge. The Côte d'Azur is heavily urbanized on the coast, as well as with a certain peri-urbanization and an urban sprawl of the plain in the hinterland. However, there is a discontinuity between the sparsely populated highlands and the densely populated lowland, "we speak of an anisotropic region built from a coastal axis and some perpendicular inland axes" [HEY 92, p. 41]. Also, although urbanization has filled coastal areas between the original resorts and spread inland, tourism is concentrated on the seaside.*

Other tourist conurbations can be identified in the world: The Costa del Sol in Spain, the Flemish Coast in Belgium and Florida's Gold Coast in the United States of America. In France, other cases, on a smaller scale than the Côte d'Azur, have also been the subject of terminology relating to tourism conurbation by researchers. This is the case of the Côte d'Émeraude in the French region of Brittany, where some authors will speak of a "Malouin conurbation" because of the continuity of residential and commercial centers that diffuse tertiary activities in a rural area, mainly for Saint-Servan, Saint-Malo, Paramé and Rothéneuf [MEY 69]. Others widen the space by defining a "Tourist conurbation of the Rance" by integrating Saint-Malo, Dinard and Dinan due to the structuring of the communication network and the isolation of roads and railways [LAR 82].

The *tourist metropolis* is a place that is considered to be multifunctional and not only based on tourism, such as a resort, a resort complex or a tourist city [JAC 17]. The city's tourist practices, mainly oriented around the promenade along itineraries of historical monuments, remarkable architecture and department store districts, are particularly true in metropolitan areas [STO 17a]. Some districts or centers have higher concentrations than others [DUH 07]. On the one hand, there is a plurality of tourist practices, and on the other hand, there is an interweaving of tourism with metropolitan life. The practices go beyond the simple visit, since they are confronted with business mobility, shopping or festive practices organized as part of events [JAC 17]. Paris and its region correspond in fact to a variety of urban spaces and whose boundaries remain unclear. On the one hand, there are inhabited areas, and on the other hand, there are the mobility of people working in Paris and its region whose place of residence is located outside the urban area, the Paris region and sometimes beyond, as shown by the tilting links provided by high-speed trains (TGV) between Paris and the cities of Nantes, Angers, Tours, Le Mans or more recently Reims, Strasbourg, Bordeaux or Rennes. We are talking about the temporal limit of urban space. Thus, in the face of Paris' influence, the notion of agglomeration, which has the advantage of associating urban space with people and their activities, is no longer sufficient, leaving room for the notion of metropolitan region [GIL 05]. This urban space means the area that Paris is likely to polarize an entire area, or about 21 million people [BOI 03]. Thus, around Paris, mobility plays a considerable role in the construction of an urban region, through polycentrism [AGU 06]; it makes it possible to play on distances and proximity: "mobility has the capacity to make distant what is close, and conversely, to make close what is distant, [...] mobility does not only have the consequence of stretching more than it is the urban fabric, it has the interest of making fragmented spaces adjacent [...]" [CHA 00, p. 106]. In addition, the metropolis also applies to leisure activities, linking leisure spaces according to a peri-urban dynamic. In Paris, the system includes a central metropolis and a rather rural peripheral area [LAZ 95]. Peri-urban leisure spaces are confused with tourist spaces which consist of several dimensions: the intramural, pericentral or suburban, the metropolitan dimension including, for example, Disneyland or the *Château de Versailles* and finally the perimeter including other territories such as the Val de Loire or Champagne [DUH 07]. Tourists may also have to cross national borders, particularly as part of excursions, for example, to Belgium, accessible for one day [STO 17a]. Within tourist metropolitan areas, a specific spatial organization can be identified. First, most tourism is concentrated in the Central Tourist District [DUH 07] and then evolves towards peripheral areas. In the case of Paris, Philippe Duhamel dissociates several parts. First, the Central Tourist District, which corresponds in the Parisian metropolis to the inner city with the extension of certain sites accessible by the metro or the regional express train transport network, such as the *Stade de France*, the *Saint-Denis basilica* or the *La Défense* district. Then, a second, more distant area includes sites such as the castles of Fontainebleau and Versailles. Finally, a last area includes various places, tourist places, villages and towns that have been visited, by excursion from Paris, such as the castles of the Loire, Normandy, or Burgundy and Champagne [DUH 18]. The result is an archipelago organization of the metropolis around the Central Tourist District and more distant places [FOU 17].

Finally, the *tourist district* corresponds to a space organized around tourist places and attractions that are more or less interdependent on each other due to a certain proximity [KNA 97a]. Some places are sometimes more unifying, and group attractions according to a principle of internal non-competition [GAI 02]. Tourism practices create complementarity between attractions, whether it is rest through accommodation in one, visit and discovery and shopping in others. Despite the specialization of each one, an energy of the district comes from the whole system of constituent attractions [ÉQU 11]. Some examples can be cited: mountain resorts in the Alps of Haute-Savoie, in the Tarentaise Valley, Périgord or Lubéron [ÉQU 02].

1.5. Conclusion

Living in the world reflects an appropriation of space, whose actions by individuals more or less visibly reflect their intentions. The tourist movement that induces a change of place (from every day to temporary) is characterized by a specific intention, that of breaking with routine, of relaxation and of recreation. The spatial listing of practices testifies to the development of tourism in spaces, which specialize according to the intensity of tourism; resorts and closed complexes live exclusively from tourism, while cities benefit from multiple activities whose tourism is not necessarily dominant. Thus, the typology of elementary places at the local level informs us of the tourist practices that take place in a rather well-defined space that constitutes the visible and materialized boundary of the resort complex, and visible and implicit by a discontinuity marked by the urbanization present or not for the site, resort or city. The local scale makes it possible to lay the foundations for a spatial reading. The place where tourism is included takes many forms, depending on the degree of appropriation of the place by tourism or the co-presence of multiple actors. The association of several elementary places of tourism has made it possible to reveal forms of regional scale. However, this scale remains poorly explained, as recognized by the researchers who proposed this typology of elementary places of tourism, "our approach would be incomplete if we limited ourselves to this typology isolating places on a local scale" [ÉQU 02, p. 230]. Also, in the effort to differentiate places built on a regional scale, the characterizations do not seem to be successful. They note that with regard to the type of place (i.e. the tourist district), "known examples are rare" [ÉQU 11, p. 258]. Concerning the tourist metropolis, even if the presence of sites and places of stay is identifiable in the context of an excursion, "it is not always so easy to understand" [STO 17a, p. 419]. The limit of the exercise is explained by the need to define what a tourist region is and to appreciate it by the spaces that characterize it.

2

The Tourist Region, a Localized Area and Localizer

In geography, the region is considered as a whole that forms a unit according to criteria of homogeneity or strong interaction [PUM 97]. By homogeneity, we refer to similarities between spatial units (by structure, function or distribution) that differ from neighboring units [CIA 07]. The region can be distinguished from other units by its specialization and thus by the discontinuities formed by neighboring units since it is a "portion of the contiguous land surface", and this "contiguous portion of the land surface is appropriated by a group" to form a territory [PUM 97].

Thus, a spatial unit is specialized if it responds to a specific type, function or use that differentiates it from other units. Specialization individualizes the unit and can create synergies with contiguous units through links [CIA 07], as is the case in the industrial region, for example. Also, although specialization makes it possible to identify a region, the links that connect other units (place, region) can highlight a new homogeneity. Also, it is the discontinuities that will make it possible to circumscribe this unit. Discontinuities are the expression of a transformation concerning a structure, a physical or social environment and create a rupture, which is manifested in a concrete way by "thresholds" such as boundaries, limits, breaks, or contacts and interfaces [DIM 02]. The threshold is an idea that makes it possible to express a change of state, thus juxtaposing two areas with different systems (whether they are social, political or economic) [DIM 02]. We will see how the analysis of the notion of region in geography has evolved, and then we will see to what extent the regional scale is relevant in the analysis of the tourism phenomenon.

2.1. How to define the tourist region?

2.1.1. *The region in geography*

Contemporary geographers consider the area to be truly discontinuous, as evidenced by observations of discordant surfaces, slope breaks, shore lines, ecumene or cultivated landscapes [BRU 67]. The Vidalian geography has also focused on identifying portions of homogeneous areas [GAY 95]. This is a naturalistic approach that consisted of countering historical or administrative boundaries at the end of the 19th Century, for example the provinces, as Vidal de la Blache testifies:

> "It would be unreasonable to use historical or administrative divisions as a geographical guide [...] When we look back at the historical incidents, the chance of succession, the necessities of circumstance that have influenced the formation of these territorial groupings, we see some doubt as to the agreement that may exist between a province and a natural region" [VID 88, p. 3].

Geographers gradually broke away from the natural border at the beginning of the 20th Century, as shown in the same author's book in 1917 on Eastern France, where he saw a "limit" to the natural border. He takes the example of Lorraine and Alsace, which were linked to France rather than with the Rhine river, but for historical and political reasons. With this turnaround, a debate arises. On the one hand, some criticize a centralizing reading. Thus, Jean-Christophe Gay notes that by the uncertainty and naturalness given to the word "region", Vidal de la Blache's disciples affirmed a centralizing and unifying republicanism seeking to banish opposition to power [GAY 95]. On the other hand, Marie-Vic Ozouf-Marignier observes that Vidal de la Blache's work has served the regionalist cause by seeking an intermediate scale between the centralized power of the government and the local power of the departments [OZO 92]. Also, at the beginning of the 20th Century, historically aware geographers brought another concept from historical regions, namely "heterogeneous regions that human wishes have shaped" [NON 04, p. 77], for example the Picardy plains or Flanders in France [DEM 05, BLA 06]. To summarize, we understand that the boundary of the region corresponds to territorial boundaries of any consistency (whether it is political or cultural) [WAC 02], where a human community recognizes itself under a common identity.

However, there is a contradiction since some borders are fixed and intangible, while others are evolutionary and modifiable [CIA 07]. We will see later that it is through this complexity that in France, after World War I, during debates in French society on the redistribution of competences between the central government and local authorities, the question of the "region" has returned to the heart of the debate in society [CLA 06].

Figure 2.1. *Boutique of regional products in Sologne, France (source: J. Piriou, October 2010). For a color version of the figures in this chapter, see www.iste.co.uk/piriou/tourism.zip*

COMMENTS ON FIGURE 2.1.– *This souvenir shop is located near a very popular Loire castle in Sologne. The presence of these shops is justified by the search for the continuity of a "sightseeing ritual" [ENZ 12], i.e. the movement to contemplate what is "to be seen", then to carry out ostentatious practices testifying to the fact of having gone there [CAS 67]. The souvenir is part of the journey [URB 93]. Its function is to make sense because it is "subject to a certain number of formal, social, and symbolic constraints" [PER 08, p. 117] and participates in a symbolic form of appropriation of places [ÉQU 02]. We also note that the souvenirs sold in these shops are signed with the effigy of the tourist place or region [PER 08]. The "regional products" panel informs visitors of the quality of the products available and refers to a certain regionalism, that of the Loire Valley, and, in particular, Sologne. In regionalism, there is a form of claim to a small homeland, which contributes to production and consumption through an identity factor [THI 91]. This regionalism developed particularly at the beginning of the 20th Century as an alternative to a dominant ideology, a cultural centralism of the nation-state, advocating a regional exception, a particularism. We will even talk about folklore [LOY 01].*

2.1.2. The tourist region

Research conducted in a geographical approach to tourism, which began in the 1980s and 1990s, shows caution in defining what a tourism region is. They prefer to use less ambiguous terminologies, such as regional tourist area types [LOZ 85], regional tourist areas [CAZ 92], spatial structures of tourism in the region [PEA 93] and spatial forms at the regional level [KNA 97a]. This is due to the fact that the region has a classical geography that has evolved since the 1970s [STO 17a], as well as because the epithet region is often misused [DUH 18].

However, there are some earlier definitions, particularly in the 1970s, that guide the geography used (whether it is regional, economic or human). Yvette Barbaza in her analysis of the spatial organization of tourism on the coast considers the tourist region as a homogeneous and continuous area "entirely dominated by the tourist function" [BAR 70, p. 460]. Also, solidarity between tourist places, according to her, does not systematically justify the presence of a tourist region. In 1972, Roger Brunet considered that the tourist region constituted a group of places with the characteristic of a tourist activity. For him, the tourist region cannot be an area of extension of a phenomenon; it can "be only the grouping on a map of points where tourism is an apparent significant activity". It distinguishes it from a region briefly named "tourist" that is "defined then by a certain climate and a certain natural environment, a position in relation to cities, the real importance of tourist activity, its facilities, a commercial, industrial, agricultural activity more or less influenced by tourism, a certain demographic, social and even political behavior, a certain rate of transformation, all linked to each other and forming a complex different from neighboring complexes, tourist or not" [BRU 72, pp. 6–7]. It is therefore understandable that the so-called "tourist" region is characterized in two ways. It is noted by a significant presence of tourism within an area, as well as by the influence of tourism within a given region. Homogeneity is therefore a key component of this approach. Roger Brunet considers the region as an area that has overall features and differs from its neighbors: "It is an area that is defined by common characters, related to each other, such that the variations of these relationships within the area considered are less than their variations outside the area" [BRU 72, p. 6]. In 1975, Alain Reynaud also perceived that the notion of a tourist region implies that in a given area, tourism is the dominant activity. Like Roger Brunet, he admitted that revealing criteria make it possible to objectively determine from the tourist regions. But he specifies that it is possible to "subjectively" determine the tourist regions experienced and perceived by the inhabitants, as well as by the outside population [REY 75]. According to him, the preconceived, pre-perceived and specified image during the tourist stay contributes to the constitution of tourist regions. In addition, he nuanced this approach to the tourism region experienced. He notes that during itineraries, tourists add up the areas and therefore the sum of the tourist images [REY 75]. Alain Reynaud's approach to the tourist region was more interested in the practices of tourists. It should be noted that the tourist region, which benefits from a significant presence of tourism, is concomitant with the tourist region perceived and practiced by tourists. Corna-Pellegrini (1968) considers the tourist region as an area that can be delimited by its own characteristics, attracting flows of people who spend part of their free time and income earned elsewhere [COR 68]. He has worked on several tourist regions in Italy. For him, the tourist region corresponds above all to the notoriety of an area, to the reception infrastructures and to the density of stay [ROG 81]. It is also in this sense that Jean-Pierre Lozato-Giotart defines the tourist region, more particularly as a multipolar network and a socio-spatial structure [LOZ 85].

Recently, the definitions proposed by teachers in tourism geography manuals, in the context of the 2017–2018 higher education competitions, reflect the recurrent complexity of defining the tourism region. In his book *Les espaces du tourisme et des loisirs* published in 2017 by Dunod, Anthony Simon uses the definition of Jean-Michel Dewailly and Émile Flament (2000), "the tourist region is an area that brings together tourist places of a larger scale in such a way that tourism is indeed the main (but not the only) agent of spatial organization" [DEW 00 quoted by SIM 17a, p. 55]. We can see that this approach still considers the region as an area, but it includes tourist places, and tourism is not necessarily a single activity.

The definition therefore becomes very broad. Alexandra Monot and Frank Paris, in a book entitled identically, but published by Bréal, consider that the region applied to tourism must reveal a multiple homogeneity, "the term region is understood here in the cultural and identity sense, not administrative, and refers to a territorial framework marked by landscape frameworks and homogeneous socio-economic conditions" [MON 17, p. 202].

These different approaches and difficulties in defining the tourist region can be explained by a poorly defined geographical scale. Indeed, the region can be both a subnational and an infracontinental territory.

2.2. Regional spatializations of the tourism phenomenon

2.2.1. *The world's major tourist regions*

The world tourist area is organized in concentric halos with a frequentation that decreases according to the distance that can be physical, economic, cultural and political [DUH 99, p. 58]. As a result, the area is classified into "basins" or "World holiday areas" [CAZ 92] that we qualify as "regions" at a geographical level higher than that of the states [VIO 13]. These regional groups are coherent given their number of visitors. The World Tourism Organization tracks international tourist arrivals (see Table 2.1). But this method of statistical calculation can be discussed since a visitor can cross a border several times or mobility can be ensured for a reason other than recreational, for example migration [DEH 03]. We can identify the major tourist regions on the planisphere that are the Euro-African, Asian and American zones:

– the *"Euro-Mediterranean" regional basin* concentrated more than 59% of international tourist arrivals in the world in 2017, integrating Europe, the Middle East and Africa;

– the *"Asia-Pacific" regional basin*, which accounted for 24.5% of international tourist arrivals worldwide in 2017. It should be noted that the eastern part of Asia is experiencing significant tourism development;

– the *"Americas" basin*, which accounted for 15.6% of international tourist arrivals in the world in 2017. North America and the Caribbean are the most affected by these international tourist arrivals.

	2017		2016		2015		2005	
	Millions	**%**	**Millions**	**%**	**Millions**	**%**	**Millions**	**%**
Europe	671	50.7	620	50.1	609	51.4	442	54.7
Asia and Pacific	324	24.5	303	24.5	277	23.3	155	19.2
America	207	15.6	201	16.2	191	16.1	134	16.6
Middle East	58	4.3	54	4.3	54	4.5	39	4.8
Africa	62	4.6	58	4.6	53	4.4	37	4.5
World	1,322	–	1,236	–	1,184	–	807	–

Table 2.1. *Distribution of international tourist arrivals by continent [DEH 03, OMT 10]*

These regional basins highlight discontinuities in the world tourist area and have common characteristics. They are dominated by regional clienteles that represent two-thirds to three-quarters of the attendance. Foreign destinations are largely frequented by travelers from countries close to those in which they reside [GAY 10]. We are talking here about a logic of regionalization.

Intraregional tourist movements correspond to movements within these basins. The latter are particularly concentrated. Philippe Duhamel and Isabelle Sacareau explain this phenomenon because of the contiguity of countries and the weight of historical ties, geopolitical legacies and socioeconomic relations [DUH 99, p. 58]. There is therefore a strong regionalization in the form of regional polarization. According to the model of the world tourism area, we note that regional basins are made up of tourist territories classified by rank of importance [DEH 03]:

– *First-level international tourist territories* are the world cities such as New York or Paris, which emit and receive tourist flows. Exchanges take place between these international tourist territories within the same world tourist regional basin, as well as between international tourist territories that are part of other international tourist regional basins.

– *Second-level international tourist territories* correspond to the high places of international tourism such as the Island of Hawaii in the USA,

Mont Blanc in France or the Côte d'Azur in France. These territories, unlike those of the first tier, are unique in receiving international tourist flows.

– *Regional tourist territories* are those that receive flows from the same regional tourist world basin, as is the case of Djerba in Tunisia. Smaller flows are concentrated within the same regional tourist basin worldwide. It is essentially a regional clientele that frequents these territories. One example is American winter sports resorts that are unlikely to attract European tourists. Despite their quality, a sufficient number of resorts are located in Europe.

The world tourist area is therefore organized on the basis of a regional, discontinuous and networked framework within which tourist territories are included [DEH 03]. There is a process of peripheral tourism diffusion. It creates a reticular form on a global scale and areal forms on a regional and local scale [GAY 10].

2.2.2. Regional approaches to tourism within a country

In regional and local approaches, several authors have developed their analysis on the structures of an area. We will focus our remarks on the context of France. Alexandra Monot and Frank Paris, in their book preparing for the higher education competitions on *Les espaces du tourisme et des loisirs* published by Bréal distinguish areas according to their topographical interest for tourists, following the French example of the côte d'Albâtre in Normandy, which "presents chalk cliffs, including the famous site of Étretat, valleys (small coastal valleys offering a sheltered site, but which remain elevated compared to the beach) and small pebble beaches, a setting that does not have much in common with seaside resorts, but which seduces the property owning populations of the Belle Époque" [MON 17, p. 203]. In response to this type of inventory, Philippe Violier has compiled a bibliography of various works from the last 30 years, which have focused on the regionalization of tourism in France [VIO 17]. It notes that few authors have dealt with this subject [CAZ 86, KNA 97a, CLA 93, BAR 99, MES 15]. He notes a great diversity in regional approaches to tourism in France. First, several works focus on the division of areas into classical categories of geography, such as rural, urban, coastal and mountain. The main criticism of this approach is that it is difficult to classify certain municipalities. This is the case of cities located on the waterfront, which is complex to categorize as urban tourism or coastal tourism. Alain Mesplier differentiates tourism by regional aspects, but sometimes by focusing on administrative regions, sometimes grouped together or by taking natural regions from classical geography [MES 15]. The portrait of tourism in France proposed by Rémy Knafou is of particular interest to us because it clarifies the difficulty of the exercise "difficult to depict because of the lack of precise data on actual tourist flows" [KNA 97a, p. 96]. He proposes to focus on the places where tourists reside and pass through. The tourism that defines the functional character of the French tourist area shows an unequal distribution. Unlike other authors, he argues that a large part of the French territory can be considered as not including tourist areas, even if these parts can accommodate some tourists on the margins. However, he differentiates between the absence of tourism and low tourist population densities, which reduces the reading by geographical concentration to zero. It proposes a typology that differentiates the areas by their tourist intensity from the French metropolitan territory:

– *Tourist areas formerly made up of major international reputations*: some specific areas are concerned, such as Paris or the Côte d'Azur. It should be noted that the western extension of the Côte d'Azur to the Esterel ledges in the Var department is considered to be a recent development without decisive government intervention. Always formerly constituted, but with major national renown, the coastal coasts (Brittany, Normandy, Basque Country, etc.) are presented, as well as certain French mountain areas such as the Puys in the Massif Central or the Pyrenees Central. With the exception of Mont Blanc and the central Pyrenees, formerly constituted and of major international renown, the mountain complex of the French Northern Alps or the Pyrenees are considered as tourist areas of major national renown without decisive intervention by the State. Unlike the Languedoc-Roussillon coast in the South of France, where the State has intervened by creating *ex nihilo* tourist resorts that have given the area an international reputation, it should be noted that the Aquitaine coast has also been the subject of a decision by the State to create tourist resorts, but this area is only nationally renowned.

– Other *tourist areas* have been *identified*: those that concentrate internationally renowned sites (i.e. in France: Alsace-Lorraine, Burgundy, Loire Valley, Périgord, Quercy, Causses-Cévennes, Bas-Rhône, Haute-Provence) and those characterized by diffuse tourism, which, despite the presence of sites, have only a small reception capacity (Massif Central, Southern Alps, Gers, Corbières).

– The rest of metropolitan France has *little or no tourism*, with the exception of certain areas with limited activity such as the Champagne vineyard, structuring cities (Lyon, Toulouse) or recreational sites (Futuroscope near Poitiers or Disneyland Park near Paris).

This portrait, although interesting, does not integrate the practices of tourists. Philippe Violier offers insight into tourist France that associates areas with practices. According to him, this approach is justified since "modalities, such as food and accommodation, are ubiquitous and linked to any travel, and therefore they are not or little discriminatory in the context of a regional approach" [VIO 17, p. 271]. The proposal consists of favoring the dominant practices that correspond to tourists' plans, and this is confirmed by their movements. Regional groups are identified [DUH 18, p. 85]. France, which is not or only slightly touristy, is an area characterized by rural landscapes that are not represented in society in a way that is conducive to the presence of tourism. These include areas around the Parisian metropolis, with the exception of the departments of the Loire Valley; along the Saône and around the Lyon conurbation, apart from some mountain areas. France "really tourist" corresponds to the southern part of the country with some coastlines and some inland departments:

– *Relaxation practices* take place on the coasts and in rural areas, rather in the summer season. In the Mediterranean coast, except for the mouth of the Rhône, and the entire Atlantic coast are concerned, with a high to very high number of visitors. These resting practices are also found, but with a medium intensity of use on the coasts of the Channel and the North Sea.

– *Discovery practices* are localizable with a high or very high number of visitors in the Parisian metropolis. Other cities such as Nantes, Le Havre, Lille, Lyon, Marseille, Bordeaux or Toulouse have a high to average number of visitors. There is also a coastal hinterland concerned by discovery practices with high to average numbers of visitors on the various coasts, particularly in the Mediterranean. Finally, in the countryside, there are discovery practices with very significant or important frequentation in the Loire Valley, with a decrease in intensity relative to the distance from the river, or in the Périgord, with also a decrease in the intensity of frequentation by distance to the Gers and the Massif Central. A significant to average number of visitors can also be seen in Alsace.

– The *game's practices* are limited to mountain areas. A very large or important number of visitors are concentrated in two regions: the Northern Alps, with an extension to the Jura mountains and south of the Alps, as well as in the Pyrenees. On the fringes of these areas, particularly in the foothills of the Alps and the Pyrenees, a medium to large number of visitors are concentrated, as well as in the Vosges and the Massif Central.

This reading of the "tourist regions of France" highlights the importance of taking into consideration practices correlated to geographical environments. Seasonality and the intensity of tourist numbers make it possible to focus on regions that are really affected by tourism (tourist regions) and on others that are not but can be specialized in other sectors, for example the steel industry in northern Lorraine constituting an industrial region or cereal cultivation in Beauce which makes it an agricultural region. Moreover, tourism is not present or very weakly present in these areas.

2.2.3. *Localized regional tourist areas*

Georges Cazes pointed out in 1992 the existence of a "selection of tourist areas", works that present comprehensive typologies allowing a satisfactory arrangement of the figures observed. He criticizes those that consist of a morphological description, photographed and mapped. He argues that socioeconomic considerations must be an integral part of a trilogy of fundamental factors such as the degree of planning, scale and the type of supporting environment [CAZ 92, p. 96]. Does it still need to be clarified what a tourist area is? Philippe Duhamel and Isabelle Sacareau consider that a tourist area must concentrate tourist places whose location in the area is not contiguous, creating a threshold below which it is not possible to speak of a tourist area [DUH 99, p. 67]. In which case, it would be a type of elementary place on a local or regional scale (see Chapter 1). Thus, Michel Chadefaud, based on the case of Southwest France, analyzes that since 1931, there have been several coastal and thermal resorts on the tourist map with a peripheral area that is beginning to spread tourism with forms of accommodation outside the tourist places developed in the 19th Century [CHA 88]. Then, the image of the area must be deeply touristic in order for it to qualify as such (see Figure 2.2).

Figure 2.2. *Village of Montrésor in Touraine (France) (source: J. Piriou, May 2008)*

COMMENTS ON FIGURE 2.2.– *The French village of Montrésor is located in the south of Touraine. Saskia Cousin evokes an "identifying image" of Touraine that is organized around the figure of the Loire castles, and in particular the village of Montrésor, around the image of the "typical French village" [COU 06]. This image was built by an investment by local actors to transform Montrésor into a small medieval village, currently labeled one of the "most beautiful villages in France". However, tourists perceive the village differently thanks to an explicit staging, differentiating itself from "inter-self" events for the inhabitants [COU 11].*

However, this does not mean that the entire tourist area is driven by tourism, but this policy must be an important factor in the local economy and society. Thus, in Alpine resorts, there is a difference between the French model with the development of ski resorts and satellite accommodation units in old villages, converting an agricultural and pastoralist activity to a winter sports activity, and the Austrian model where in Tyrol, the development of hotels in resorts has been consistent with the development of local agriculture [PIC 61]. The tourist area consists of multiple elementary places such as sites, resorts and cities linked by routes that operate as a network or stand out as an isolated area. For example, since the beginning of the 20th Century in Upper Egypt, tourists have been visiting Luxor, an essential stop on a Nile cruise, particularly for a visit to the temple, supplemented by visits to the pyramids of Giza [GAM 06]. Tourist resorts, especially on the coast, are rarely isolated and create coastal units. Geographer Daniel Clary explains that Deauville was created thanks to Trouville on the Normandy coast of France. Indeed, the high society of Paris, seeing the arrival of a "middle" bourgeois class, gradually left Trouville to join Deauville on the western bank of the river "La Touques". The development of "secondary resorts" gradually became widespread with the arrival of the railway, such as Granville, Saint-Valéry-sur-Somme and Le Tréport [CLA 77].

Within non-tourist areas as we have seen precisely, mainly in rural areas, there is a more diffuse tourism that takes "different non-concentrated forms of tourism that exist in non-tourist areas, within multi-purpose economies whose dynamics can be declining or rising" [KNA 95, p. 15]. The Périgord is a territory in southwestern France that has a large number of visitors. Michel Genty and Régis Delbru proposed in 1986 a map of the favorite tourist places in Périgord [GEN 86]. This map differentiates between high-traffic, medium-traffic and low-traffic areas. In addition, they provide some information on the number of visitors to museums, prehistoric caves, castles and medieval urban centers. This study shows that the south-east of the department of Dordogne, commonly known as the "Périgord Noir" in reference to the presence of cork oaks which give a dark color to the landscape, concentrates most of the tourist places with high visitor numbers. Organized around the city of Sarlat-la-Canéda, and on the banks of the Dordogne and Vézère rivers, several castles, museums and caves have a medium to large number of visitors (Lascaux cave, the Prehistory Museum in Les Eyzies-de-Tayac, etc.). This high-traffic area is expanded by a medium-traffic area down the Dordogne, including the town and vineyard of Bergerac, as well as away towards Quercy. Separated by a transverse band of low traffic, another much smaller area concentrates a high traffic around the city of Périgueux. The intensity of the traffic becomes less important by going up along the Isle and Auvézère rivers, as well as by going down the Isle river towards Bordeaux. Finally, the last area is marked with many visitors, located in the north of Périgord, including the village of Brantôme and the Villars cave. This area is extended to the west in the Ribérac sector with a small number of visitors.

Also, despite the identification of these localized regional areas, it is necessary to understand their functioning, since situations of synergies or competition exist between tourist places within the framework of tourist practices. We will then look at the different geographical approaches that have made it possible to better understand the tourist area on a regional scale (see Chapter 3).

2.3. Construction of a regional tourism area

Other regional tourist areas can be identified, but they have often been built and developed by the decision of a government. Regional development involves the development of infrastructure, in particular transport systems to allow tourists to travel, equipment, and the supply of energy, water and waste management, sometimes in public, with several resorts. There is a desire to structure localities that become tourist destinations in the region [WIL 98].

In France, in the 1960s and 1970s, both coastal and mountain resorts were developed as tourist regions due to the dominance of tourism over other activities, as well as to the number of visitors. In 1963, the *Mission interministérielle pour l'aménagement touristique du littoral Languedoc-Roussillon* (MIATLLR) [Inter-ministerial Mission for the Tourist Development of the Languedoc-Roussillon Coast] created new resorts and marinas[1] on a 210-kilometer coastal area, composed of a sandy shore associated with lagoons. It was under the impetus of the State Councilor, Pierre Racine, who was responsible for promoting the overall development of this regionally important tourist area: "It is not a question of building large urban complexes but holiday towns, created for the relaxation and pleasure of people. The objective is to make this coast a modern region of great tourism. The development will therefore be global" [RAC 80, p. 38]. This large-scale and regional-scale development will have the particularity of ensuring green breaks and vegetated areas between resorts, which are linked by a motorway, allowing access to

---

1 The eight resorts are La Grande-Motte, Carnon, Port Camargue and Cap d'Agde in the department of Hérault, Gruissan in Aude and finally Port Leucate, Port Barcarès and Saint-Cyprien in the Pyrénées Orientales, but see, in particular, the remarkable case of La Grande-Motte presented by Jean Rieucau [RIE 00].

the main emitting basins [CLA 77]. It can be seen that this tourist region is ensured by a set of connected units whose discontinuity is located at the limits of the agglomerations of Montpellier and Perpignan.

In the mountains, the "Snow Plan" developed between 1964 and 1977 made it possible to develop existing integrated resorts in the Alps or to create new generation resorts with a capacity of between 20,000 and 30,000 beds (see Figure 2.3). However, unlike the development of the Languedoc coast, the creation focused on the resorts in isolation; there was no pre-established regional plan. Thus, it is mainly in the Tarentaise valley, a high French alpine valley, that a concentration of accommodation has increased, reaching one third of the offer[2] of the 28 leading French resorts over the period 1986–1987 [KNA 87]. All these resorts are installed perpendicular to this "great valley of the Tarentaise". Also, the staggering of these resorts on several levels of altitude and their secondary centers give rise to satellite groups [MER 08] or constellations unified by "a commercial name", such as La Plagne, divided into 11 resorts at various levels of altitude; or sometimes unified by "the same commune" such as *Les Menuires and Val Thorens*, both located in Saint-Martin-de-Belleville [PRE 82]. These constellations, or satellite groups, are interlinked by a ski area creating a massif unit [KNA 87] that allows good skiers not to get bored as with the Three Valleys ski area, which extends over 600 kilometers. These satellite resorts or groups, although concentrated, still leave room for discontinuities, mainly agricultural.

In addition to the creation of new resorts, the institutional actors of tourism have been led to create "tourist regions". In order to spread tourism throughout their territories, the official authorities have divided them into tourist regions in order to ensure that people visit their entire territories.

In France, each administrative region has defined the administrative level for the promotion of tourism as the territory of action. The Regional Tourism Committees were created during the Vichy regime between 1940 and 1944 to ensure various regional tourism developments. Their missions were confirmed by the law of January 3, 1987, by becoming a mandatory

---

2 There are 32,430 beds in Courchevel, 30,000 beds in La Plagne, 24,800 beds in Tignes, 20,000 beds in Les Arcs, 19,300 beds in Méribel, 18,500 beds in Les Menuires, 17,210 beds in Val d'Isère and 14,000 beds in Val Thorens. The resorts of Courchevel, Méribel and Val Thorens are located in tributary valleys to the Tarentaise valley, including those of Saint-Bon, Allues and Les Menuires.

technical body of the decentralized regional authority and by its effective functions and an important place in the territorial organization of tourism. They differ from the regional tourism delegations, establishing a direct link with the government [VLE 06]. Only the Côte d'Azur has a regional tourism committee in Nice. Provence and the southern Alps being represented by another regional tourism committee located in Marseille.

Figure 2.3. *Avoriaz resort in the French Northern Alps (source: J. Piriou, June 2016)*

COMMENT ON FIGURE 2.3.– *The Avoriaz resort located in the commune of Morzine in the Chablais of the Haute-Savoie department was opened in 1966. This resort was designed ex nihilo thanks to Olympic champion Jean Vuarnet who helped launch the resort [BOU 04]. But Avoriaz is also one of the first French resorts to be granted almost entirely to private individuals. Also, Gérard Brémond, current president and CEO of the Pierre & Vacances-Center Parcs group, was in charge of developing the business [MAN 07]. This resort was one of 23 new resorts in the "Snow Plan" with a developer. The world-class resort enjoys a very good occupancy rate and is one of the leaders in winter sports resorts [SCA 97].*

In Quebec, the objective of the so-called "tourist" regions is to make tourism the dominant activity through appropriate development and planning [GRA 00]. On the other hand, these regions are based on rather varied and vague criteria, "Quebec tourism regions have generally been defined on the basis of regions already established: natural regions, economic regions, administrative subdivisions or groupings, regions corresponding to the old notion of countries, urban centers" [CAZ 99, p. 18]. However, tourist attendance is very uneven between tourist regions, with some regions even being in the shadow of others. François de Grandpré also notes that below these tourist regions, there would exist a regional tourism model that does not necessarily correspond to the official administrative divisions, and sometimes straddles two tourist regions according to important criteria of "touristicity" such as location in relation to an emitting zone, the landscape allowing regions to be defined as "relatively homogeneous areas" [GRA 08, p. 134].

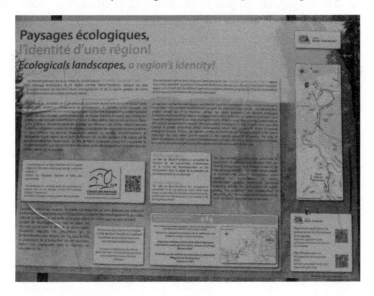

Figure 2.4. *Information panel on the regional landscape in the village from Mont-Tremblant (Canada) (source: J. Piriou, June 2016)*

COMMENT ON FIGURE 2.4.– *In Tremblant, the Laurentian Mountains, the lake and the village created ex nihilo provide representations of nature. Located north of the city of Montreal, in the heart of the Laurentians, these tourist structures are among the oldest in the tourist region [BEA 96]. The Quebec imagination of "Pays d'en haut" (the symbols of the social history of French Canadians) contributes to a social construction of nature by Quebecers [JOL 07].*

Finally, this approach of composing "tourist regions" is similar to what Claude Raffestin calls a territorial imposition [RAF 80], insofar as the division consists of a transposition of the administrative network that does not consider the real practices of tourists as we have shown previously.

2.4. Conclusion

The region is a complex concept in geography. Understanding its size, limits and characteristics is, in fact, part of each sectoral approach. Indeed, an agricultural region cannot be assimilated to an industrial region. As a result, the tourist region appears as a multiple territory, both by the geographical scale and by the perception of the actors. Spatial practices still seem to indicate the orientation given to the meaning of the tourist region, but a reading by a geographical approach will allow us to clarify the social and spatial issues that complicate this well-known concept of geography.

3

Geographical Approaches
of the Tourist Region

The study of tourism, with a geographical focus, has been the subject of various approaches that have followed the evolution of the discipline. First of all, we will see that regional geography has emerged as a means of accounting for the phenomenon within arbitrarily delimited territories. Next, we will present the influence of economics in the analysis of the functional region of tourism. Through the center–periphery model, several researchers have sought to better explain the phenomenon by the polarity of the places. Then, at the end of the last century, in a phenomenological trend of geography, the tourist region was approached by the practices of the actors as a *lived space*. Finally, we will note that the geography of tourism has shifted towards contextual and relational modeling, proposing a link between tourist places and the practices of stakeholders.

3.1. A regional geography of tourism

Unlike physical and human geography, regional geography is a branch of geography that provides an analysis of unique places [STO 17a]. As we have seen, Paul Vidal de la Blache shows how groups exploit the environment in which they live in a context of natural regions[1] (see Chapter 2) with

---

1 The natural region refers to the popular distinctions of area born at the end of the 18th Century, including elements such as the subsoil, altitude, climate, vegetation and countries named by the natives, constituting a common reality with historical depth and lived dimension [NON 04, CLA 06]. One example is Elisée Reclus' book on universal geography, published in 1976, which borrows terms from physics and physiology [REC 76].

geographical explanations in a regional approach [CLA 06]. Following on from Emmanuel de Martonne's proposal to study the structuring of a region by the physical, economic or political phenomenon in his book on Wallachia [MAR 02], Paul Vidal de la Blache, in his *Tableau de la géographie de la France en 1903*, facilitates geographical description and develops the principle of regionalization which highlights homogeneous groups, which is often based on nature and precise fields created by cultural centers [VID 03]. Also, until the 1970s, regional geography was a dominant way of doing geography, with the "region" being a research subject [STO 17a]. At that time, tourism was addressed by some authors from the 1930s onwards [MIÈ 33], and more consistently in the 1960s [BUR 63, GIN 63, PRE 68, CRI 65], in works consisting of a description of the tourism aspect. They observe the effects of tourism in different regions by focusing on the main natural and structuring characteristics that allow the development of a specific economy. Let us take a closer look at two articles published around 1960, one in France, on a portion of the northeast coast of Brittany, the other on the province of Quebec in Canada.

3.1.1. *Example of the analysis of the tourism phenomenon in the Saint-Malo region (France)*

In 1956, Denise Delouche, Associate Professor of History and Geography at the Geography Laboratory of the Rennes University in Brittany, proposed a regional geography of tourism applied to the Saint-Malo region in Brittany, which she defined as follows: "The Côte d'Ille-et-Vilaine is part of a vast tourist association, the Côte d'Émeraude, which extends from Granville to Cap Fréhel, but it is the center and most active point with the large seaside resort of Dinard and the 'tourist gateway' of Saint-Malo" [DEL 56, p. 439]. Here, the author delimits the "Malouin region" at the coastal portion of the department of Ille-et-Vilaine, which is part of a larger area that extends, to the west, from the department of Côtes-d'Armor, more precisely from Cap Fréhel and to the east to Cotentin in Normandy in the department of La Manche, more precisely in Granville. In her description of tourism in the "Malouin region", Denise Delouche first identifies the conditions of tourism development which, according to her, are due to the physical geography of the area (coasts, beaches, tides, climatic conditions), as well as to the "human conditions of tourism" which use these physical conditions [DEL 56]. Then, it divides this space into zones according to the level of development from the tourist resort of Dinard (which would constitute the center of tourist activity) to the coastal river "la Rance" which flows into the Channel Sea at the gates of the seaside resort (which would provide a demarcation): "The development of small resorts in the western Rance", "East of the Rance, development is slower". This distinction is made by ranking tourist resorts with "the most or least important place" in summer activity.

Figure 3.1. *Beach cabins on the beach of l'Écluse in Dinard (France) (source: J. Piriou, July 2011). For a color version of the figures in this chapter, see www.iste.co.uk/piriou/tourism.zip*

COMMENT ON FIGURE 3.1.– *Dinard is one of the tourist resorts located on the Emerald Coast of Brittany. The name Côte d'Émeraude is given by Eugène Herpin, a local lawyer and historian, to describe a coast with carved relief and rocky bottoms reflecting an emerald color [HER 16]. The name Côte d'Émeraude is derived from the name of the coast. This name was mainly given in response to the name Côte d'Azur, which refers to the more eastern part of the French metropolitan coastline. But photographs and postcards have helped to maintain the name "Côte d'Émeraude" featuring seaside practices [TOU 00]. The resort of Dinard experienced its main expansion in 1930–1935 with the development of multiple facilities (yacht club, tennis, casino) and became the "urban center" of the Côte d'Émeraude. This centrality is also reflected in the fact that employees come from the hinterland [AND 51].*

In this regional geographical approach, the author distinguishes (based on the number of rooms and the communication axes identified) the places according to their tourist activity and their place among other activities:

"– tourism is an essential resource for Dinard, Paramé, Saint-Lunaire, and Saint-Briac;

– tourism is an important resource among other activities in Saint-Malo, Saint-Servan, and Cancale;

– a category of tourist places formed by villages and hamlets with disadvantageous natural conditions, such as the coast of the wetlands or the Rance" [DEL 56, pp. 441–442].

The categories of tourist places show us a heterogeneity of tourism within this area explained by the infrastructures, as well as by the presence of tourism. A social significance of the tourism phenomenon appears, which modifies the qualities of a given region [STO 17a].

3.1.2. *Example of the analysis of tourism in the province of Quebec (Canada)*

At the same time, geographer Roger Brière proposed *Les cadres d'une géographie touristique du Québec* in 1961, where he developed an inventory of tourist areas, activities, and infrastructures. According to him, tourism is a sufficiently relevant field of exploration to exploit a geographical approach, as evidenced by his introduction:

"From the sole point of view of geography, does tourism not give rise to a pattern of land use, particular types of habitat, circular or alternative population movements? Does it not transform the landscapes of high-traffic areas? Are the natural or cultural attractions that explain a person's holiday movements, these movements themselves as well as the accommodation and recreation equipment, not measurable and mappable elements whose distribution, intensity, direction, and seasonal variations can be studied?" [BRI 61, p. 39]

To explain the phenomenon of tourism in Quebec, it is based on classic geography categories such as physical (relief, climate, vegetation) and cultural (tourist facilities including accommodation) attractions. But it is also interested in the tourist function of areas according to their private, public, commercial and other uses. It distinguishes tourist regions by the density of equipment and the intensity of use. It describes as a tourist region "areas where tourist life is fairly widespread homogeneous" [BRI 61, p. 59]. To define them, it uses a variety of criteria: the density of accommodation facilities over a large area; the proportion of the working population employed in the production of tourist services; tourist traffic; the place of sedentarism and nomadism in tourism and the type of accommodation (chalets and hotels or cabins and motels); total population growth in season; and existence of small urban centers whose important function is to meet tourists' needs [BRI 61]. Moreover, with the application of these criteria, he distinguishes only two "true" tourist regions in Quebec: first, the Montreal Laurentian Mountains, which are a homogeneous group of mountains and lakes, punctuated by cottages and resorts; then in the southwestern part of the Eastern Townships, a much less important area.

Regional geography appears to be a convenient means of spatial delimitation for studying tourism. However, the regional description of tourism as a scientific objective was the subject of much criticism in the 1960s. The regional paradigm poses problems both in terms of the heterogeneity of the scales behind the regional delimitation, and in the absence of an understanding of how these areas work.

3.2. The functional region of tourism

At the limits of geography and spatial economics, a functional geography will focus on spatial structures. It was following the pioneering work of Johann Heinrich von Thünen in 1826 and Alfred Weber in 1909 that great founding models were born, such as the theory of central places, which later inspired several geographers. The *central place theory* explains the size and number of cities and their spacing. It distinguishes between centers, where goods and services are located, and peripheries where the user demand for these goods and services resides. The centers are prioritized according to multiple levels of services according to the distance that the consumer agrees to travel to acquire this good or service and according to an appearance threshold that depends on the clientele required to make the service offer profitable [MER 03].

Walter Christaller introduced a model in 1933 that described the distribution between central and dispersed locations. Central locations correspond to a "significant surplus", since they have central functions and serve a complementary area. They are central in relation to the presence of dispersed inhabitants in the complementary area. The centrality of the place shows its importance in relation to its complementary area, particularly in terms of the degree of exercise of central functions. The dispersed locations are not distribution locations and are located in this complementary area and residents must move to the central locations. Central goods and services are produced for consumption at a large number of dispersed points [CHR 55]. Tourist places are therefore considered as "peripheral places", they are accessible for tourist practice against urban centers [CHR 55]. He considers that tourist places operate inversely to central sites. Indeed, central places attract for their goods and services, while tourist places attract for themselves [STO 17b]. August Lösch refuted Christaller's theory in 1943, considering that the geometric model was incorrect [LÖS 43]. Lösch has a greater diversity of scope of goods and hierarchical levels. In addition, it considers that higher-level centers generally offer services of lower scope. Mathis Stock points out that Reinhard Paseler remarked in 1984 that tourist places are not places that can be integrated into the urban hierarchy conceived in the central place model, since they would be "a new type of central place of a low or medium hierarchical level" [PAE 84, p. 59 cited by STO 17b]. He also argues that tourist places can be considered as central places if they are part of a regional system of cities, following the idea of Alfonso Pagnini and Cesare Battisti (1979) who consider that non-central places can become central places [PAG 79 cited by STO 17b]. Several authors have used the center–periphery model to explain a tourism phenomenon at the local and then regional level. We can mention the Italian Umberto Toschi who identifies the region on the basis of functional relationships according to the homogeneous presence of tourism and with a spatial organization influenced by the use of tourist resources [TOS 57]. The tourist region for Italian authors corresponds to an area composed of several centers of attraction, which are linked by interactions and reciprocity [NIC 65].

3.2.1. *The use of the center–periphery model to explain the tourism region in French-language literature*

In 1977, the French researcher Jean-Marie Miossec quoted Walter Christaller to explain a functional model of the tourist area located on the periphery of work and power centers, "these are peripheral areas that today have a powerful tropism effect" [MIO 77, p. 42]. In a "complex and disordered" area, he perceives a hierarchy of resorts from international to local. This hierarchy is explained by a change due to multiple factors (international tourism situation, improvement of communication routes and resort evolution). It explains the evolution of tourist areas on a variable scale from micro-region to vast area in five phases:

"– a *pre-touristic phase* with an area crossed or not visited, without resort and without specific request;

– a *phase* where a *pioneering resort* born with a weak tourist function, tourists have only a summary perception;

– a *phase* where *resorts multiply* and development appears accompanied by an increasing volume of tourists;

– an organizational *phase* where *resorts specialize* and competition is born, a dualism is born between an area where the tourist function is strong and the rest;

– a *saturation phase* or a pyramidal system of hierarchical resorts within an area that has become 'banal' and makes the inhabitants, sometimes even tourists, lose their bearings" [MIO 77, p. 46].

Jean-Marie Miossec illustrates this framework of dynamics of the tourist area with cases which, in his opinion, are in a phase of saturation, since they are successful situations of tourist development and corresponding to tourist regions: Florida in the USA, the Côte d'Azur in France and the Costa Brava in Spain.

Figure 3.2. *Rosas, Costa Brava in Spain (source: J. Piriou, November 2015)*

COMMENT ON FIGURE 3.2.– *The Costa Brava, in the northeast of the country, has been the subject of numerous municipal urban planning projects with "extremely permissive control by the provincial delegation of the Spanish Ministry of Housing" [CAL 77, p. 201]. While tourism was born in the 1930s on the Catalan coast within traditional urban centers (Tossa, Lloret, Platja d'Aro), general urban development plans developed until the 1970s, creating major expansions. The resort of Rosas claims to be the tourist capital of the Costa Brava. However, tourism establishes relations between small towns that have become denser and more diversified, constituting a real functional tourist area [BAR 70, pp. 450–451].*

This model, illustrated mainly by coastal areas, was adopted by Jean-Pierre Lozato-Giotart in 1985 in his manual on the geography of tourism, which analyzes various regional geographical combinations by polarity and according to geographical areas. He considers a tourist region as such:

"The tourist region seems to be defined when the organization of transport, services and the economy in general is partly or totally due to the impact of the flows, attendance, and hostels specific to the tourist function" [LOZ 08, p. 195].

It also proposes a typology of spatial forms based on the spatial distribution of tourist resources, flows, activities, facilities and the level of specialization of the local area. It distinguishes between highly polarized regional tourist areas and slightly or not polarized regional areas.

First, the *highly polarized regional areas* correspond, for the most important, to "tourist regions" and reflect a high concentration of hubs and hostels and a certain geographical continuity of the tourism phenomenon [LOZ 08, pp. 195–216]. On the coast, it distinguishes several types of highly polarized regional areas:

– The *dense and diversified regional multipolarity seaside resort type*, for example, the Côte d'Azur in France with open multipurpose seaside resorts and specialized seaside resorts that are more or less multipurpose and multinuclear [LOZ 08, pp. 196–197]. Some regions are even considered as "specialized and multipolar", for example the Algarve coast in Portugal, and others are "diversified and have a dense multipolarity", for example the Côte d'Opale in France [LOZ 08, pp. 202–203].

– The *specialized seaside resort type with discontinuous regional polarity*, for example the Languedoc-Roussillon coast in France, which is a model with separate tourist centers or centers of non-tourist intermediate areas [LOZ 08, pp. 203–205]. Islands are also considered as tourist regions [LOZ 08, p. 208]. Then, in urban areas, it defines other highly polarized regional areas. It is a type of multipolar urban tourist area that is divided into two sub-categories.

– *Tourist regions with urban polarity centralized in a large city*, such as Rome, Madrid or Prague (see Figure 3.3). These capitals are at the head of regional areas that they dominate, giving only a complementary place to other cities located in their regional area of influence [LOZ 08, p. 211].

– *Tourist regions with urban multipolarity* that are organized around cities with cultural assets. In Tuscany, a regional tourist area is organized around Florence in the center, Siena in the south, Lucca in the north and Pisa [LOZ 08, pp. 211–212].

Figure 3.3. *Old Town Square in Prague (Czech Republic)*
(source: J. Piriou, August 2017)

COMMENT ON FIGURE 3.3.– *Staroměstské náměstí which means "Old Town Square" in Czech corresponds to the touristy hypercenter of Prague. The center has the characteristic of having a set of streets and squares of the same baroque style, without any building that stands out [VEY 63]. The city of Prague receives approximately 4 million tourists per year, including 60,000 tourists per hour on the famous Charles Bridge [BOU 98].*

Then, in the mountains, two categories of highly polarized regional areas are identified:

– The *multipolar "white" type*, which can be found in the mountain ranges of developed countries, through the presence of multipolar strings of sports resorts in the French, Austrian, Swiss or German Alps. However, Jean-Pierre Lozato-Giotart points out the complexity of the delimitation in the mountains, "the relief imposes a partitioning which makes any precise delimitation of the regional tourist area delicate, each valley-massif forming a kind of sub-regional tourist unit" [LOZ 08, p. 214].

– A *bipolar type*, the mountain is a factor of continuity rather than a rupture between two complementary tourist areas characteristic of regional bipolarity, as in Marrakech and the High Atlas in Morocco [LOZ 08, p. 215].

Finally, a last type of *highly polarized regional areas* concerns *polarized cultural tourist regions*. They are structured around a major central cultural and urban center and other hubs visited are satellite hubs ensuring geographical coherence, particularly for one-day trips facilitated by good infrastructure [LOZ 08, p. 215]. The classic model would correspond, for example, to the Loire Valley with its castles and the central model with satellite would correspond to Paris, which satellites peri-urban cultural centers, such as the Château de Versailles, as well as the castles of the Loire Valley constituting a "megaregion" [LOZ 08, p. 216].

Second, regional tourist areas with little or no polarization are characterized by a discontinuity in the tourism phenomenon. They correspond to island areas (e.g. Corsica), protected areas (a nature reserve in Africa) or more or less connected cultural centers [LOZ 08, pp. 217–219].

Jean-Pierre Lozato-Giotart acknowledges that a simple reading by the center–periphery model is not sufficient to explain a geographical and social phenomenon of tourism within a region: "The notion of a tourist region therefore corresponds to a territory in which the intensity of tourist activities gives it a strong geographical and sociocultural specificity" [LOZ 08, p. 223]. Jean-Michel Dewailly and Émile Flament also integrate (2000) the idea of associating a distinctive image and notable climatic and landscape characteristics to a vast space [DEW 00]. However, they also use polarity and centrality models by distinguishing between linear regions and nuclear or massive regions. The linear region is defined around a major axis that structures tourism activity. There are some of them on the coast (e.g. rivieras), as well as in large valleys (e.g. along the Rhine between Mainz and Cologne in Germany). The nuclear or massive region corresponds to a stretched region where flows are less dependent on a structuring axis. They can be found in mountainous areas, in metropolitan areas, in regions whose historical and administrative unity is reflected in a strong image (e.g. Scotland), and finally in archipelagos establishing relations (e.g. the Channel Islands) [DEW 00].

3.2.2. The use of the center–periphery model to explain the tourist region in English literature

The English-speaking authors also borrowed the theory of central places to explain the functioning of tourist regions. Clare A. Gunn sees tourism as a system involving five elements: individuals who want to move; attractions that offer activities; services and facilities; transportation that move individuals to and from attractions; and information that helps individuals [GUN 65]. Spatially, tourism can be broken down into three parts. First, a place of origin is identified, and according to her it is a region generating tourists from home. Second, it specifies that tourists stay temporarily in a "host locality" or "destination region". Finally, a road or "transit region" connects the place of origin to the host locality or region of destination, through which tourists travel [GUN 65]. In 1970, Charles Stansfield and John Rickert proposed the concept of the *recreational business district*, which they presented locally as a linear accumulation of services to satisfy the consumption needs of visitors: "Seasonally oriented linear aggregation of restaurants, various specialty food stands, candy stores and varied array of novelty and souvenirs shops that cater to visitor's leisurely shopping needs" [STA 70, p. 219]. Then, following on from Thorstein Veblen's work in sociology focusing on leisure [VEB 99], Dean MacCannell provides some clarification to the "destination regions" model. He considers that they are chosen according to "tourist attractions" that are characterized by markers. These markers come in various shapes and provide information to tourists about the attractions. It may be a landscape as well as a completed development (e.g. a scenic road) [MAC 76]. According to Leiper, these attractions are located in tourist destination regions, and others are located in transit regions. According to him, tourist destination regions are places that attract tourists temporarily, thanks in part to these attractions. But these attractions can be located in the destination region as well as on a "transit route". Transit routes connect tourist areas, including stopover points. They contribute to the importance of tourist flows [LEI 79].

In the 1980s, research on attraction was completed. Jan O. J. Lundgren endeavored to better understand the phenomenon of tourism on a regional scale via an analysis of the functions of tourist places and flows, taking into account the intensity of tourism, the degree of centrality, or the place of attractions and supply in the local or regional economy. It distinguishes four types of destinations: metropolitan areas integrated into international transport networks generating significant tourist flows, suburbs of metropolitan areas, rural areas and finally natural environments far from the main tourist flows (e.g. natural parks) [LUN 84]. Also, the destination constitutes a system within the tourist system [MIL 85]. These are the attractions, which Lew believes lead people to move around [LEW 87]. Clare A. Gunn describes the very structure of the destination region. It is organized by nodes or points of interest, which consist of attractions, infrastructure and services in the core [GUN 88]. Nodes can be local sub-destinations or isolated attractions. For Leiper, the destination region is similar to a relationship between an amusement complex and the core. In addition, a night in another place creates a new destination region [LEI 90]. Dianne Dredge completed this work in 1999 with a proposal for a hierarchical arrangement of the destination region [DRE 99]:

"– *single node destination region*: tourists travel from the place of origin to the single node of the destination region. This node has a nucleus or possibly an attraction complex comprising several nuclei. All services and infrastructures are accessible and do not require leaving this destination region;

– *multiple node destination* corresponds to a destination that has more than one node. There are three levels of nodes, primary, secondary and tertiary. A district may appear encompassing one or more nodes in a similar form of tourism;

– *chained destination region* is built from the connection of single node and/or multiple node destination regions. A tourist trip includes two or more destination regions in which at least one night is spent in each of them. Dianne Dredge pointed out that it could be tourism in the Loire Valley in France. The markers are of interest for the attraction of the destination region, in particular they allow the increase in the number of nights spent" [DRE 99, pp. 787–788].

We understand that according to these models, the spatial dimension is very heterogeneous. First, the single-node destination region would correspond to a spatial dimension of local scale such as the tourist resort or tourist closed complex. Second, the multi-node destination region could be similar to the tourist conurbation or tourist district because of the multipolarity and existing relationships. However, the chained destination region model could also correspond to the proposed definition of a tourist district. There is therefore confusion about changing the "region".

The center–periphery model, and in particular the theory of central places, is criticized as it applies to tourism. It should be noted that, in 1972, Roger Brunet challenged the idea that a tourist region could be an extension area of a phenomenon [BRU 72]. Also, the typology involving the polarity of the places proposed by Jean-Marie Miossec (1977) and Jean-Pierre Lozato-Giotart (1985) is questionable [MIO 77, LOZ 85], especially since it is based on geographical environments. A certain geographical determinism cannot explain a social phenomenon such as tourism. For example, how can we explain the international tourist tours that integrate Paris, the landing beaches in Normandy and the valley of the Loire castles? For tour operators, the proposal corresponds to a French or even European regional area. Mathis Stock denounces the fact that tourism is seen as an antagonism of centrality, "interpreting tourist places using the central place mode is problematic" [STO 17b, p. 271]. It is not enough to use a model to have it verified in different fields of geography. However, geographers have tended to use the center–periphery model for ease of use, as Jacques Lévy points out, "because of its simplicity, robustness, and explanatory power, the center–periphery model seems to be the very example of the efficient model, having found the right balance between the strength of meaning and the ability to adapt" [LÉV 03b, p. 143]. But the initial condition of the central place model is that there is a "complementary area" at the regional level. However, Mathis Stock points out that the scale is not relevant to the movement of tourists from a place of daily living to a place of temporary living for recreational purposes, "so the site's network of reference places is not the region, but virtually the whole world" [STO 17b, p. 271]. Moreover, a place is only central if it polarizes other places. Centrality is expressed by a convergence of flows from adjacent areas. According to Mathis Stock, the non-central or peripheral nature of tourist places would be relevant based on the classic model of central places in its initial version, considering a regional spatial system of cities whose relationships are established by commercial or administrative activities. The system of centrality would emerge through the *in situ* practice of temporary inhabitants who give meaning to centralities, in particular by differentiating tourist places from other places [STO 17b]. Thus, Leiper's proposal concerning transit roads that contribute to the inclusion of tourism in areas [LEI 79] can also be called into question. Indeed, in her thesis in 1977, Micheline Cassou-Mounat shows that it was tourists who first went to the Arcachon coast, taking advantage of fishing facilities alone, before any development of accommodation infrastructures or communication routes [CAS 77]. However, in these approaches, there has been an evolution that takes into account the view of tourists, as well as their movements.

3.3. The tourist region, a lived space

3.3.1. *The region as a lived space*

At the end of the 20th Century, although Armand Frémont found the functional region attractive because it was quantifiable, he was not satisfied with the economic definitions, nor with the naturalistic or administrative definitions of the region, "too objective and reductive, the economic region, like the natural region, did not properly define the human area [i.e.] the reality of the relationships that unite people at the place" [FRE 99, p. 56]. However, it does not refute the idea of a region-system as a structure of relations that unites people to places in a specific area, but insists on the need to deepen the analysis of the quality of these relations. According to him, man is not a neutral object in the constitution and perception of the region, but he perceives the surrounding area unequally and makes a judgment on the place [FRE 99]. We will talk about a region of a lived space. A new phenomenological approach to geography is emerging. According to this current approach, the a lived space includes the area of daily practices (living area) and the area of social interrelationships (social area) as objects of perception and mental representation that an individual or a group can construct itself. The geographical level at which the region is located among other spatial units seems rather vague, as Armand Frémont's definition shows: "An average area, less extensive than the nation or the great area of civilization, larger than the social area of a group and *a fortiori* of a place" [FRE 99, p. 188]. Also, the region, as a lived space, is an area balanced by regulations as well as by superior, national and international relations, relations of production and elementary exchange or located between the familiar and the known domain and that of the foreign and the exceptional [FRE 99]. However, the regional area is also an image, the result of one of the most fundamental relationships between people and the areas where they live, defined by perception and psychological behavior in relation to a lived space [FRE 99]. The image is the essential element of the regional combination, i.e. the psychological link of people to an area. According to Frémont, people do not live in an area as it is, but in a represented area that they invest from a psychological point of view; it is the lived space. Thus, it distinguishes the lived space from the living area, i.e. all the places frequented on a daily basis, from the social area, i.e. the living space completed by all the social relationships maintained. The region thus integrates a lived space and social areas according to a certain coherence and specificity forming a certain idea of the region and which is distinguished by representations, regional images, in the perception of endogenous and exogenous actors [BAI 95].

Armand Frémont proposes a distinction between the three regions [FRE 99]:

– *fluid regions* are characterized from the outset by a lack of anchoring or homogeneity in natural or polarized regions, and they also do not take into account natural, humanized or lived-in places. Fluidity corresponds to a connection that exists between people and places;

– the *rooted region* is mainly justified in the context of peasant civilizations where there is a particular attachment of people to the land in the sense that places belong to people and people belong to places;

– the *functional region*, in the sense of Frémont, corresponds to the organization of an area by industrial society, at a high point of growth. This society attributes to the function the highest level of the value scale, modifying the conditions of communication between people as well as the relationship to people's area (distance-time, transport, urbanization, etc.).

Finally, let us remember that the region, a lived space, "is not an object with some reality in itself has taught us A. Frémont" [DIM 91, p. 170]. These representations cannot be summarized as "neither the economic region, nor the administrative region, nor the natural region" [DIM 91, p. 169]. Also, to the question "why this area attracts rather than another?",

Émile Flament proposes mobilizing the significance of the places and the recreational value of the area [FLA 75]. It takes up the idea of Marc Boyer who considers that the success of a region depends on the representation of the company [BOY 72]. Also, according to Émile Flament, "a portion of an area becomes tourist if it coincides with its [society's] tastes and rhythms" [FLA 75, p. 616].

3.3.2. *Representations as a tool to define the tourist region as experienced*

In this trend, Claude Raffestin considers the tourist place as a projection of historicity, a product of society. Only individuals create existence in places, "there is no tourist place except because there is a cultural model and landscape needs. During the journey, a relationship is forged between humankind and the earth that is not concrete in the sense that it has been prepared by a representation" [RAF 86, p. 14]. The representation directs the tourist gaze and attributes to places the interest that individuals have in their tourist practices. Spatial representations and the value attributed to the sites will be the subject of several research projects from the 1980s onwards. Bernard Debarbieux and Hervé Gumuchian conducted a study in 1987 on spatial representations and names of territories, focusing on the case of the toponymic inscription of recent tourist developments in the Northern Alps. Representations are a relevant means of spatial analysis, "reading area in terms of representations is to admit that there is no truth about spatial reality; it is to privilege the view of the users of this area by considering their constructions of spatial reality as relevant for analysis; it is to understand – perhaps a little better – the logic of area-producing groups" [DEB 87, p. 182]. According to them, the name generated by the representation makes it possible to name the places. This reflects an appropriation of an area of a social group. And the process of territorialization contributes to social and spatial reproduction. They specify that "the repeated inscription in an area, in the form of neotoponyms, of stereotyped, trivialized, and strongly connoted images that accompany tourist practices can only reinforce these practices and the social actors who organized them" [DEB 87, p. 82]. They mention the case of the La Plagne ski lifts, which organize a series of satellite resorts with names based on local toponyms (e.g. La Plagne Bellecôte) and evoking a particular topographical feature (Les Crêtes) or toponymic inventions [DEB 87]. Still concerning mountain ranges, Jean-Pierre Lozato-Giotart criticizes the fact that the different altitudes are not taken into account in the same large regional tourist complex. It justifies the fact that a lived space contributes to the evolution of the appreciation of the area, "this is the whole problem of defining the notion of tourist region: a lived space that is seen, experienced and organized at the same time. Only the lived space can in the long run change the traditional cliché of a 'tourist region'" [LOZ 08, pp. 214–223].

3.4. Tourist places and mobility in a regional dimension

The geography of tourism then opened up to contextual and relational modeling, particularly through tourism practices [STO 17a]. We will see that these are not only seen as mobilities, but also as contributing to the development of geographical places. The *hubs and spokes* model was born of the geographical phenomena of society linked to the increase in mobility, a concentration of an area as well as the ability of cities to anticipate and innovate. This model, considered as an alternative to Walter Christaller's [ROO 93] central location model, involves a new approach through the network. Flows (of goods, but especially of people as in the case of air transport) are directed more towards *hubs* that actually correspond to complete multimodal junctions than towards the periphery. Also, the operation does not correspond to the "center–periphery" model. *Spokes* allow *hubs* to be connected directly to each other without intermediate relays; in this case, we speak of a tunnel effect [LER 00]. In transport geography, Jean Varlet has identified three fundamental principles of the hub and spokes model [VAR 97]. First of all, this network operates according to a completely new morphology, since it is a star-shaped functional network. Second, it makes it possible to respond to economic concerns by directing stakeholders towards a search for competitiveness and profitability. The network allows economies of scale to be achieved. Finally, a logic of power operates because of the search for a dominant position. It was also noted that there is a logic of concentration of flows on a few radiating axes and on one point, as well as a logic of semi-isolation and territorial sharing that is created insofar as the traditional organization is disrupted by a diffusion of flows between the hubs and spokes [VAR 97].

Concerning the tourist space, C. K. Campbell proposed in 1967 a model that integrates the movements of individuals [CAM 67]:

– first, he distinguishes the movement that connects the place of daily life to a place of leisure with a return by the same route. He considers that these are places identified around the city; it may be similar to a recreational metropolitan hinterland;

– second, he considers that a trip that connects the place of daily life to a place of leisure can be part of a region that is the subject of small trips that connect other places. It is a regional recreational complex;

– third, round trips can create new links between recreation centers and other places on the route. This corresponds to holiday regions with services.

In 1969, Mariot took up three itineraries that linked places of daily life to those of tourism: the access and return route to a tourist place; the roads that served other tourist places; and finally the recreational route that offered a series of itinerant tourist places [MAR 69]. Neil Leiper identifies distinct geographical elements through movement sequences. According to him, traveling from a place of daily life is prepared by motivation, planning and organization. Then the transit route between the place of daily living and the place of tourist stay can be the subject of the use of services, in particular accommodation and catering or visits, during stops. Then during the stay, there are interactions between the main attractions, services within a region. Finally, upon return, memories and a return to daily life occur [LEI 79, p. 398].

Mobility is a visible spatial practice. Tourists register their actions on a local or regional scale. In geography, mobility is a preferred object of study, as it corresponds to a "form of movement that is expressed by a change in position" [BRU 93, p. 333]. Some authors who are part of a trend of mobility turn thinking will go beyond the notion of mobility. The English sociologist John Urry appreciates mobility not only as a spatial effect, but also as a social effect. For him, tourism is organized of *scapes and flows* by distance from a place by contemplation of landscapes different from those of everyday life [URR 00, p. 35]. Spatial movements are facilitated by various technologies, including transport [URR 05]. Thus, travel is no longer considered as a waste of time; it stimulates other activities of stay and can also constitute an activity in its own right as a tourist excursion [LYO 05]. Rémy Knafou points out that tourist mobility, which corresponds to all the movements made by individuals registered in space–time outside daily life, constitutes an element of a general system of mobility [KNA 00a, p. 85]. Geographer Tim Cresswell analyzes mobility from three angles: observable movements, representations of movement and experiences related to the journey of the world [CRE 06].

The spatial dimension of tourist mobility is global in scope. However, the stay is part of a local or regional scale. By passing through and staying in the region, Rémy Knafou identified in 1997 models of tourism development characterized by the importance of a housing park and tourist attendance, "at the regional level, spatial tourism organizations are of great variety, in that they combine tourist and non-tourist places, as well as spatial structures of a very different nature and form" [KNA 97a, p. 119].

First of all, the *tourist pole* is remarkable for its own attendance as well as for its role as a pivot point, providing an international welcome and then a redistribution to external sites [KNA 97a]. Based on the model of the *Central Business District* known in major metropolitan areas, the concept of *Central Tourist District* is used, characterized by hotels, tourist infrastructures and different territorial units that participate in its delimitation [BUR 91]. Based on Donald Getz's (1997) approach (which considers that *Tourism District Business*, and in particular *Central District Business*, corresponds to the heritage areas of the oldest cities) [GET 97], Gregory John Ashworth and John E. Tunbridge define a critical mass of historical attractions, tourist visits and secondary tourism services, a polycentric model applied to large cities [ASH 00, p. 93]. For Philippe Duhamel and Rémy Knafou, the *Central Tourist District* is rather revealing of a visited area [DUH 07]. The Parisian metropolis makes it possible to identify a *Central Tourist District* delimited by the number of tickets sold to museums and sites, in two areas: the historic center and 19th-Century Paris. *The Central Tourist District* then extends along the banks of the Seine [DUH 07]. Then, other centers are identified in the *metropolis* (e.g. Versailles or Disneyland), to which satellites from the center are added (e.g. the Stade de France and the Saint-Denis basilica or the La Défense district). Finally, the Parisian metropolis also appears as a tourist *pole* "from which the tourist who stays there can easily reach the tourist attractions of the surrounding regions" (e.g. Mont-Saint-Michel or Champagne) [FOU 17]. We note a spatial organization in the archipelago.

Then, among the other models of tourism development, Rémy Knafou distinguishes between several *types of tourism networks* [KNA 97a]. These networks consist of tourist places frequented by tourists passing through, and tourist places characterized by tourist habitats. The areas are structured according to the tourists' itineraries:

– In the mountains, *rings of places surrounding a mountain massif* and connected by ski resorts can be noted. We can mention the Tarentaise valley in the French Alps, which gathers the first French group of winter sports resorts among which are Méribel, Courchevel, Les Menuires, Val Thorens, La Plagne, Les Arcs, Tignes, etc.

– Another type of *network includes comparable sites*. This is the case in the Loire Valley, which includes castles of varying ages, but whose fame makes it possible for some to benefit others with a large number of visitors. The château de Cheverny, located geographically on the tourist routes between the château de Blois and château de Chenonceau, benefits from the flow of tourists visiting the Loire Valley castles.

– The *combination of picturesque sites of various types* constitutes another tourist area with a reticular structure. This is based on local hubs. We can mention the case of the perched villages located in the southwest of France such as the village de Conques (see Figure 3.4).

– The final type includes a tourist space with uncertain contours, which does not really operate in network mode, but has the characteristics of *a "seedling"-type device*. We can mention the Massif Central in France with the presence of former thermal resorts and some visited sites.

Figure 3.4. *Conques en Rouergue in the South of France (source: J. Piriou, May 2018)*

COMMENT ON FIGURE 3.4.– The village of Conques located in Aveyron is an important stop on the Route of Santiago de Compostela, a religious pilgrimage route. Conques doubled its attendance between 1985 and 1995, reaching 500,000 visitors per year, including 90,000 for its treasure museum in Sainte-Foy [DEH 99]. This increase in the number of visitors can be explained by a redevelopment of the village, the renovated building, renovated facades and flowered streets [DEH 97], leading the municipality to be classified as one of the "Most Beautiful Villages in France" network in the year the association was created (i.e. in 1982). In 1998, the Abbey Church of Sainte-Foy and the Pilgrims' Bridge were included on the UNESCO World Heritage List. Finally, in 2008, the Midi-Pyrénées Regional Council designated the village as a "Grands Sites", a symbol of regional tourism policy, renewed in 2017 by the Occitane region.

3.5. Conclusion

The evolution of geography, and more particularly the study of the "region", has allowed an important exploration of the regional dimension of the tourism phenomenon. The regional geography has favored a local knowledge of the places visited, as well as an identification of the facilities and services necessary for the presence of tourism. However, the determinism relating to spatial delimitation, whether based on natural or administrative criteria, could not explain the functioning of these areas. In this sense, the functional region has had the merit of enhancing the hierarchical relationships between tourist places according to their polarities. But here again, apart from a more precise reading of the whole set of places, few explanations are given as to why places are linked. The administrative, command or connection role for its communication axes of a particular place does not systematically make it a tourist place. In this sense, the region as a *lived space* has highlighted a discrepancy between the places practiced by the different actors. Tourists make choices of places, which turn out to be places that can be different from the places visited by the inhabitants according to their lived regions. Thus, taking into account the mobility associated with tourist places has contributed to a proposal to explain the tourist region. The justification for the travel of tourists combining places with visits has made it possible to identify tourist regions [VIO 17]. Yet even if the tourist has the main role, they do not act alone. Other actors are involved in the choice of location practices, which generate mobility and shape tourist regions. We will then study the logic of actors to practice a tourist destination of regional dimension.

Stakeholder Logics in the Practice of a Tourist Destination in a Regional Dimension

Introduction to Part 2

Tourism uses the concept of destination to characterize a receiving territory. The destination is a subjective territory, since it is difficult to give it a stable dimension or to define it precisely. Indeed, a place can be a tourist destination in its own right, for example a city or a resort, but a region can also be a tourist region composed of several places. The tourist destination would therefore be both what is promoted by tourism professionals and what is perceived by tourists [MON 07]. The tourist destination takes a regional form depending on how all stakeholders, including the tourist, organize the system. In other words, the tourist destination takes on a regional dimension if necessary [VIO 09]. Therefore, focusing the reflection on the role of the actors seems relevant to us in order to understand the delimitation and construction of a tourist region, "to put the actor at the center of the analysis, whether it is tourists, entrepreneurs, administrations, etc., is essential if we want to understand the logic of how tourism works as a system: Indeed, it does not only include markets or areas, within the framework of their own strategic competences, and which act within the framework of their intentions according to standard legal and social standards" [STO 03, p. 167]. Moreover, the consideration of the actor, in the sense of an actor with a subjective interiority and intentionality, as well as their practices, constitutes the very center of our discussion. We have identified four stakeholder logics that lead them to practice a tourist destination with a regional dimension. These logics are related to their intentions, whether they are professional, political or recreational.

First of all, we will start from the peregrination logic of tourists who choose places and visit them through tourist mobilities according to their own recreational plans. This information helps to draw the spatial dimensions of the territories used and informs us about the tourist regions. In particular, we will focus on a field study, in which we interviewed tourists whom we met in several tourist places around Lake Geneva in France and Switzerland (see Chapter 4). Then, we will see that public or private investors through their creation of facilities (through their spatial planning) contribute to creating a tourist region in a top-down strategy. Indeed, they structure the area so that tourists go beyond the scale of the elementary place and visit in a regional dimension (see Chapter 5). Next, we will present the bottom-up strategy of developers, which consists of enhancing the value of their territories and mobilizing local actors (see Chapter 6). Finally, we will explain the role of advisors, who are actors who encourage tourists to visit multiple places. By various means of information, they propose places and itineraries to be used in order to spread and limit the concentration of tourism (see Chapter 7).

4

Tourists and their Territories Practices in a Regional Dimension

The quest for recreation is justified by a need to restore the body and mind as a result of the constraints and routines of daily life. The less time available for daily "restoration" contributes to a "destructive" daily lifestyle [ELI 94]. Recreation includes most of the activities required to carry out a recreational project; it is a "set of recreational activities that can be carried out both in the local space and time of daily life and in the space–time of tourism" [KNA 03, p. 581]. The recreational project can be set up in your home or in your daily environment. Tourism is a social practice that is characterized by spatial mobility outside time and space of daily life, and "if there is mobility, it is because restoration will be more effective in a space or place other than the place of daily life" [VIO 07, p. 160]. There is a proven effectiveness of the change of location, with tourist mobilities favoring the recreation of individuals. Mobility, which can be defined as a "form of movement expressed through a change in position" [BRU 93, p. 333], reflects a spatial action of the individual since it is "all the manifestations linked to the movements of social realities in space" [LUS 03, p. 622]. Spatial mobility is not uniform. Thus, in the analysis of work–home mobility, we define "peregrination" as the way of managing the multiplicity of trips due to the fragmentation of a territory of life "based on the optimal combination of routes and stops between destinations whose one of the terms is inevitably the home" [PIN 01, p. 23]. This peregrination is reflected in a structuring home–work axis around which are grafted stages of peregrinations or circular movements [HER 07].

This travel logic therefore seems interesting to mobilize in the context of tourist travel. Indeed, we will see that tourists put in place a strategy, in their travel, relating to space skills. It is important to distinguish the tourist who chooses a monotopic destination (one will qualify his/her strategy as "homely") from the one who looks for a polytopic destination and will make day trips or a route throughout their stay (one will call their spatial action of peregrination). Then, we will see that these movements can be analyzed to understand the choice of spatial directions followed and the tourist places practiced within a space of regional dimension. Finally, we will propose a distinction of tourist mobilities to understand the relationship between elementary tourist places and spatial practices with a regional dimension.

4.1. Spatial skills linked to tourist mobilities within a space of regional dimension

Moving around for recreation purposes involves a movement that requires organization. Practicing places other than those of everyday life translates into a tourist's confrontation with otherness, which can be relative depending on the knowledge of the place and become a familiarity. It is advisable to control the space during the touristic stay [STO 17a]. Also, once a first trip has been made between the daily place of residence and the first tourist place of stay, tourists must understand the relevant tourist space (according to physical, financial, temporal availability, etc.) and the places that compose it. Space control requires a spatial competence that is established by measuring distances, location, route, crossing boundaries in space or cutting and delimiting portions of spaces [LUS 13]. Michel Lussault distinguishes *six elementary spatial skills* that we will apply to the peregrinations of tourists who, in their tourist stays, make optimal combinations of routes and stops between tourist places:

– The competence related to the *mastery of metrics* allows individuals to "discriminate between the near and far and to evaluate the right distance to keep between themselves and other social realities [...] since the spatiality of humans always unfolds from the person" [LUS 13, p. 45]. The perception of distances evolves from that of everyday space and may prove to be a challenge, requiring the mobilization of this spatial competence. Thus, the distances to be covered in a country like China for French people require a specific organization and adapted means of transport during the stay. The study carried out by Philippe Violier in his study of tour operators' offers for

China shows the need for adaptation [VIO 11]. In the circuit entitled "China of Eight Treasures" offered by Nouvelles-Frontières, after arriving in Shanghai, customers travel to Xian on the second day, i.e. 1,400 kilometers (869 miles), requiring the use of a plane, which reduces the 14-hour bus journey time to a maximum of 4 hours by plane. On the fifth day, they use the train to go to Luoyang, Dengfeng and Longmen Caves on excursions. On the seventh day, they travel to Beijing by train to complete their stay in the Chinese capital. After a day in the city of Beijing (Forbidden City and Temple of Heaven), two days of excursions are proposed[1]. One proposes to discover sites in the outskirts near Beijing at the Summer Palace residence (about 20 kilometers) and at the Lamas temple (about 10 kilometers). The other is further away from the city as it includes a discovery of the Great Wall of China (see Figure 4.1) at the Badaling site (70 kilometers or 43 miles) and the Ming Tomb site (50 kilometers or 31 miles).

Figure 4.1. *Great Wall of China in Badaling (China) (source: J. Piriou, December 2014). For a color version of the figures in this chapter, see www.iste.co.uk/piriou/tourism.zip*

---

1 We consider Tiananmen Square as the central point of Beijing city. It is also the city's tourist center with the main access to the Forbidden City.

COMMENT ON FIGURE 4.1.– *The Great Wall of China and more particularly the Badaling site is a major tourist attraction in China. This great wall, 3,000 kilometers (1864 miles) long, connected sections between the 15th and 16th Centuries under the Ming dynasty. It materializes a space policy and projects a hierarchy of society onto the territories [SAN 18]. Tourist guides, such as travel agencies, list this site as a reference to discover China [LI 12]. However, most Chinese tourists who visit the Great Wall go there by their own means without going through a travel agency, while "nearby" Western and Asian tourists make their first excursion through a travel agency [WAN 08].*

– The *placement and arrangement of competence* corresponds to a choice made by tourists in the practice of one or more tourist places to implement their project. Take the case of Chambord Castle in the French tourist destination of the "Loire Castles". Despite an estimated attendance of approximately one million visitors per year, the municipality of Chambord has only 39 rooms. Also, to compensate for this lack of capacity, tourists will stay in the surrounding areas. The Tours region thus has a significant hotel capacity of more than 3,000 rooms. Chambord is not a monotopic destination, but a site that makes up a polytopic destination: that of the Loire castles. Chambord Castle, as a high town (see Figure 4.2), reflects excellence but, because of its limited accommodation capacity, the site is only an aggregate of the "Loire Valley Castles" destination, which is inseparable from other surrounding areas [PIR 11a].

Figure 4.2. *Tourists in front of Chambord Castle: (France) (source: J. Piriou, October 2008)*

COMMENT ON FIGURE 4.2.– *Chambord's image far exceeds that of the other Loire castles. Thus, an exhibition made in Chambord was organized from June 2007 to May 2009 on the castle site to illustrate the importance of the exploitation of the castle's name and image by brands, advertisers and the tourism industry for commercial purposes. There are many media, such as lithographs and postcards, that appeared at the end of the 19th Century, which contributed to a "touristification". As early as 1880, images of high places were used to decorate consumer product packaging. The distribution of these products has had a propaganda effect, encouraging consumers to come and observe the places represented on the packaging [BER 07].*

– *Scalar competence* corresponds to the ability to "discriminate between the small and the large and to appreciate the absolute and relative size of social objects" [LUS 13, p. 47]. The tourist metropolis can thus be understood both by the Central Tourist District and by its periphery. In the case of Paris, only a few places are included in the Central Tourist District. The analysis of tour operator brochures produced by Laurie Lepan in 2013 shows that only the Château de Versailles is present in the "Paris" destination, while the Château de Fontainebleau and Disneyland are almost absent. On the other hand, there are other places on an "extra-metropolitan" scale, such as Mont-Saint-Michel or the castles of the Loire Valley, but which are part of larger circuits and are not part of the Paris destination [LEP 13].

Figure 4.3. *Tourists taking pictures of the clear view of the riverbanks from the Bir-Hakeim bridge in Paris (source: J. Piriou, March 2017)*

COMMENT ON FIGURE 4.3.– *Tourists identify places that match their images and knowledge. However, in metropolitan areas, such as Paris, the familiarity of these places of otherness is more difficult, with fewer familiar landmarks with the exception of the touristified districts, including the Central Tourist District [COË 08]. As part of the photographic practice, tourists look for the point of view that will allow them to obtain the best image of the place. The tourist photo is located between the reportage photo and the family photo, "it documents places, lists them, as in the case of travel reports and at the same time, it refers to a practice of testimony and appropriation, as in family portraits" [DON 07, p. 23]. So, there is a staging of affections, through memory, and experience, through testimony [DON 07].*

– The *division and delimitation of competence* consists of "cutting the space into relevant elementary units, [...] delimiting, setting spatial boundaries between the different discriminated entities" [LUS 13, p. 46]. Hong Kong is a polytopic metropolis whose spatial practice of neighborhoods is chosen according to the tourists' plan and according to their knowledge of the place. First-time visitors visit the urbanized spaces of Hong Kong Island and Kowloon, while repeaters tend to be more selective in their spatial practices [MCK 12]. For tourists, Kowloon, the New Territories and the island of Hong Kong are not separated since they are attached to the destination name Hong Kong, which corresponds both to the name of the Special Administrative Region attached in 1997 to the People's Republic of China. In addition, tourists group the name "Hong Kong" by going mainly to the northern shore of Hong Kong Island, to Causeway Bay for first-time visitors to the Central and Wan Chai districts for all tourists, first-time visitors and repeat visitors and further west to Scheung Wan for return visitors. Only a few districts on the Kowloon peninsula are subject to tourist practices (Tsim Sha Tsui and Hung Hom) and a few other peripheral places (Disneyland and Ocean Park) [MCK 12].

– The *franchising competence* "gathers all the techniques and habits that we have acquired and that allow everyone to cross, the airlocks, the thresholds, the borders, the security gates, the limits of all kinds that now punctuate our daily lives" [LUS 13, p. 46]. Techniques and habits acquired to escape from everyday life can be presented in the means of transport that allow mobility. The cruise is an "all-inclusive" product that includes accommodation, food, activities and whose tours offer an alternation between stopovers and days at sea. In the Caribbean, a classic stay offers several stopovers during a week of navigation to private islands or parts of islands, some of which are privatized by cruise lines constituting an archipelagic regional grouping. These places embody by this exclusive access by boat a "terrestrial paradise" with a luxuriant vegetation and fine sandy beaches [GAY 17b].

– *Progression competence* refers to "the ability of an individual to compose and provide an itinerary" [LUS 13, p. 46]. Controlling mobility, which combines a combination of "other" places, requires adaptation to the mobility known and acquired in everyday places. Three elements can explain tourist mobilities: the preparation of the trip and stay, the "ability" to travel and finally the ability to manage unforeseen situations [TSA 10]. In a survey of tourists conducted in 2003 and 2004 in Marrakech, Morocco, Stéphanie Leroux explains that among tourists who plan an itinerary individually, the role of planners is important in the suggestion (car rental agencies, travel guides). Moreover, their tours often correspond to the places practiced with the same stopovers by those offered by tour operators. The road is part of the adventure because of the high number of kilometers traveled, between 1,000 and 1,500. Advice and help in the organization are necessary according to free time, as evidenced by the quotes of the interviewees: "Perhaps we will not do all of the itinerary that has been proposed to us to do; if we like a place, we will stay there. If we don't like it, we'll set the course. We have a week to discover the South and the desert, we'll see" [LER 07, p. 278]. The tourist's ability to adapt their movement is perceived by their "way of approaching space in a reticular way by interpreting and identifying connections (links in a network of places) in addition to contiguity" [STO 17a, p. 130]. In this degree of ease in organizing, Alain Decrop and Dirk Snelders (2005) identify several behaviors [DEC 05]:

    - tourists who are rational and cautious by trusting the same travel agent;

    - tourists who are hedonists, dreamers and optimists;

    - tourists who are opportunistic and whose vacations are not a real subject of organization;

    - vacation planners who think about the choice and make their final decision at the last minute.

We will now look at the routes and journeys taken that give particular forms of tourist mobilities as long as they are on a regional scale.

4.2. Itineraries and routes according to tourist mobilities on a regional scale

Tourism mobilities are mainly studied in the literature concerning a shift from a place of daily life to an "off-daily" place. There are a few authors who have begun analyses of spatial practices with a regional dimension (see Chapter 3). Thus, Neil Leiper (1979) goes beyond the main distinction of a generating region which corresponds to the place of departure and return of a tourist stay; from the destination region that temporarily attracts tourists by attractions, he also observes transit routes with stopover points as well as extended routes in the form of a tourist route, such as the Scenic road created in 1913 in the United States of America [LEI 79].

As early as 1967, C. K. Campbell wanted to examine the modes of recreational travel that differentiated between day trips, trips to resorts, trips from a base with excursions, self-drive tours, rail and bus trips, and round trips by car [CAM 67]. In Great Britain, the precise analysis of tourist routes in the Highlands and Scottish Islands was conducted by M. R. Carter. It differentiated between two main connecting routes and some secondary routes [CAR 71]. On the island of Jersey, C. P. Cooper interviewed tourists about their first five days of vacation. He notes a hierarchy of places in the choice of visits, which he defines as "a wave of visits that spreads from top to bottom and decreases as the number of sites increases" [COO 81, p. 365]. Thus, high places or those known by tourists are practiced first before going to other places.

In another methodology, P. C. Forer and D. Pearce (1984) study the itineraries of tour operator brochure tours on New Zealand. This study shows a reticular approach of New Zealand and tourist regions by the presence of primary and secondary nodes according to the places proposed for the night by the coach operators. This highlights two main centers in New Zealand: Queenstown and Rotorva. Then, a regional scale of other nodes is added to these centers. The importance of nodes is defined by the number of nights and its connexion, i.e. the number of links with other nodes. Thus, the large cities of Christchurch and Auckland have only a few nights' accommodation but a strong connection due to the communication networks. In contrast, the small town of Te Anau has more overnight stays because it is a starting point for day trips to other places (including Milford Sound Fjord) [FOR 84]. This model of nodes was already developed by Peter Haggett (1965) and then taken up by Jay W. Vogt (1976) concerning gathering places on holiday routes and finally by Pryer (1997) who was interested in studying the practices of international tourists on the road [HAG 65, VOG 76, PRY 97]. Thor Flognfeldt Jr. used this work as a basis for studying tourist routes in Norway (see Box 4.1) [FLO 05].

Thor Flognfeldt Jr. distinguishes the places according to the distance traveled from a starting point, as well as according to the distance traveled from the tourist place used. It describes the route of a coach tour to visit the Maihaugen Open Air Museum in Lillehammer, Norway [FLO 05].

Evolution of the places covered according to the chronology of a day

– Site 1: wake-up and breakfast, transport.

– Site 2: visit to the museum, lunch at 1 pm and then shopping until 4 pm.

– Site 3: break, transport.

– Site 4: arrival at the new accommodation at 8 pm.

Possible locations of places on tourist routes

1) The place visited on the way from home to the place of stay.

2) The between home and the place of stay.

3) The place of excursion from a place of stay.

4) The resort being directly moved from home.

Box 4.1. *Study of tourist itineraries in Norway [FLO 05]*

In short, all this work makes it possible to characterize several types of tourist mobilities (see Figure 4.4) [PIR 09]. First of all, a *primary mobility*. This occurs when an individual or a group of individuals move from their place of residence to a first place of stay (even for a short period of time), allowing them to reach their tourist destination. Then, we can identify two types of *secondary mobility*, i.e. trips made as part of a tourist stay. *Diffusion* consists of making trips from an accommodation location to which a return will be ensured, without changing accommodation. Finally, the *continuation* corresponds to movements in which places, including at least two places of accommodation, follow one another, forming intermediate stages, sometimes in the form of a loop, i.e. with a return to the starting point. We will now report on the itineraries made by tourists, according to mobility, and represent our results schematically.

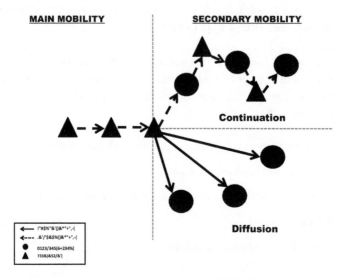

Figure 4.4. *Types of mobility carried out by tourists during their stays [PIR 09]*

4.3. Reading tourist mobilities to understand spatial practices with a regional dimension

In order to understand the tourist mobilities involved, we interviewed tourists within a tourist area of regional dimension: the Lake Geneva Region. In the fall of 2009, we conducted about 57 interviews with tourists in tourist destinations. We interviewed them in the form of a stay account and then produced schematic maps to report on the routes taken by tourists.

4.3.1. *A space laboratory: the Lake Geneva Region, a diversity of tourist places in a homogeneous lake landscape*

The Lake Geneva Region is the space that extends around Lake Geneva. Also known as Lake Geneva, this pocket of water formed by the Rhône River occupies a depression created by an overburden of an ancient glacier. The significant relief that surrounds it between the Jura to the northwest, the Mittelland plateau to the north and the Prealps du Chablais to the south gives this area a certain landscape homogeneity. This space, which we use as a study site for our research, is relevant because of the presence of various tourist places. There are tourist resorts (Evian-les-Bains, Divonne-les-Bains, etc.), cities with a tourist function (Geneva, Lausanne) and even touristified villages (Gruyères, Yvoire). The number of tourists is significant since the Swiss Vaud state recorded 2.5 million overnight stays, to which can be added 2.8 million Geneva overnight stays, and 3.4 million overnight stays on the neighboring French departments, for a total of 8.7 million overnight stays[2].

The shores of Lake Geneva are inhabited by tourists for both the landscape and the climate. Montreux, located on the eastern end of the lake, went from a group of villages consisting of a few boarding houses and small hotels to a real social resort between 1850 and 1905 (see Figure 4.5). The development was achieved by increasing the density of hotel establishments on different altitude levels, all accessible by cable car [BAR 87]. Montreux plays the card of the hotel resort of comfort and modernity to satisfy a wealthy and demanding clientele until the beginning of World War I [RIN 06]. The proximity of the resort, picturesque sites and villages has also helped to establish Montreux as a center for excursions. Finally, Montreux has also benefited from the rail connection with German-speaking Switzerland, an important factor in the development of tourism, with the creation of a line of national and international importance, the Montreux Oberland Bernois (MOB) Railway Company, whose construction began in 1893 and ended in 1902 [TIS 06]. Then, other places developed in order to treat patients for medical purposes such as Evian-les-Bains, Thonon-les-Bains and Divonne-les-Bains spas. These resorts have the advantage of benefiting not only from sports and cultural facilities similar to seaside resorts but also from the proximity of the lake, promoted as a climatic quality. Evian-les-Bains has experienced a real tourist development following the discovery of the Cachat spring in 1789 and the creation of a bathing establishment in 1826. The development of the resort was such that it spread a model of bourgeois resorts to small peripheral towns on the shores of the lake such as Maxilly, Publier and Neuvecelle [SCE 74]. Today, Évian-les-Bains is positioned as a top high-end resort, thanks in particular to the conservation of monuments and Belle Époque décor, such as the Royal hotel establishment and the casino [DUR 09].

2 Sources: Federal Statistical Office 2007, Geneva Cantonal Statistical Office and Savoie-Mont-Blanc Tourism Agency, 2007.

Figure 4.5. *View from Lake Geneva of Montreux (Switzerland)*
(source: J. Piriou, June 2009)

COMMENT ON FIGURE 4.5.– *Montreux is originally a group of about 20 hamlets which since the middle of the 19th Century have grouped together to become a city [RIN 06]. The city was put into tourism by the creation of large hotels in the middle of the last century, a long walk along the lake or a flowering of the shore of Lake Geneva. It is a microcosm whose social characteristics have been described by Jean-Pierre Gaudin (1993), including rich English Londoners fleeing the gray and foggy city in search of the sun [GAU 93]. Indeed, the climate is rather mild, the place is exposed to the south and one evokes the Lake Geneva adret. The vegetation is reminiscent of the Mediterranean Riviera (umbrella pines, cypresses, palm trees), hence the name "Riviera vaudoise" attributed to this bank of Lake Geneva on the shore of the canton of Vaud of the upper lake [GUE 12]. Tourism has also contributed to changing the places in Montreux as well as in different places located within the Lake Geneva Arc, allowing this area to become prosperous [HUM 14]. Two global industries are represented: the Société des Eaux Minérales d'Evian located in Amphion-Publier (France) or the Nestlé agri-food group located in Vevey (Switzerland).*

In addition, cities play an important role in the tourist situation of the Lake Geneva Region. Geneva has a strategic geographical position, not only for its views, as evidenced by the hotels that boast a view of Mont Blanc, but also by the communication routes offered to travelers. Indeed, this city is both a gateway to the Alps for tourists traveling by train and also a crossroads on a European route or excursions to Switzerland, France or Italy:

"From Paris, the choice depends on the destination in Switzerland: Basel and Geneva are generally the busiest border cities. While they are relatively well connected to the French network, they offer the possibility of quickly reaching privileged destinations: for example, Chamonix from Geneva" [TIS 00].

Geneva has been positioned since the 18th Century as a scientific and literary center, justifying the arrival of artists, scientists and the installation of clinics and schools. Then, during the 20th Century, the headquarters of international institutions such as the League of Nations or the United Nations Organization were established. Geneva also has an airport since 1920 [TIS 07]. The city of Lausanne, for its part, already enjoyed a high level of notoriety thanks to its educational establishments and health centers [HUM 07]. It therefore seized the opportunity of the development of the railway between 1855 and 1865 by connecting to an international rail network. Indeed, as early as 1864, Thomas Cook proposed Lausanne in all his offers for Switzerland [TIS 00].

Today, these cities concentrate the highest hotel capacity with a Geneva dominance with 14,738 beds in its canton, a figure to which we can add the 1,336 beds located in France on the border communes. While cross-border relations between France and Switzerland were still cautious in the 1970s, both for commuters and for tourism, studies carried out by researchers in the 2000s revealed a metropolis structured by a polycentric network based on three conurbations (Geneva, Lausanne and Vevey-Montreux) and small- and medium-sized cities (Thonon-Évian, Nyon and Morges) located in pericentral areas whose economic, social and cultural activities are linked to the three major conurbations [POS 01]. The polycentric metropolis formed around Lake Geneva is made up of nuclei that are characterized by their metropolitan functions such as the financial and geopolitical functions of Geneva, sports and medical functions of Lausanne, cultural functions of Martigny and Montreux, or scientific and leisure functions for the country of Gex [DUR 09].

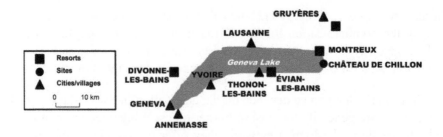

Figure 4.6. *Interviews with tourists around Lake Geneva (October–November 2009) [PIR 12]*

COMMENT ON FIGURE 4.6.– *In our selection, we have chosen different types of elementary places (resort, site, city, village). We interviewed a total of 57 tourists, 38 of whom were in Switzerland and 19 in France[3]. In France, we interviewed three tourists in Annemasse, three tourists in Divonne-les-Bains, three tourists in Yvoire, four in Thonon-les-Bains and six in Évian-les-Bains. In Switzerland, we interviewed five tourists at the entrance to the Château de Chillon, six tourists in Montreux, seven tourists in Lausanne, nine tourists in Geneva and we extended our study area to the Prealps by interviewing seven tourists in the city of Gruyères and finally four tourists in the small mountain resort of Moléson-sur-Gruyères.*

4.3.2. A methodology: spatialization of a life story and representation by schematic maps

In our space laboratory, we randomly met tourists at selected tourist places and interviewed them to provide us with an account of their stay (see Figure 4.6). The methodology of the life story allows us to better understand the complexity as well as to analyze the subjectivity of social phenomena. The life story is "a particular form of interview, the narrative interview, during which a researcher asks a person, hereinafter referred to as the subject, to tell them all or part of their lived experience" [BER 05, p. 11]. From a methodological point of view, this method constitutes a

---

3 During the doctoral work, we also conducted an additional interview with a tourist in Chamonix Mont-Blanc, but we chose not to include it in our analysis because of the small number of interviews conducted in this place.

comprehensive, narrative interview and highlights the representations of the lived experience. This approach can be found in the work on home–work mobility [HER 07, BER 17].

This exercise limits objectivity. Indeed, the story takes place with a given person, at a given time and in a given place. This gives a selection of the information collected.

Moreover, the reliability of the narrative cannot be verified, and the reading of spatial practices and choices made are only an overview. Hence, the need to have a common denominator of experience for individuals, by interviewing them in the same place, and by randomly selecting people to be interviewed. This choice is not elaborated by "standard profiles" but by the spatial practice of the same place. After identifying the people (status, age, origin and context of the stay), we sought to understand the travel choices as well as the relationship between geographical places made by tourists during their stay. Our only question was: "Could you tell us in chronological order what you did during your stay (places of visit, places of accommodation and others, etc.) and explain your choices?"

We were thus looking for a spatialized life story in order to realize a schematic map representation of this story by geometric codes related to spatial symbolism, circulars for places and features for mobility [LÉV 08]. These spatialized life stories allow us to better understand the spatial logics specific to the tourist stays of the tourists interviewed.

4.3.3. One observation: an insertion of places into networks of more or less important spatial dimension according to tourist mobilities

In addition to primary mobility between home and the place of stay, tourists also engage in secondary mobility. As mentioned above, we have identified two main ones: the diffusion mobility from a main accomodation, and the continuous mobility that is subject to a systematic change of accommodation during the trip. Stays can also be hybridized with a long process integrating several diffusion mobilities.

First, some places are practiced only by diffusion mobility, integrated into networks of places that are not very extensive, as is the case of Divonne-les-Bains and Moléson-sur-Gruyères. These two places are resorts where tourists stay, from which daytime mobility can be organized. In Moléson-sur-Gruyères, tourists will visit nearby places located in the Pre-Alps or on the Vaud Riviera, the eastern part of Lake Geneva (see Figure 4.7), as a French couple on holiday in the resort (survey no. 4):

"We stayed in Moléson on Monday and Tuesday, Wednesday we went to Gstaad (to see the chalets and luxury shops) and Château d'Œx, Thursday we went to Gruyères, and Friday we went to the shore of Lake Geneva in Montreux and Vevey. The tourist office recommended the magnificent view of the lake over the mountains".

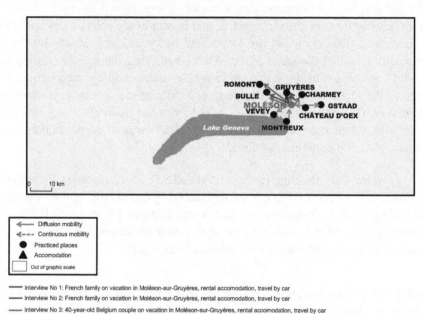

Figure 4.7. *A schematic map of the mobility of the tourists interviewed in Moléson-sur-Gruyères: (Switzerland) [PIR 12]*

COMMENT ON FIGURE 4.7.– *In Moléson-sur-Gruyères, half of the four tourists interviewed are families and couples. All stay in the resort and travel around the resort by car. We note that the distance per kilometer visited is rather small, being limited to places of the Gruyère (Bulle, Charmey, Gruyères) and by extension some places of the Pays d'en haut (Château d'Œx, Gstaad) and some places located on the shores of Lake Geneva (Vevey, Montreux).*

Second, other places are on the other hand practiced by continuous mobility and are part of very extensive networks (as far as Central and Eastern Switzerland). Lausanne is a city crossed mainly by secondary mobility in continuation (see Figure 4.8). This group of Germans is on a tour with Geneva as the arrival and departure point (interview no. 5):

> "We arrived in Geneva on Monday, we had a fondue in a restaurant in the center. On Tuesday, we visited the Geneva center with a guide and we visited CERN[4] in the afternoon with engineers, we had a conference on CERN projects, we were very interested. This morning, we went to the Swiss National Museum and had lunch in Lausanne in Ouchy. This afternoon we visited the Olympic Museum and tonight we have a theatre evening. Tomorrow, we will go to Lutry to discover the wine of Lavaux and then we will go to the castle of Chillon. We sleep in Villeneuve. On Friday, we will go to the Gianadda Foundation and Sion. Then we will return by bus to Geneva to return to Berlin".

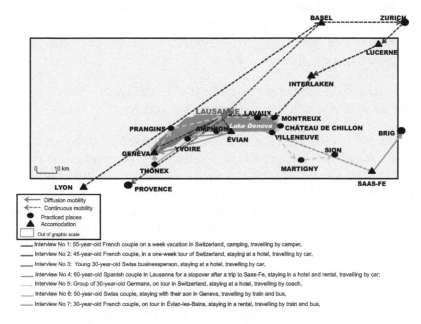

Interview No 1: 55-year-old French couple on a week vacation in Switzerland, camping, travelling by camper,
Interview No 2: 45-year-old French couple, in a one-week tour of Switzerland, staying at a hotel, travelling by car,
Interview No 3: Young 30-year-old Swiss businessperson, staying at a hotel, travelling by car,
Interview No 4: 60-year-old Spanish couple in Lausanne for a stopover after a trip to Saas-Fe, staying in a hotel and rental, travelling by car;
Interview No 5: Group of 30-year-old Germans, on tour in Switzerland, staying at a hotel, travelling by coach,
Interview No 6: 50-year-old Swiss couple, staying with their son in Geneva, travelling by train and bus,
Interview No 7: 30-year-old French couple, on tour in Évian-les-Bains, staying in a rental, travelling by train and bus,

Figure 4.8. *A schematic map of the mobility of the tourists interviewed in Lausanne: (Switzerland) [PIR 12]*

---

4 The European Organization for Nuclear Research.

COMMENT ON FIGURE 4.8.– *In Lausanne, the tourists interviewed have different profiles (couples, individuals, groups). Some are accommodated in Lausanne and others are in Lausanne on an excursion from a fixed place of stay or are in Lausanne as part of a longer itinerary. It should be noted that the distances traveled by the tourists interviewed in Lausanne are greater and the places mentioned are national (Basel, Zurich) and European (Lyon, Provence).*

It should be noted that, according to our interviews, Lausanne is also part of a few networks of places in terms of diffusion mobility. Indeed, the Swiss city benefits from a good boat connection from Evian-les-Bains on the French shore (see Figure 4.8). Excursions are possible to Lausanne as specified by this couple staying in Evian-les-Bains (interview no. 7):

> "We arrived Saturday afternoon, we didn't move until Monday. Monday, we went for a walk in the afternoon in Yvoire. In fact, we asked the Evian tourist office what we could do by using public transport as we came to Evian by train. On Tuesday, we visited the Evian bottling plant. Today we are in Lausanne. Tomorrow, we may go for a walk in Evian by the lake. On Friday, we have planned an excursion to Geneva and on Saturday we will return to Paris".

Lausanne would therefore be a stopover in the various tourist routes to France, as well as to northern and eastern Switzerland.

Third, we have observed places that are traversed by diffusion mobility and continuous mobility and that are part of very geographically extensive networks. The village of Gruyères in Switzerland is in this configuration (see Figure 4.9). The village is part of networks that integrate various European tourist places, as evidenced by the route taken by this French couple who travel by camper van and enjoy a trip to Gruyères on their way between Rougemont in the Pays d'en haut and Neuchâtel (interview no. 1):

> "We crossed through the Auvergne. We slept near Puy de Sancy and then we went along Lake Geneva. We slept at the border and passed through Aigle, the Col des Mosses, Château d'Œx and Gstaad. We spent a night in Rougemont and here we are in Gruyères. Afterwards, we will go to Neuchâtel and finish in the Jura before returning to the Basque Country".

But there are also other tourists who come to Gruyères by day as part of an excursion; such is the case of this German couple, staying in Murten, whom we met in the village (interview no. 5):

"We stayed a lot around Murten, but on Tuesday we went to Neuchâtel and today Gruyères. If the weather is bad tomorrow, maybe we'll go to Bern to visit the Swiss capital, we know the symbol of the bear, but that's all".

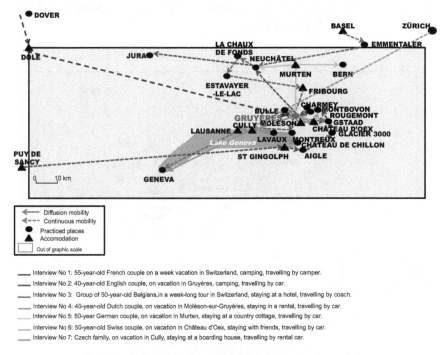

_____ Interview No 1: 55-year-old French couple on a week vacation in Switzerland, camping, travelling by camper.
_____ Interview No 2: 40-year-old English couple, on vacation in Gruyères, camping, travelling by car.
_____ Interview No 3: Group of 50-year-old Belgians, in a week-long tour in Switzerland, staying at a hotel, travelling by coach.
_____ Interview No 4: 40-year-old Dutch couple, on vacation in Moléson-sur-Gruyères, staying in a rental, travelling by car.
_____ Interview No 5: 50-year German couple, on vacation in Murten, staying at a country cottage, travelling by car.
_____ Interview No 6: 50-year-old Swiss couple, on vacation in Château d'Oex, staying with friends, travelling by car.
_____ Interview No 7: Czech family, on vacation in Cully, staying at a boarding house, travelling by rental car.

Figure 4.9. A schematic map of the mobility of the tourists
interviewed in Gruyères: (Switzerland) [PIR 12]

COMMENT ON FIGURE 4.9.– _In Gruyères, the profiles of the tourists interviewed are varied (couples, groups, families). There are two major elements. On the one hand, some tourists travel within a short distance (this is the case of respondents no. 4, a Dutch couple staying in Moléson-sur-Gruyères and visiting places in Gruyère); on the other hand, other tourists travel a greater distance (this is the case of respondents no. 7, a Czech family staying in Cully between Lausanne and Vevey, who travel as far as Geneva or Zurich)._

Fourth, we note places that are also practiced by the two forms of secondary mobility, i.e. in diffusion mobility and in continuous mobility, but diffusion mobility tends to dominate, reducing the geographical extent of the network of places. Evian-les-Bains is mainly among the interviewees, a place of stay (for four of the tourists interviewed out of six). Among the mobility of tourists staying in Evian-les-Bains, we note that the movements are mainly towards the shores of the lake (Yvoire, Amphion-les-Bains, Aquapark) as well as in the Chablais massif (Abondance, Boëge) or further south to Annecy (see Figure 4.10).

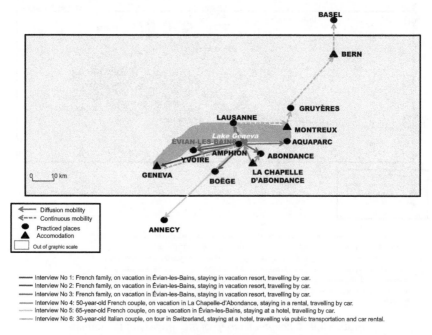

Figure 4.10. *A schematic map of tourist mobility interviewed at Évian-les-Bains: (France) [PIR 12]*

COMMENT ON FIGURE 4.10.– *In Évian-les-Bains, four out of six tourists interviewed are accommodated in the spa resort. This situation explains the diffusion mobility from Evian-les-Bains with a short distance traveled. It should also be noted that Évian-les-Bains can be the subject of an excursion from another place of stay (La Chapelle-d'Abondance in the case of respondents no. 4) or a stopover during a more important tour (in the case of respondents no. 5).*

In this case, the mobility used is the diffusion (for five interviews out of six) as evidenced by the story of this French couple, on family holidays in Evian-les-Bains:

> "Yesterday morning, we went to Yvoire to walk with the children and today we went mountain biking between here and Abondance. Tomorrow, we will spend the day in Lausanne, we will take the boat. And on weekends, if the children are good, we will go to the water park in Switzerland, you know... at the Aquapark".

4.4. Conclusion

Through their travels, the tourist builds, according to choices that reflect a recreation project, a network of tourist places. We have also observed differentiated tourist mobilities between a primary mobility from home to tourist destination and a secondary mobility in terms of diffusion or continuation within the destination. In some cases, the spatial dimension can be very important, even on a continental scale, as part of organized tours that cover tourist places throughout Europe in a week. In other cases, the spatial dimension of the network of tourist places will be smaller, particularly in the context of excursions to places around a place of stay limited to a single day. In our opinion, the change of accommodation is carried out only through mobility along the way. Staying in the same place and taking part in day trips reflects diffusion mobility. Also, some places are characterized by dominant spatial practices, or even fit into networks of tourist places with a more or less large regional spatial dimension.

5

Investors and their Structuring of Regional Tourist Territories

To create tourist places, tourists have either visited existing places or promoted the creation of *ex nihilo* sites. However, it was only possible to set up tourism thanks to the support of several actors who invested in the territories. Investment consists of the mobilization of capital by an actor in a business in order to increase the means of production. The top-down strategy corresponds to an intervention, by a major actor, within a given territory. This actor is at the same time accelerator, catalyst and pillar of this strategy. This may be a developer building a resort, a company installing accommodation or leisure facilities, or the government that structures and provides a framework for tourism orientation within the territories. We will see how investment (whether from a public or a private actor) is made in specific types of basic places (mainly closed complexes and resorts). We will also analyze that the investment goes beyond the scale of the place and benefits a territory in a regional dimension.

5.1. The private investor and their creation of regional tourism territories

5.1.1. *From the creation of equipment to the multiplication of tourist places*

A regional deployment of tourism can be observed as soon as tourist places are created with the resorts as their nuclei, initially put into tourism from the middle of the 19th Century. As a result of these creations, entrepreneurs have contributed to the creation of various facilities to accommodate tourists, sometimes of major tourist intensity, making it possible to coordinate the tourist operation of a regional group of places.

On the French coast, the company Barrière has contributed to the development of resorts and, by extension, coasts for tourism. In Normandy on the Côte Fleurie, two resorts will be equipped thanks to investors who will enable Deauville-Trouville to expand its influence. Eugène Cornuché, director of the Trouville casino, became director of the Deauville casino, which was built in 1912 and completed with a hotel (the Normandy).

Following him, François André took over the management of the Deauville hotels and casino company [HÉB 05]. He created the Lucien Barrière group. In 1927, the Hôtel du Golf was built and then an adjoining golf course was built in the town of Saint-Arnoult, bordering Deauville. Then, it was his nephew, Lucien Barrière, who developed new equipment with the help of the then mayor Michel d'Ornano, including an Olympic swimming pool, a congress center, horse races and a film festival. In 1931, the mayor created an airport in the neighboring town of Saint-Gatien-des-Bois on a land parcel belonging to Deauville [ROL 04]. Later, in 1957, the Barrière group acquired the Trouville casino. Also, on the Côte Fleurie, more particularly around the Deauville-Trouville core, the Barrière entrepreneur has contributed to the development of facilities that have structured a tourist region. At the same time on the Atlantic coast, François André invested in La Baule [VIO 02]. He first bought the casino and the Royal Hotel, which existed in 1923. The price of the land was low, and he undertook the construction of two new palaces and sports facilities, the Hermitage and Castel Marie-Louise, 200 meters apart. Later, Lucien Barrière obtained from the municipality the exclusivity of pedestrian practices in front of his establishments on the waterfront, allowing privileged access to the beach. Lucien Barrière then created new facilities "in the countryside", on the outskirts of La Baule in the commune of Saint-André-des-Eaux. A golf course was built in 1976, then the hotel company of the Lucien Barrière chain built a hotel and a set of villas in the mid-1990s.

Today, the Barrière group remains a major player in tourism, on the one hand, because it employs between 600 and 800 people all year round and, on the other hand, since the municipal council of La Baule-Escoublac unanimously voted at its meeting on September 22, 2017 to delegate a public service to the Barrière group to manage the casino over a 12-year period, bringing in over one million euros per year to the municipality.

Figure 5.1. *Esplanade of the Deauville International Center (France) in front of the Normandy Hotel (left) and the casino (right) (source: J. Piriou, June 2005). For a color version of this figure, see www.iste.co.uk/piriou/tourism.zip*

COMMENT ON FIGURE 5.1.– *The casino and Hotel Normandy are both located on Eugène Cornuché Boulevard, the name of the famous entrepreneur who was the casino's director. These two establishments are also separated from each other by rue Lucien Barrière, the name of the famous contractor who developed many facilities in the Deauville resort. Tourism boosted the creation of Deauville in 1860 by the Duke of Morny who had perceived the interest in sea bathing as well as business and congress activities [AUG 15]. Deauville is a real estate project that was built on dry marshes and whose architectural ambition at the time made it possible to classify 550 buildings since 2005 under a heritage conservation plan[1] [FAB 15]. Today, the city is seeking to deseasonalize tourism activity, in particular by developing event activities, requiring overall management, as Philippe Augier, Mayor of Deauville, points out: "As you can see, a city*

---

1 Classification under the Urban, Architectural and Landscape Heritage Protection Zone, which has become an area for the enhancement of architecture and heritage since 2010.

where the tourist economy represents 90% of the activity must be managed as a business" [AUG 15, p. 340].

The creation of a place *ex nihilo* also reveals an investment that goes beyond the tourist place. For the past 50 years, Center Parcs has been creating resort complexes with a theme focused on nature and leisure. The establishment of the first Center Parcs in France, in Normandy in 1988, gave a rural area the opportunity to benefit from a large number of overnight stays (about one million per year), with particular attention to the nearby Paris region. This territory would not have benefited from such an attendance if the company had not set up shop there. Indeed, the tourist concentration in Normandy is mainly located on the coast. In 1993, a second Center Parcs was opened on the outskirts of Paris, in Sologne. The geographical situation is characterized by its immediate proximity to the castles of the Loire Valley. Moreover, the tourist offer of the surroundings constitutes an argument for promoting the Center Parcs located in Sologne as evidenced by its website since, on the one hand, it uses a photograph of the Château de Chambord as a welcome band, and, on the other hand, one finds in the section "to see, to do in the surroundings of the park"[2], several places referenced within a radius of less than 50 kilometers (31 miles): the Château de la Ferté Saint-Aubin (11 km, 6.8 mi), the Château de Cheverny (36 km, 22 mi), the Château du moulin Conservatoire de la Fraise (37 km, 23 mi), the Royal Château de Blois (45 km, 28 mi) and the Beauval Zoo (68 km, 42 mi). This regional dynamic is therefore attracting the interest of many territories that are seeking to take advantage of the driving effect of such equipment to develop tourism in a vast area. More recently, in 2015, the Pierre & Vacances group, owner of the "Center Parcs" brand, was convinced of the political arguments of the actors in the Vienne department to build a fifth resort in the northwest of the department in the Loudunais in 2015. One year after the opening, the general manager of this Center Parcs insists on the ideal geographical situation, bordering other territories with high tourist intensity, such as the Loire Valley, Futuroscope, the Atlantic coast, sought after by customers, "the enormous work that has been carried out for more than thirty years in the Vienne, with emblematic figures like Futuroscope that our customers want to find and find again when they arrive here [...] We become a complementary actor to their holidays. It's like an itinerary that

2 Available at this website: https://www.centerparcs.fr/fr-fr/france/fp_CH_vacances-domaine-les-hauts-de-bruyeres/guide, accessed June 1, 2018.

is organized around us"[3]. Partnerships are in place, as can be seen on the Center Parcs website under the heading "What to see, what to do around the park"[4], which lists the Futuroscope, the Bioparc zoo of Doué-la-Fontaine, or the abbey of Fontevraud, both located in the neighboring department of Maine-et-Loire and belonging more to the destination of the "châteaux de la Loire".

5.1.2. *Organization of a regional tourism offer*

Some private investors create tourist places that immediately constitute a tourist offer with a regional dimension. Thus, at the beginning of the last century, railway companies offered a cascade offer combining train travel, transit to a station and accommodation in a hotel, all to a promoted destination. This was the case towards the mountains, in Savoy with the service provided by the *Compagnie des chemins de fer Paris–Lyon–Marseille* (PLM) to an important tourist center including the city of Aix-les-Bains and Mount Revard, which dominates it within the Bauges massif. During the 19th Century, Aix-les-Bains was a flourishing spa resort, particularly following the annexation of Savoy in France in 1860 and thanks to the development of various activities complementary to the spa, such as climate walks or boat trips on Lake Bourget [BEL 14]. In 1890, Dr. Jean Monard, a member of the Aix medical society and also of the French Alpine Club, launched a concept of an "Aix-Revard climate valley" including the shores of the lake, the center of Aix, the Revard balconies and Mont Revard. To access Mount Revard, a rack railway linked the city center of Aix, a chalet-restaurant and then chalet hotels between 1892 and 1894. But in 1923, the *Paris–Lyon–Méditerranée* company bought the entire estate through a subsidiary of the Revard company and further developed winter sports at the beginning of the 20th Century with the creation of ski lifts, including a cable car in 1932 [FOU 04]. It is becoming a major player in tourism and controls the various tourist offers. The Grand Hotel PLM will be part of the work of a campaign carried out in 1924 and 1925. By promoting through advertising posters in resorts, on Aix and Mont Revard, the

---

3 Excerpt from the Bruyère Philippe regional daily press article, (2016), "Center Parcs : pari gagné pour son premier anniversaire" *La Nouvelle République*, available at: https://www.lanouvellerepublique.fr/actu/center-parcs-pari-gagne-pour-son-premier-anniversaire, online on 25 July, 2016, accessed April 1, 2018.
4 Available at the website: https://www.centerparcs.fr/fr-fr/france/fp_BD_vacances-domaine-le-bois-aux-daims/guide, accessed June 1, 2018.

Paris–Lyon–Marseille company is affirming a regional tourism center that condenses the various possibilities of tourist practices in the mountains (rest, sport, comfort).

More recently, the arrival of the Disney company in 1987 in the Seine-et-Marne department, in the countryside east of Paris (an area without initial tourist activity) was a real success from the first years of operation[5]. Today, the Euro Disney SCA subsidiary is a major player in the region. In addition to the initial park, it operates another Walt Disney Studios park, a Villages Nature park in partnership with the Pierre & Vacances group, as well as six hotels, a ranch, "Disney Village", a commercial entertainment and entertainment space, and a conference center and golf course, creating approximately 14,000 permanent jobs [FAB 13]. The complex covers 22.30 square kilometers in the municipalities of Bailly-Romainvilliers, Chessy, Coupvray, Magny-le-Hongre, Montévrain and Serris. Through an agreement with public authorities, including the government, Disney participates in the development and urbanization of the Val d'Europe, the eastern part of the new urban area of Marne-la-Vallée. Housing, shopping centers and cultural facilities have been created thanks to the presence of the American company. The government has also provided connections with the main modes of transport (TGV station accessible from Roissy International Airport, regional express train station accessible from Paris, motorway interchange). Public and private stakeholders gathered around the major player "Disney" within a tourism cluster in the Val d'Europe.

5.2. The public investor and its regional spatial planning through tourism

5.2.1. Government investment for tourism diffusion

The role of the government is preponderant in the diffusion of tourism, which is also in the linking of places through tourism. In France, in the heart of the Ardèche gorges, the construction of a road in 1887 along the Ardèche river gave access on foot to a site previously admired by an elite population, the Pont d'Arc [DUV 06]. Faced with the influx of vehicles in the 1950s, a tourist road was built in 1969 to secure traffic conditions along the gorges. It

---

5 According to the figures in the history of key financial data for the financial years 1993–2014 provided by Euro Disney SCA: 8.9 million visitors in 1993 and between 12 and 13 million from 1997 to 2001.

was also connected to other transversal axes connecting villages located on the plateaus. This route is supposed to capture tourist flows from the Rhone Valley to cover a tourism route along the Ardèche gorges, dotted with various caves, whose flows are concentrated between the Pont d'Arc and the town of Vallon. Recently, the discovery of the Chauvet cave has strengthened a pre-existing regional tourism organization, but focusing along the established road axis:

"…by opening just opposite the Pont d'Arc, [the Chauvet cave] reinforces the tendency to hyper-concentration of tourist traffic at an already very popular point and risks going against all efforts to spread tourist flows to the surrounding plateaus or to the 'hinterland' of the gorges" [GAU 09, p. 90].

Figure 5.2. *Bridge of the Arc in the gorges of the Ardèche (France) (source: J. Piriou, June 2009)*

COMMENT ON FIGURE 5.2.– *The Ardèche gorges are a destination of both tourist and sporting recreational practices. Since the beginning of the 20th Century, people taking the waters in Vals-les-Bains spa have been coming to see the gorges of the Ardèche, and more particularly the Pont de l'Arc, in particular by a boat trip down the gorges [DUV 06]. Tourists also stroll and drive along the roads along the gorges, enjoying panoramic views (especially of the Pont de l'Arc) but they also practice various outdoor activities in the gorges [DAU 86]. The activity of canoeing to descend the gorges is particularly popular and is the subject of an ancient commercial activity. But there are also caving activities [MAO 05]. It is estimated that one million visitors a year visit the gorges of the Ardèche, including about 20,000 visitors who canoe and kayak from the village of Vallon Pont d'Arc [BAC 95].*

In China, the government is acting to control the country's image and has been able to identify places of interest for tourists, an action reinforced in particular by the monopoly of government travel agencies or by public intervention in investments in tourist infrastructure. Along the Li River, two cities, Guilin and Yangshuo, are tourist destinations, thanks in particular to the landscape readings they offer of karst mountains, commonly known as "sugar loaves" that are reflected in the river. Politicians, artists and writers have promoted these two places [LEI 08]. In 1973, Guilin and Yangshuo were among the first places to be reopened to foreign tourists, and the Li River was one of the first places considered as *mingsheng*, defining exceptional places in 1982. The public stakeholders have chosen to strengthen Guilin's role within this regionally important tourist area, in particular by widening roads and renovating bridges, as well as by creating new projects (in particular the "two rivers and four lakes" project, which consists of linking two rivers and four lakes surrounding the center of the city of Guilin) [TAU 08].

Figure 5.3. *Cruise on the Li River between Guilin and Yangshuo (China) (source: J. Piriou, November 2013)*

COMMENT ON FIGURE 5.3.– The cruise on the Li River from Zhujiang, about 30 kilometers (18 miles) from Guilin to Yanghuo, is an important tourist excursion lasting about 4 hours. On the way, the landscapes of hills and "sugar loaves" that karst reliefs constitute have inspired many Chinese artists. Moreover, the 20-yuan banknote shows an engraving of one of these landscapes. Tourists do not fail to take pictures of the image that corresponds to what they seem to perceive on the 20-yuan banknote. At the end of the cruise, 1.75 million tourists cross the village of Yanghuo on foot and then return to Guilin by coach with stops at picturesque sites [LEI 08]. An estimated 1.75 million tourists disembark in Yangshuo following the cruise on the Li River [LEI 08]. The village of Yangshuo is the tourist center on the outskirts of the city of Guilin. The infrastructure has been modernized, with the rebuilt buildings giving way to multiple shops. Chinese actors are investing in the construction of hotels and residences in the countryside that benefit other villages within a 20-kilometer radius (12 miles) around Yangshuo, making the village a center of a secondary tourist periphery [TAU 12].

5.2.2. Tourism planning in a regional dimension by public institutions

Regional tourism planning has several objectives: to improve the spatial structure of a well-defined area, stimulate the regional economy and employment, develop infrastructure to improve water and electricity supply, and create a transport system to make the area accessible and fluid for visitors [WIL 98]. However, these regional tourism development plans have environmental concerns, whether in controlling urbanization or regulating visitor flows through traffic systems. In several countries such as Spain, Bulgaria and Romania, as well as France, the government is planning new tourist regions [WIL 98]. On coasts and mountain ranges, regional areas made up of tourist resorts appeared in the 1960s and 1970s.

As early as 1963, in France, the Interministerial Mission for the Development of the Languedoc-Roussillon Coastal Region (MIATL) under the direction of Jean Racine developed an urban plan of regional interest approved by decree in 1964. The French Government has acquired a land reserve of 1,200 hectares through its *Fonds national d'aménagement foncier urbain* (FNAFU) at the location of future resorts. But the purchase of an additional 3,000 hectares, or about 700 hectares per resort, will be necessary.

Then, by declaration of public utility, the French Government created deferred development zones around the acquired land (i.e. approximately 25,000 hectares), also exercising its right of pre-emption [CAZ 72]. Under the authority and financed by the inter-ministerial mission, an inter-departmental agreement for the control of mosquitoes along the coast was made in 1958 (chaired by the Hérault General Council), and stagnant water, certain reforested plots of land and water purification, water and electricity networks were installed. Major equipment works were undertaken, in particular through the creation of road linking expressways and secondary roads allowing access to future resorts. The Regional Interest Urban Plan provided for six tourist units (TUs), but the one at the mouth of the Aude at the level of the municipality of Fleury will be abandoned [SAG 01]. The five TUs are on an axis linking the cities of Montpellier and Perpignan from north to south:

– TU of Grande-Motte integrating the existing communes of Grau-du-Roi, Carnon and Palavas, allowing the creation of La Grande-Motte resort and the port of Port-Camargue with a total capacity of 63,000 beds;

– TU of the Thau basin integrating the existing municipalities of Agde (Grau district), Balaruc-les-Bains and Marseillan, allowing the creation of the Cap d'Adge resort with a capacity of 52,000 beds;

– TU of Gruissan integrating the existing municipalities of Saint-Pierre-sur-Mer, Narbonne and Gruissan, allowing the development of the Gruissan resort with a capacity of 42,000 beds;

– TU of Port-Leucate and Port-Barcarès integrating the municipality of Leucate (including the district of La Franqui) and Le Barcarès for the creation of the ports and resorts of Port-Leucate and Port-Barcarès with a capacity of 82,000 beds;

– TU of Saint-Cyprien integrating the municipalities of Sainte-Marie-de-la-Mer, Canet-en-Roussillon, Saint-Cyprien and Argelès-sur-Mer and increasing the existing capacity by 24,000 additional beds.

However, despite a regional layout with a global plan, the resorts have differentiated themselves, in particular because of the allocation of the construction of each of these TUs to different architects: for example, Jean Le Couteur for the Cap d'Adge and Jean Balladur for La Grande-Motte. La Grande-Motte is certainly the most emblematic resort; it embodies truncated pyramids seen by the architect in Teotihuacan near Mexico City, which best embodies the landscape rather than the parallelepiped towers or buildings fashionable in the 1960s [BAL 94]. The regional development project is intended to be organized and reconciling natural areas and beach life under government control rather than anarchic private development: "It was a disorderly and continuous occupation of a Mediterranean coastline of France, still untouched, following the example of what was observed on the Côte d'Azur, on the Italian, Greek, and Spanish coasts. It was also necessary to preserve the outstanding natural and historical sites and to establish large areas between the areas dedicated to the reception of vacationers of large cuts left to the state of nature" [BAL 94, p. 20–21]. A total of 12 billion francs (1,829 billion euros) have been invested, two-thirds of which comes from private investors [VLE 96]. Work began in February 1965 with the creation of La Grande-Motte, dredged millions of cubic meters of displaced sand and mud, and the addition of soil to create the port in July 1967. The government that financed the major infrastructure works sold the land to semi-public companies in charge of equipping the resorts and finding developers.

At the same time, in the mountains of the French Alps, the control of public institutions, this time at the departmental level, to limit private speculation will constitute a reason for public investment. An excerpt from the Sibue report of the meeting of November 26, 1945, of the 3rd Commission of the General Council of Savoie summarizes the context and the willingness to invest in a project with a regional dimension: "The aim we propose is to put an end to such a situation and to cut short all speculation. To this end, we propose that the department fully develop an entire region, not only by carrying out road works, but also by taking possession of land that could constitute residential areas, build ski-lifts or cable cars, establish trails; in short, develop a winter sports resort that will provide our community with income opportunities and increase its heritage" [KNA 78, p. 21]. Some resort successes exist, such as Val d'Isère, which integrates winter sports facilities into a traditional village. But on a design of the Savoie department, the resort of Courchevel was born in the town of Saint-Bon on May 3, 1946. The idea is to design a global development of a complex in a greenfield site for which the department has developed the new resort model as well as the tools and means to be implemented [MAR 12]. This will be a new concept with public funds and will be a model for the development of other resorts. In 1961, the *Société de gestion des équipements de la vallée de Belleville* (SOGEVAB) was created to seek financing other than that of the department in order to reproduce the "Courchevel" model. It was supported by the *Caisse des dépôts et consignations* in 1959 [MAR 12]. As part of its fourth development plan, the Inter-ministerial Commission for Mountain Development was created in 1964, which developed a model for tourism development in the mountains, often referred to as the "Snow Plan", although it does not have the same dimension as that of the Languedoc coast. Indeed, the government wanted the mountain development policy to be a means of combating the desertification of mountain territories. Also, with Courchevel, the Savoie department demonstrated a real legitimacy, particularly in the accumulation of know-how and the creation of an innovative environment around the Tarentaise valley. But the land issue is now a tripartite one between the government, the municipality and private actors within the framework of a 1958 ordinance that allows municipalities to request expropriation for public utility purposes for projects granted to a private actor. Also, developer-designers will create integrated "third generation" resorts, some of which are located on the Vanoise massif. In the territory of the Société des Trois Vallées ski area, in addition to Courchevel (which has existed since 1946), the villages of Méribel (Les Menuires with 26,000 beds built in 1964 and Val Thorens with 20,000 beds built in 1971) were created. A significant concentration of resorts is located on the Vanoise massif following the regional development policy developed in the 1960s and 1970s. From west to east, you can locate the ski areas separated by about 30 kilometers, each grouping together the resorts with the highest accommodation capacity in the French Alps: Les Trois Vallées (Méribel, Courchevel, Les Menuires, Val Thorens, La Tania, etc.), Paradiski (Les Arcs and La Plagne) and l'Espace Killy (Tignes, Val d'Isère). The 6th Development Plan (1971–1975) intensified the government's effort but abandoned the resort's design as it had been previously deployed. An increasing environmental sensitivity led the President of the Republic to commit himself to the protection and development of the mountains according to precise urban planning rules defined by the procedure of new TUs adopted by decree. Also, the project of 350,000 beds to be built was reduced to 150,000 beds. It is in this context that Val-Thorens was born, but above all Valmorel was perceived as a correction of errors, allowing the role of local actors and the resort's place in spatial planning to be replaced [MAR 12].

5.2.3. *Intervention of public actors in the creation of tourist places for regional diffusion of tourism*

Tourism is a means for public actors to diversify the economic activity of a territory and to maintain local populations. Also, all (or almost all) means are good to create the tourist place that would "save" a territory in loss. A model of creation above ground has been a real success in the Poitou countryside near the city of Poitiers (France), in the Vienne department: the creation of the Futuroscope. Who would have imagined a theme park on image and sound technologies in an agricultural territory dotted with architectural monuments of Romanesque art? It was the idea of René Monory, originally mayor of Loudun since 1959, who, through his political career, took on many local and national functions. Elected General Councillor of the Vienne Department in 1961, he became its President in 1977 and was then appointed by the President of the Republic Valéry Giscard d'Estaing, Minister of Trade and Crafts Industry in 1977, the then Minister of Economy in 1978 and became Minister of Social Education under the presidency of François Mitterrand during the cohabitation with Jacques Chirac as Prime Minister in 1986. Also, despite his many hats, the professional car mechanic imagined a big project for his department. In a rural department whose tourist numbers are in the shadow of a concentration on the Charente-Maritime coastline and the rural tourist parks of the Marais poitevin in the Deux-Sèvres or the banks of the Charente river, the General Council of Vienne decided in 1983, under the presidency of René Monory, to create a major economic and tourist center: the Futuroscope park which will open its doors in 1987 (see Figure 5.4). In fact, a whole development strategy is planned and managed by the department. The investment program is worth approximately one billion French francs (more than 264,534,071 euros), for which the department has financed 600 million French francs (more than 158,720,442 euros), with participants from the region contributing 100 million francs [CAZ 88]. The Vienne General Council is the prime contractor, but the management is entrusted to a semi-public company under the majority control of the General Council (70%), with the remaining 30% being private actors in the energy and hotel sectors. The project is colossal and risky, but faced with the influx of visitors; the Futuroscope is becoming a tertiary and tourist center [DEH 98]. The 250-hectare site located between the national road and the highway was completed with tertiary activities (training organizations, service companies).

Figure 5.4. *Futuroscope park (near to Poitiers, France) (source: J. Piriou, June 2018)*

COMMENT ON FIGURE 5.4.– *The Futuroscope is a successful ex nihilo creation of a tourist site. This theme park, designed against the backdrop of local identity, rural landscapes and Romanesque art and dedicated to new image and sound technologies, receives more than one million visitors per year [VIO 08]. The initiator René Monory has given a boost to the national and international reputation of the park, but the Vienne department is struggling to spread the flow of visitors to other tourist places.*

However, tourist interest prevails. The desire behind this project is to capture tourist flows by this hub and then redistribute flows throughout the department. There is a challenge in creating a regional tourism area. The department council funding to support structuring tourist facilities in the department that would act as a relay for the Futuroscope cluster. In 1998, the Vallée des Singes park was created in Romagne south of Poitiers (about 60 kilometers (37.28 miles) south of the Futuroscope, almost an hour's drive), with public funding from the General Council and the community of municipalities to the tune of 6 million euros for the arrival of primates. In August 2008, crocodiles from all continents arrived in Civaux in the south of Vienne, a town that saw the commissioning of a nuclear power plant in 1997. Inspired by the model of another similar park in the Rhône Valley, Planète des Crocodiles cost €8.5 million and was financed to the tune of €900,000 by the Vienne General Council, €750,000 by the *Fonds national d'aménagement et de développement du territoire* and also by the municipality through the business tax it receives from the presence of the *company Électricité de France* (EDF) via the nuclear power plant. However, the attendance figures for these peripheral leisure parks differ significantly from those of the Futuroscope cluster. According to the latest available figures from the Poitou-Charentes Tourism Observatory, in 2014, when the Futuroscope welcomed 1,650,000 visitors, La Vallée des Singes received only 12% of its attendance, or 201,000 visitors, while the La Planète des Crocodiles received only 3% of the Futuroscope's attendance with 50,000 visitors. The other facilities receiving the most visitors in Vienne are the aquatic centers of Poitiers and Civaux with 152,800 and 141,000 visitors, respectively. In the end, there is no regional tourism area that includes facilities that have been invested by public actors. It would seem that the Futuroscope site is limited to a passing tourism linking a Futuroscope-Atlantic coastal axis [DEH 98]. This does not prevent many public actors from setting up their projects with a regional tourist "vocation", a term that Philippe Violier disputes and indicates that it is an abuse of language to evoke a function of place since the function is socially constructed (the opposite of a vocation decreed by heaven) [VIO 07]. Examples include the Vulcania park near Clermont-Ferrand (France), 85% funded by the Auvergne Regional Council for a total cost of 123 million euros, and the Terra Botanica park created near Angers (France), which will cost the Maine-et-Loire department 75.2 million euros for a total of 115 million euros.

Another scenario of regional structuring of tourism by public actors is emerging through the creation of linear axes. The idea is to link tourist places by a structuring axis in order to bring them out of a regional tourism space. This is the case for developed tourist routes. As we have seen in the case of the Ardèche Gorges, public actors can intervene after the presence of tourism in order to secure access to tourist places of intense frequentation, but nowadays, many public actors are trying to capture the flows of important routes to spread tourism in regional areas that are the subject of public development policies. In France the Loire à Vélo (Loire by bike) itinerary is a project born in 1995 by the commissioning of a study on the development of the banks of the Loire for cycle tourism practices, at the initiative of the *Centre* and *Pays de la Loire* regional councils [COU 15]. A €52 million investment has been made to develop infrastructure, signage and security. The regional councils (*Centre* and *Pays de la Loire*) finance 60% by agreement with the contracting authorities, who finance the remaining 40%, namely the six urban and urban community councils (Angers, Blois,

Nantes, Orléans, Saumur and Tours) or the six departmental councils (Cher, Loiret, Loir-et-Cher, Indre-et-Loire, Maine-et-Loire and Loire-Atlantique), studies and signage (see Figure 5.5), monitoring and maintenance, security services, information, and tourism development, the deployment of the quality charter and assistance with advice and expertise. A section links the two regions between Angers and Tours in 2012 with a total route of 670 kilometers put into service out of the 800 kilometers (416 miles) planned. According to a study carried out in 2010 for the regional tourism council of *Centre-Val de Loire* and for the *Pays de la Loire* regional public company and co-financed by the Regional Directorates of Enterprise, Competition, Consumption, Labor and Employment of the two regions, we know that an estimated 736,000 cyclists use the Loire by bicycle per year, but the vast majority come from the regions concerned by the development (45% from the *Pays de la Loire* region and 36% from the *Centre-Val-de-Loire* region).

Figure 5.5. *Tourist information road sign on the Loire by bike (source: J. Piriou, July 2018)*

COMMENT ON FIGURE 5.5.– *La Loire à Vélo, initiated in 1996 with the signing of a general protocol for interregional cooperation between the Pays de la Loire and Centre regional councils, will open a first section in the*

Chalonnes-sur-Loire sector from 2001. This cycle route project was an opportunity for the two regions to collaborate in the field of tourism, while cooperation already existed in other sectors (agriculture, transport, etc.) [COU 15]. On their routes, cyclists find developed or semi-developed trails, signage as well as shops and services adapted to their practices (accommodation, restaurants with bicycle shelters, parking facilities at tourist places, etc.). The success of the Loire à Vélo goes beyond the simple interest of developing the bicycle sector, since this project has "made it possible to bring together the actors, beyond the administrative limits, in favor of a new tourist sector, which is a challenge given the complexity of the French 'administrative and territorial millefeuille'" [COU 15, p. 37].

A quantitative survey conducted on 16 survey points along the route reveals that only 24% of cyclists use it for tourist itineraries and 54% for leisure activities; the average distance covered being 43 kilometers (26.7 miles). A limited practice per portion is confirmed by the length of the trip, which is mostly one or two hours for the inhabitants of the region (58% of respondents) and a maximum of half a day for tourists (52% of respondents). Finally, the presence of 20 automatic meters (automatic meters) along the route indicates that some portions are much more frequented than others. Thus, the portion between Saumur and Tours is the most frequented with 60,000 passages per year, followed by the portion between Tours and Blois, between Nantes and Angers and the Orléans area with 40,000–60,000 passages. We can see that these are portions corresponding to the outskirts of large urban areas, which are certainly the subject of excursion practices. Nevertheless, the most frequented portion reveals, beyond a practice of excursionists, tourist practices given the more important passage than elsewhere. The spread of flows is probably due to the concentration of castles along the Loire and its tributaries (Villandry, Ussé, Langeais, Chinon, Montsoreau, etc.). Also, to support local actors in welcoming these cycling-related practices, development work is carried out by the *Val de Loire Mission*, an organization created in March 2002 on the initiative of the Regional Councils of the *Centre* and *Pays de la Loire* in charge of the Loire Valley, a site registered as a World Heritage Site by UNESCO in 2000. It is in charge of steering and expertise with local authorities and coordinates 185 service providers located less than 5 kilometers (3.1 miles) from the itinerary, including accommodation providers, bicycle rental companies and visiting sites.

5.3. Conclusion

Investment by private and/or public actors does not clearly make it a tourist destination and, moreover, a regional tourist area. However, it should be noted that these major actors act as a reactive strategy within a territory, crystallizing the organization of tourism around a project (park, route, resort, etc.). For these actors, the need to create an equipment, a tourist place is only established if the geographical context is favorable to the capture of tourist flows. But the capture of tourist flows is only possible if tourists see an interest in it. In the case of the Ardèche Gorges, the road was developed as people were already going there to contemplate the area. For the Loire à Vélo, we can see that the busiest sections already correspond to the areas with the highest tourist numbers, i.e. in the presence of castles on the banks of the Loire. But creations can also constitute new tourist poles, as is the case with the resorts created on the Languedoc coast, whose Mediterranean climatic conditions close to the Spanish coast but above all the flows of tourists who came to them met the conditions for success without too much risk. The same is true in the Alps with the increase in accommodation capacity in the massifs, particularly in the Vanoise, at the risk of creating a landscape of "ski factories" that was contested at the end of the developments. On the other hand, creating a site within a non-tourist area is a much higher risk. However, the Futuroscope has been a real development success for the Vienne department, attracting approximately 2 million visitors each year. The difficulty of attendance experienced by theme parks created in the south of Vienne, despite the participation of public funding, testifies to the impossibility of creating a regional tourism area where tourists do not want it. In the case of the Vienne, they certainly go to Futuroscope, but then go to other tourist destinations, whether it is the coasts of the Atlantic and Channel coasts or the Loire Valley with its castles. We will then see that development can help encourage tourists to discover places they would not have considered visiting.

6

Developers and Local Actors Mobilization for Promotion of their Regional Territories

Developers are actors whose practices consist of promoting local development. The practices of these actors within these territories consist of promoting local development. According to Paul Houée's definition, local development is "a global process of synergistically setting in motion local actors for the development of human and material resources of a given territory, in relation to the decision-making centers of the economic, social, and political groups of which it is part" [HOU 96, p. 293]. Local development mobilizes local actors in non-market resource development linked to proximity [PEC 96]. Also, bottom-up strategies are identified in this development logic. Both public and private actors work in tourist areas for local development. Unlike the top-down strategy led by investors, the bottom-up approach, by developers, includes a regional dimension from sites or cities in its action. We will also see that development through tourism goes beyond the scale of the place and is part of a territory with a regional dimension.

6.1. Public actors and the collective interest of a territory in a regional dimension

The developers are seeking to propose a relevant territory so that tourists can carry out their recreational plans there. The territory can have multiple spatial dimensions ranging from the continent to the neighborhood. Also, to attract the attention of visitors, developers act to reveal places and to localize of them within a tourist destination of regional dimension. Specific locations are generally abstract and often invisible in the landscape to exogenous visitors and must be marked either physically or not physically [TIM 98]. We will see the case of a city whose metropolitan dimension of tourism development has gone beyond the framework of the place, creating a multipolarity within tourism development that takes place in a regional dimension. Then, we will present the case of territories where the mobilization of public and private actors leads to the identification of a territory by the landscape and the development of a tourist destination of regional dimension from multiple sites, villages and cities.

6.1.1. *The case of the urban tourism development of Nantes (France) and its regional extension*

In France, the Nantes region has experienced tremendous growth since the 2000s, encouraging people to "take the journey". The city of Nantes, located about 60 kilometers (37 miles) upstream from the Loire estuary, is a city characterized by a rather dark past due to a significant slave trade activity from the 17th to the 19th Century in the city's trade and also because of the industrial slowdown in shipbuilding until the closure of the last shipyards in 1987. In terms of tourism, at the end of the 20th Century, there was a low tourism presence in the city, more oriented towards business activities. Nantes is, above all, a thoroughfare for tourists coming from the Paris region and heading towards the Atlantic coast, Brittany or Southern France. In fact, Nantes is a short-stay destination, and tourists go there "opportunistically" in order to make a stopover [VIO 98]. Also, faced with a lack of positive image following multiple communication attempts in 2007, 20 years after the closure of the last shipyards, an urban project permanently modified the city's anchoring and resulted in a change in the city's tourism policy. The development of the island of Nantes, an abandoned warehouse district dating back to the industrial era, has been entrusted to a new public-private organization, the *Société d'aménagement de la métropole Ouest Atlantique* (SAMOA) (Western Atlantic Metropolitan Planning Corporation), which has chosen to opt for an artistic and recreational facility with a strong cultural and tourist dimension. The Great Elephant (see Figure 6.1), straight out of the workshop of the company *La Machine* on July 1, 2007, is one of the mechanical machines produced in this project; it wanders on the esplanade and under the naves of the former shipyards to anchor the city around a new theme, "the journey", while keeping a link with the city's past (including trade to the West Indies). One of its creators, François Delarozière, defines it as "a possibility to combine urban planning, dreams, and poetry. We create urban postcards and unforgettable memories. It is the very history of Nantes, marked by the navy, the great explorers, and the large-scale popular cultural events, that made this crazy project possible. The *Machines de l'Île* [Machines of the Island] could not have been created elsewhere, even if many cities wanted to do so"[1].

Figure 6.1. *The Great Elephant on the esplanade of the former shipyards from Nantes (France) (source: J. Piriou, July 2016). For a color version of the figures in this chapter, see www.iste.co.uk/piriou/tourism.zip*

COMMENT ON FIGURE 6.1.– *The institutional actors of the urban community council of Nantes have reallocated industrial buildings along the Loire River to develop residential, business and tourism functions [BAR 09]. In the summer of 2007, in one of the large naves of the former Dubigeon shipyard, François Delarozière and Pierre Oréfice launched the Machines de l'Île project. The first machine will be the 12-meter-high Great Elephant, which carries about 30 passengers on its back for a walk on the esplanade. The Machine Gallery is also open to visitors. It is here that other achievements have been created, such as the carousel of the Marine Worlds or the Heron Tree with a dimension of more than 20 meters in height [MOR 09]. On the site of the former banana hangar located at the tip of the island of Nantes are now housed in the cells of bars, theaters, discos and restaurants [BAR 09]. In addition, the edition of the contemporary art biennial "Estuaire" launched in 2007 demonstrated the city of Nantes and Saint-Nazaire's stated strategy of developing a metropolitan area in the Loire with a European influence with approximately one million inhabitants [MOR 09].*

1 Excerpt from the journal *Communauté urbaine Nantes Métropole*, No. 10, July/August 2007, p. 11.

In Nantes, local authorities were fully involved[2] in this project by relying on private companies[3]. In addition, tourism development will go beyond the city limits and integrate the municipalities bordering the Loire River between Nantes and the estuary. In 2007, 2009 and 2012, the biennales of contemporary art called "*Estuaire*" took place, creating about 20 works over the 60 kilometers (37.2 miles) that separate the city from the estuary from the river. Some works have settled into the landscape and contribute to the image of the destination. We can mention "*La Maison dans la Loire*", half engulfed in the Couëron river created by Jean-Luc Courcoult, founder and director of Royal de Luxe, the "Ocean Serpent" of the Chinese artist Huang Yong Ping, a skeleton beached at the mouth of the Loire on the beach of Mindin in Saint-Brevin-les-Pins or the "*Villa Cheminée*" of the Japanese artist Tatzu Nishi located near the power station in Cordemais. But the relationship between developers is difficult: on the one hand, the actors of tourism and, on the other hand, the actors of culture who are structured in a double organization [GIR 09].

On January 18, 2011, the urban community council of *Nantes Métropole* awarded a public service delegation to a new structure, a local public company "*Le Voyage à Nantes*"[4] in order to ensure the management of cultural, technical and commercial facilities, as well as to position and affirm an identity at the destination while giving it a regional scale dimension with inter-municipality and partnerships with other territories on the coast or in the Loire Valley. This structure has strengthened the city's anchoring around cultural facilities by taking over the responsibility of the Nantes Metropolitan Tourist Office, the Nantes Culture and Heritage mixed economy company and the "*Estuaire*" biennial. To mark this new stage, the "*Voyage à Nantes*" event was born in the summer of 2012. It offers an animation of the public space through a tour organized in the city, crisscrossing ephemeral works of art and Nantes heritage sites. At a press conference held on August 23, 2012, the Director of "*Voyage à Nantes*,"

---

2 The urban community council of *Nantes Métropole* owns the Machines, and the financing is the subject of an agreement between the city of Nantes, the Loire-Atlantique department, the Pays de la Loire region, Europe via European Regional Development Fund (ERDF) funds.
3 For example, EDF, *Siemens France Automatisme*, SFCMM (*Société de Chaudronnerie*) Chailloux, ArcelorMittal.
4 It is 72% owned by the *Nantes Métropole* urban community, 18% by the city of Nantes, 5% by the Loire-Atlantique department and 5% by the Pays de la Loire region.

Jean Blaise, announced that there would be 1.8 million visitors and that air traffic would increase by 16% in July compared to the previous year. In 2014, the *"Voyage à Nantes"* event is extended to the vineyard with stops on a route between Nantes and the city of Clisson. The following year, it was the town of Saint-Nazaire at the mouth of the Loire that used the term "voyage" in the city's tourist communication, calling it the "port of all journeys".

6.1.2. The case of natural parks, creation of a territory of regional dimension with a view to developing tourism through a landscape

Regional culture can also be found in the construction of a landscape. Landscape can be defined as "a portion of land seen by the observer" [LEC 07, p. 47]. Also, the landscape representation depends not only on the characteristics of the environment but also on the subjectivity of the observer. From this point of view, the landscape can be compared to a painting since it passes before its eyes even before it has had time to be clearly identified [BER 96b]. The landscape, beyond a contemplation of the eye, is a construction of the mind that passes through a representation that poses the problem of "encoding" and "decoding" according to individuals [DEL 01]. The regional landscape "is part of a more general development work with a standardized collective perception of the national space" [BER 96b, p. 31]. Regional nature parks make it possible, under the supervision of the regional councils and the public-private governance, to establish a charter with the territorial authorities concerned (local, departmental or regional), to pay attention to territories of fragile balance and to the natural and cultural heritage protected [CHA 93]. There are 53 regional nature parks in France, the last of which, the Aubrac Regional Nature Park, a mid-mountain plateau located in the Massif Central, was validated by a decree of the Prime Minister on May 23, 2018. This classification arouses many desires in order to propose regional areas as perimeters to be protected, which are the subject of associations prefiguring future mixed unions. The national classification framework is also an incentive to develop by offering guidance through specifications of state institutions that must be respected in order to be labeled. On the northern coast of Brittany, the association *COEUR Émeraude*, whose acronym stands for *Comité opérationnel des élus et des usagers du fleuve maritime Rance et de la Côte d'Émeraude* (Operational Committee of elected officials and users of the maritime river Rance and the Emerald Coast), was created with a view to the proposal to create a regional natural park. To this end, local authorities, the government, companies, associations and residents mobilize and consult each other in order to reach a contract that is embodied in a park charter that is subject to public inquiry. The perimeter includes sites, villages and small towns characterized by a river and coastal landscape. Then, inter-municipalities and departments join them, if they so wish, and it is then the region that requests the ministry in charge of the environment for expertise. The government therefore intervenes *a posteriori* by decree of classification but the approach is indeed based on local actors.

In Great Britain, there is the same desire to mobilize actors in a regional dimension, but this time from a specific location. The county of Cumbria, located in the northern North West region of England, is divided into five districts (South Lakeland, Allerdale, Copeland, Carlisle and Barrow-in-Furness) and includes cities such as Carlisle, Lancaster and Blackpool. But in the heart of the county is the 229,000-hectare Lake District National Park, which includes the municipalities of Kendal, Windermere, Ambleside, Keswick and Penrith [POU 14]. Also, the tourism developers within the county have chosen to develop a destination of regional dimension related to this national park. Thus, the Cumbria County Tourist Office incorporates the name of the Lake District, "Cumbria Tourism is the official Tourist Board for the Lake District, Cumbria". The web page for the visitor displays "GoLakes. Official website for the Lake District. Cumbria". In fact, the board of directors of the tourist office is composed of elected representatives from the Lake District. However, the tourist office offers other places to visit than the Lake District: the city of Carlisle, Hadrian's wall, the Pennines mountains, or the Yorkshire Dales National Park.

6.2. Private actors and their territorial valuations in the interest of their companies

Private actors place their actions within a territory of regional dimension as soon as they see an interest in increasing the visibility and economic activity of their company. The sharing of a territory between multiple private actors can lead them to cooperate, shaping an identity to this territory from signs, symbols embedded in objects, things, landscapes and places [BUL 05]. The representations that actors make of space and time are called spatial markers [COË 06]. Through these demonstrations of the homogeneity of a culture or an identity, the actors testify to their belonging to a society or a territory; this is particularly true in a regional approach. We will see the case of two territories whose mobilization of private actors makes it possible to identify bottom-up strategies to define a tourism territory with a regional dimension.

6.2.1. The case of the Cognac vineyard (France) in the mobilization of spirits and tourism stakeholders to promote a region in a regional dimension

The Cognac vineyard is similar to a classic wine-growing territory, in that it is based on an area of controlled designation of origin which is divided into six vintages that extend from the islands of Ré and Oléron, located in the Atlantic Ocean, to the foothills of the Massif Central, with the Charente river as the backbone. Several cities are part of this perimeter: La Rochelle, Rochefort, Saintes, Jonzac, Angouleme, Jarnac and in particular the city of Cognac. However, the economic weight of cognac production companies plays a role within the territory (see Figure 6.2). Also, even if there are a multitude of houses, the market is very concentrated: 80% of cognac sales are made by four major trading houses (Hennessy, Rémy Martin, Martell and Courvoisier). Cognac is marketed almost exclusively for export (98%), and the major trading houses are fairly resistant to global economic fluctuations or climatic hazards thanks to their membership of multinational companies listed on the stock exchange whose headquarters are in Paris (Hennessy at LVMH, Martell at Pernod-Ricard), New York (Couvoisier at Fortune Brands) or Bermuda (Baron-Otard at Bacardi). In addition, the power of some cognac trading houses allows them to control the entire production chain, from contracting with winegrowers around a set of specifications for the cultivation of the vine to managing sales outlets and marketing bottles worldwide [PIR 18a]. Then, we observe that these large houses, located mainly in Cognac and Jarnac, open their doors to the public and offer visiting tours.

Figure 6.2. *Signage for the ecomuseum in the vineyard of Cognac (France) (source: J. Piriou, June 2014)*

COMMENT ON FIGURE 6.2.– *Tourism professionals are taking advantage of this premium product to propose a global offer that characterizes the destination of the Cognac vineyard. Thus, an association "Les étapes du cognac" is in charge of qualifying winegrowing operations, accommodation and restaurants to welcome the public at the vineyard level, mainly in the departments of Charente and Charente-Maritime. However, the process is difficult, in a context of individualism of winegrowers and a lack of organization, due to the control of the sector by the National Interprofessional Bureau of Cognac and the control of the trade on distillation and aging [BEL 75]. Indeed, in order to ensure quality, the major trading houses practice an "upstream integration", i.e. they control production and limit the power of action of the distillers. Each trading house therefore has its own production method, and through the intermediary of the distillers, each house imposes its own distillation system for the aging of alcohols [BER 96a]. Thus, the tourism of winegrowing farms is limited, due to the systemic functioning of cognac production with multiple intermediate actors.*

Some actors outside tourism are also involved in this approach to tourism development in a regional dimension (i.e. the vineyard). Among them, a manufacturer of grape harvesting machines, located in a commune bordering the city of Cognac (a producer of balsamic vinegar located in the south of the department), and an ecomuseum located in the north of the vineyard contribute to enhancing a territory of regional dimension thematized in economic discovery. Finally, an association has also been created to institutionalize cooperation between the actors involved in cognac production, in the form of a cluster, including tourism actors.

6.2.2. The case of the Santa Claus region (Lapland) in the exploitation of an imagination for a regional tourism development

Imagination and symbolism also make it possible to exploit images for investment in tourism, resulting in the creation of a regional area. In Finland, since the 1970s, thousands of visitors, mainly Scandinavians, have been coming to Rovaniemi in search of Santa Claus, particularly because of Lapland's position on the Arctic Circle. At first, there was only Santa's house. In fact, the tourist office is in charge of organizing sleigh rides, located in the city center. Then, between the airport and the city, two important places were built: Santa Claus Village in 1985 and then the Santa Park theme park which opened in 1998 [PRE 95, HAL 09]. Located 5 miles (5 kilometers) away from the center of Rovaniemi, village du père Noël, Santa Claus Village, originated from a viewpoint designed by Colonel Oiva J. Willamo to provide a stopover for tourists and take pictures of the Arctic Circle. Created in 1948, the tourist office of the city of Rovaniemi was then in charge of the management and development of the Polar Circle cabin, which became Santa Claus Village. This park offers about 50 attractions, outdoor activities (dog sleigh rides, reindeer rides, snowmobile rides), souvenir shops, hotels and a holiday village. Then, only 2 kilometers (1.2 miles) away, Santa Park offers similar activities (discovery workshops, train, show, ice gallery, etc.). It has been managed since 2009 by a couple who claim family management and develop activities around the theme of Santa Claus and the Arctic Circle (Santa Claus Secret Forest opened in 2007, Arctic Forest Spa was created in 2013 and a hotel opened in 2016). Due to a lack of patents in tourism, these creations can also be found in Sweden, as well as in Finland, where other private actors are taking advantage of this opportunity of the imagination around Santa Claus to create establishments elsewhere, not just in Rovaniemi. This is the case of Kakslauttanen Arctic Resort East Village, which includes a hotel and a Santa Claus house, in the municipality of Saariselkä (250 kilometers (155 miles) northeast of Rovaniemi).

6.3. Make the territory a shared brand to develop a regional tourist destination

The brand is a strategy for enhancing the value of work done on territorial identity. Marketing strategies to attract tourists are not new. Railway companies have also promoted the regional development of tourist places that encourage travel on their companies' trains, for example within the destination of the Loire castles in France. Thus, the Orléans railway company proposed several itineraries promoted in their promotional posters that praise the presence of castles associated with the railway stations of the municipalities served. At the disposal of the stations in a chain, a regional linear space is emerging which evolved by serving intervals by services to individuals who will take over from the train. There are entrepreneurs in the Loire Valley who offer car trips to the castles: "Local entrepreneurs rent cars by the hour or in the tourist race [...] with a group excursion car parked in front of the castle carrying at least fifteen crammed in tourists [...]" [BER 07, p. 169]. These initiatives have contributed to the development of tourism in the area. However, in an evolving context of micro-economics, marketing has had to adapt according to spatial scales [BEN 06] and based on four major facts. First of all, on a globalized economy and tourism practices that are also globalized and constantly expanding and increasing competition between destinations. We are also witnessing a return to the regional and local economy, encouraged in particular by the decentralization and local development policies implemented since the 1980s. Developers seek to enhance the value of their territory while qualifying it with an identity.

Territorial identity can be defined as "the set of values, images, concepts that define local particularity, that define the existence by a group through the delimitation of a territory" [DUB 98, p. 31]. They carry out identity analysis studies in order not only to position themselves in relation to other competing territories but also to federate local actors and, in particular, inhabitants into the project. Second, an evolution of the means of communication (whether for multimedia or travel) also offers a significant choice. Finally, the experience gained from the widespread and controlled use of marketing requires decision-makers to adopt an offensive and effective strategy. Tourism marketing is nowadays taken into account by decision-makers as a process that makes it possible to identify and anticipate tourist demand in order to propose an adapted offer in order to satisfy them [TOC 99]. Benoît Meyronin identifies three basic ingredients for successful territorial marketing, which is also aimed at tourists: "the identity that must be defined, forged, promoted, developed, and sometimes defended," "actors that must be convinced, federate, mobilized, and valued, but also attracted," "plans that must be thought of, positioned, conducted, and promoted but also attracted" [MEY 12, p. 7]. Tourism or non-tourism stakeholders can all be involved in territorial marketing. These may be traditional industries such as transport, accommodation, but the government and local authorities have become major players in territorial marketing [STO 17a]. The brand will make it easier to identify the offer and differentiate it from competitors [KEL 09]. It must concern the whole community, whether it is public organizations, private companies, residents, as well as visitors [MAU 07]. The brand is intangible, but it makes it possible to reach different categories of tourists by a declination into several individual brands [LUM 00]. We will illustrate our point with the example of two tourism brands with a regional dimension: "Loire Valley" and "Be Breizh".

6.3.1. "Loire Valley", a brand that promotes a regional tourist destination

In France, the two administrative regions of Pays de la Loire and Centre-Val de Loire were created at the end of the 1970s by Olivier Guichard, Minister of Public Works and Town and Country Planning, in order to better regulate the territory, but Claude Raffestin pointed out in the 1980s that this new link, which is the region, is a problem because it is more "said than lived" [RAF 80, p. 164]. Indeed, these two regions do not have any coherence with a former province and have been the subject of a rapprochement of departments in order to ensure demographic and economic coherence. In France, however, it is the local authorities that are in charge of promoting and communicating tourism in their territory. Also, after the Val de Loire was classified as a UNESCO World Heritage Site in 2000 (see Figure 6.3), a rapprochement was made around the "Val de Loire/Loire Valley" brand between the two administrative regions in order to jointly promote and communicate about the destination. Other brands are associated with it when they relate to an interregional project ("*La Loire à vélo*", see Chapter 5) or to territories of former provinces ("Berry", "Anjou" and "Touraine"). Also, tourist destinations in the Loire Valley use the name "Val de Loire/Loire Valley" as a shared brand created in 2014 to develop their territorial marketing and affirm their belonging to this regional space: the "Angers Loire Valley" brand was created in 2011 for this purpose as well as the local tourist offices "Blois-Chambord-Val de Loire" and "Orléans Val de Loire Tourism".

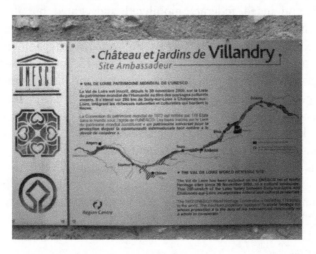

Figure 6.3. *Plaque of the "UNESCO" label at the entrance of the Château de Villandry (France) (source: J. Piriou, October 2008)*

COMMENT ON FIGURE 6.3.– *After the Château and Domaine de Chambord were included on the UNESCO list of cultural properties, the Loire Valley, over a 260-kilometer (161.5 miles) stretch between Chalonnes-sur-Loire and Sully-sur-Loire, was classified as a cultural landscape on UNESCO's World Heritage List in 2000. The heritage dimension will help to mobilize and raise awareness among the inhabitants in order to maintain a new relationship with the river [HUY 08]. Cities and tourist sites (e.g. castles) will participate in this labeling of an exceptional cultural landscape. They will become ambassadors for the label. Local authorities will also take advantage of the inscription to transform it into a tourist label. The notion of World Heritage and in particular the reference to "cultural landscape" will constitute a pretext for development and "to organize a policy of diversification of tourist flows at all scales" [COU 06, p. 25]. Signage will also be installed for visibility purposes, the label being the guarantee of the action of local authorities in the conservation and enhancement of heritage.*

6.3.2. *Brittany, between cultural territory and administrative territory, as a tourist brand?*

For the region Brittany in France, the case is different, since this region is characterized by a strong identity. Brittany has a recognized identity in the image of a French province characterized by a strong regional identity [BER 80, LEC 98]. This identity is also promoted and mediatized by the officialization of Breton as a regional language, allowing its teaching since the 1970s or by road signs in the 1990s [ABA 00]. Following the classification of the fest-noz (night festival in the Breton language) as a UNESCO intangible cultural heritage of humanity on December 5, 2012, we carried out a study on the tourism promotion of the fest-noz within the territories, which shows that the fest-noz constitutes more of an event-based programming than an intangible heritage. However, the fest-noz is constitutive to everything that makes up the immaterial tourist destination of the region "Brittany" because of codes, such as dance steps or language, since the famous song of the *kan ha diskan* is pronounced in Breton language. It is indeed an intangible spatial marker of Breton culture that contributes to the definition of the region's identity by developers. Indeed, the fest-noz is valued as a tourist resource for the purpose of animating the tourist territory [PIR 14].

However, identity does not allow the region to be delimited, particularly for its territorial marketing. Brittany has limits that are disputed between the historical perimeter including Nantes and the Loire-Atlantique department (today in the Pays-de-la-Loire region) and today with only four departments (Côtes-d'Armor, Finistère, Ille-et-Vilaine and Morbihan). Tourism professionals are more concerned about the destination perceived by tourists, since the territory of Brittany, which can be found in tourist brochures, is not the one that corresponds to the program region: "The Regional Tourism Committee is not bothered by the administrative divisions of the French government that deprive the region of Nantes, its capital, and in the brochures and maps of Brittany distributed by this organization, the Loire-Atlantique is systematically included, whether it is to present the natural heritage, traditional festivals, or artistic cities" [GAU 00, p. 305–306]. Also, in a context of developed territorial marketing, territorial competition and a study of insufficient notoriety, the Brittany region launched in 2011 a brand code, with a signature for tourism communication "Be Breizh". This approach has been pursued by other territories such as the department of Ille-et-Vilaine with the "Haute-Bretagne" brand, aimed at economic and tourism stakeholders. Finally, we note that territory brands contribute to giving an image of a territory with a strong identity and lead to the development of a sense of belonging. However, we note that the declination and multiplicity of brands, despite common elements relating to a "Loire Valley" area or a "Brittany" culture, can lead to confusion since each territory would seek to assert itself with its brand, without clarifying a recognition of the regional dimension practiced by developers.

6.4. Conclusion

Developers are the local actors who act in the development of a territory in a regional dimension. They mobilize and participate in putting the space in order, but the scope of action remains narrower than in a top-down strategy. As we have seen, the government can intervene in the development of an entire coastal complex or a major private company working to create a regional tourist area. On the other hand, local actors, in a bottom-up strategy, whether public or private, practice a more limited scale that is limited to their own place or a set of nearby places. In Nantes, the extension of tourism development extends from the city to its neighboring vineyard. Concerning natural parks, the actors involved are only those concerned by an identified landscape. In the Cognac vineyard, the majority of trading houses and other companies that offer discovery tourism are located mainly in the city of Cognac (in Jarnac and some surrounding places). In Lapland, despite the various initiatives created, development applies only to certain sites. Then, in a context of international competition, institutional actors and tourism professionals are led to widen the administrative boundaries and adapt the perimeter of the tourist destination. Territorial marketing intervenes to convince tourists to visit a regional space delimited by the tourist destination defined by the professional tourism stakeholders. It is at this moment that the prescribers act to advise and guide tourists. This may work but abusing it may lead to territorial imposition rejected by tourists.

7

The Prescribers and the Encouragement of Regional Practices

Prescribing is a term used in the medical field; it is an act of prescribing treatment on a document called a "prescription". It is therefore interesting to know that a medical prescription written by a doctor engages their professional responsibility, so it is an act of trust and guarantee for the patient. We have noted the recurrent presence of the word "prescription" in the tourist sector, whether in the case of a travel agency to advise a customer or a tourist office to inform a visitor. What meaning can we give to the tourist prescription? In marketing, it is an important strategy since it is "a person or organization that has expert status and gives an opinion that influences the process" [DEV 16, p. 23]. The prescriber then acts as an intermediary between tourists and service providers. However, let us insist once again on the fact that the relationship to a territory is above all individual [BAI 95], depending on the social identity of the individual and the nature of the territory concerned, including amenities such as accessibility or the opening of the places to tourism. Some researchers have taken an interest in the mental map to find out the practical, social or sentimental organization of the living space [GOU 74, FRE 99], but, in the case of the regional dimension of a tourist territory, the approach remains only interpretative. However, we know that tourist mobilities depends not only on the intention of each individual but also on the production of habits or systems of sustainable and transposable provisions, which would be accompanied by strategic calculations [BOU 80]. It is for this reason that tourism professionals try to influence the choices that tourists make during their stay and influence perception. It can be defined as a process of decoding information by the brain that provides answers to the suggestion of places, and also according to the psychological experience of each person. This mechanism is very important in the motivation, orientation and consumption of tourist activities [NKO 08]. We will now develop the different means of prescription available to tourism stakeholders in suggesting places and routes for spatial practices with a regional dimension.

7.1. The prescription to guide tourists in their choice of places

The tourist guide is a prescriber of regional spatial practices. It can be considered as a tool that shows what to see or do and contributes to the construction of the tourist perspective [URR 90]. This tourist gaze is built collectively in the gaze of tourist spaces. However, multiple tourist views exist depending on the culture and social class of the individuals [STO 17a]. The tourist guide can be an individual or a medium such as a book or digital data. Concerning the individual, the World Federation of Tourist Guide Associations defines a tourist guide as a person who guides visitors in a given language and interprets the cultural and natural heritage of a region. The latter normally has a qualification specific to the area usually issued and/or recognized by the competent authority [SAL 08]. In France, it is the government services that issue the professional guide-lecturer card. Nevertheless, any individual can claim to be a tourist guide, for example in the organization of excursions and organized tours. According to Erik Cohen, the role of tourist guide integrates four functions: instrumental, social, interactive and communicative. On the one hand, it provides tourists with privileged access to the reading of a territory, and, on the other hand, it is a social mediator in the relationship with the inhabitants [COH 85].

The tourist guide, as a support, was originally presented as small booklets, which, since 1830–1860, were one of the major tools to encourage regional escapades, once the traveler had arrived at the place of stay [TIS 00]. Originally, railway guides provided information on the stations served by railway lines, sometimes in the form of circular trips, but leaving few forays between services. In the 20th Century, the function of the guide evolved. For motorists, its objective was to promote the road network, mentioning only a few accommodations and tourist interests. These guides were offered by tire companies to their customers. Faced with their success, they expanded by giving recommendations for excursions in the form of diffusion mobility or tours. For example, the Michelin Guide compensated for the lack of such guides [BOY 05] and proposed a hierarchy of monuments that would allow tourists to choose their destination in full knowledge of the facts [FRA 01]. Historians have noted that these books resolutely adopt the position of advising tourists, becoming true educational guides [BER 99]. They developed as much as tourism became industrialized [TIS 00]. The regional guide describes the landscapes, identities and regional characteristics (such as gastronomy and folklore), while suggesting that you explore the area in the form of thematic tours. Tourist guides encourage escapades with a description of landscapes and identities, as well as places by suggesting going from one point to another [KNA 00b]. To do this, the guide describes and even produces a space, "if the guides willingly talk about areas, in fact their content generally concerns places presented either in the form of a simple collection that the figure of the archipelago can describe, or in the form of itineraries and it is then that the network fig is essential" explained Rémy Knafou [KNA 00b, p. 473]. It also considers the realities of society, by networking a certain number of places, places that are the subject of a selection and whose center would be the beneficiary for the benefit of the periphery. However, rather than encouraging people to travel through an entire area, it suggests moving from one tourist point to another. In order to facilitate its use, the guide is produced according to three criteria: in a space unknown to the visitor, by promoting a quick consultation, in order to prepare a trip and also during a visit. For this purpose, the information must be brief and synthetic [DEV 09].

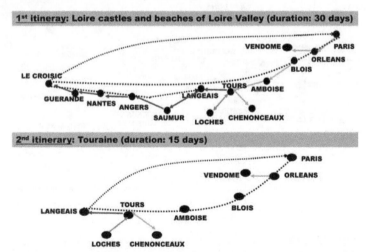

Figure 7.1. *Train itineraries proposed by the Guide Joanne "Les châteaux de la Loire" in 1907 (source: J. Piriou after [JOA 07]). For a color version of the figures in this chapter, see www.iste.co.uk/piriou/tourism.zip*

In order to understand the role of the prescription of these tourist guides, we carried out an analysis of travel guides concerning the tourist destination of the Loire Valley castles in France. These selected guides allowed us to compare tours or excursions between the beginning and the end of the 20th Century [MIC 97, JOA 07]. According to the analysis of tourist guides, we note that at the beginning of the last century, the *Guide Joanne* proposed a series of similar places (see Figure 7.1). However, the situation changed at the end of the 20th Century, as the Michelin tourist guide advocates the spread of tourism to diverse places (see Figure 7.2). Indeed, in the *Guide Joanne* of 1907, we find essentially cities (Orléans, Vendôme, Blois, Amboise, Tours, etc.), and some sites, few in number, appear. The castles of Chenonceau and Langeais were prescribed in the Loire Valley. These series of places were much more diversified at the end of the 20th Century in the 1997 Michelin Guide, which offers more complete itineraries. Many castles are proposed to the detriment of the cities in the Loire Valley.

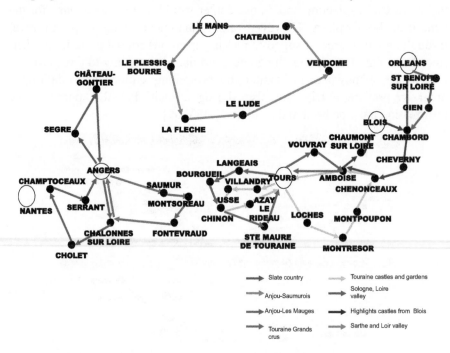

Figure 7.2. *Itineraries by car proposed by the Michelin Green Guide "Les châteaux de la Loire" in 1997 (design: J. Piriou according to [MIC 97])*

With regard to this comparison of tourist guides over these two distinct periods, we can explain this evolution. First, the areas put into tourism since the 18th–19th Centuries are now known. Second, accessibility to the site is easier thanks to the individual access of tourists to cars, which contributes to tourism development. As early as 1907, the *Guide Joanne* proposed itineraries adapted to the different modes of transport, those concerning rail travel and those concerning car travel. By car, the guide offered several main excursion centers. For example, from Tours, several routes are available depending on the time required for travel. The guide proposes to go from Tours in half a day, round trip, to Chenonceaux, Montrichard Saint-Aignan, or by adding Valençay for a total itinerary of two days in round trip. In addition, some places are mentioned as secondary, such as Cinq Mars, for the round-trip itinerary from Tours integrating Villandry, Langeais, Saumur and Angers. Blois is one of the excursion centers for car travel. Several castles are recommended, including Chambord, Cheverny and Beauregard. It is specified that these castles can be visited together in a day's drive, but that hurried tourists should not miss Blois and Chambord and possibly neglect Cheverny and Beauregard. The guides will also adapt to the tourist diffusion mobility and suggest new places to visit during a stay. The proximity of the area contributes to the suggestion of itineraries. This proximity can not only be geographical but also attractive[1]. First, the recurring element we find is that of the same places that act as crossroads, whether at the beginning or at the end of the century. Within the destination "châteaux de la Loire", we find, in particular, the cities of Tours and Orléans. From the city of Angers, excursions to Haut-Anjou, as well as to the Mauges and Saumur were offered. Moreover, despite the remoteness of a place, tourist guides may recommend that you spend a certain amount of time there to get there. In this case, the geographical proximity of the places is quite relative. Indeed, the number of places proposed for visits on the tours increased considerably between the beginning and the end of the 20th Century in these two tourist guides. While daily excursions as part of a train trip were limited to three escapades in the 1907 *Guide Joanne* (Chenonceaux, Loches and Vendôme), the number of places has increased significantly on the daily car itineraries in the 1997 Michelin Guide, since loops integrating multiple places such as Villandry, Ussé, Chinon, Azay-le-Rideau, or Vouvray and Amboise are available. We can explain this increase in the number of possible places and routes by the

---

1 As a reminder, Neil Leiper's proximity to attractions is generated by "attractive" nucleuses, towards which tourists converge, and whose agglomeration of these nucleuses constitutes nodes [LEI 95].

services provided by train or car, and, as a result, by a new distance–time ratio that allows an optimization of the stay. Over the course of a day, it is therefore easier at the end of the 20th Century to visit several places, sometimes over a longer distance, but in a limited time frame. According to our study of tourist guides, we can see that there is no real hierarchy in the proposed tours. On the other hand, some places would be more unavoidable than others since they can be found in all the circuits (Chambord, Chenonceau castles, etc.), and therefore, require a specific trip, or they are "crossroads" to reach these places (notably the city of Tours).

As we have just seen, the influence of prescription, through the information provided in tourist guides, is not recent. Historians note that these books resolutely adopt the position of advising tourists, becoming true educational guides [BER 99], and are developing as much as tourism is becoming more industrialized [TIS 00]. However, tourist guides are themselves influenced by actors who seek to control their content. These pressures exerted by tourism professionals, entrepreneurs and institutions are as old as guides and are by no means a modern perversion [TIS 00].

7.2. The prescription of the local advisors to select the places

Each actor can be a prescriber of places, of a territory. However, there is a profession of "host/hostess", which is nowadays referred to as "stay advisor", which involves informing and orienting visitors or clients. Thus, according to the definition of the French government's tourism professions, "they encourage the public to stay in the region, inform them about accommodation, tourist heritage, cultural activities"[2]. The stay advisor works mainly in tourist offices. As we saw in the previous chapter, these institutions have major funding from local authorities (municipal or inter-municipal) and include their actions within a clearly defined scope. In a prescription to tourists, we therefore find, in some speeches, an orientation given according to an administrative framework. The spatial dimension of the scope of tourist offices' skills dates back to the birth of federations of tourist information offices at the beginning of the 20th Century, the forerunner of today's tourist offices, which predisposed to regional

---

2 Ministry of Economy and Finance, Directorate General for Enterprise, definition of "resident advisor" available at: https://www.entreprises.gouv.fr/tourisme/metiers/hotesse-daccueil, online since 04/10/2016, accessed June 3, 2018.

reflection. A debate on tourism regionalism emerged at the beginning of the 20th Century, which led tourist information offices to join forces [MAN 17]. A context of cultural regionalism has enabled local actors to give meaning to a space with a regional dimension [REV 89]. Thus, the tourist information offices of the Midi were created in 1903 or the Côte d'Azur in 1905. Moreover, an adaptation of the scope of action reveals that tourist visits were taken into account, as Julie Manfredini points out, "the department was perceived at the time as an administrative division that was not specific to tourism and a framework that was too limited compared to reality" [MAN 17, p. 235]. Today, institutional managers perceive an evolution in the practices and scope of tourism that no longer corresponds to the administrative scope. However, whatever the legal status of the tourist office today, its operation in France remains twofold between an elected official close to its territory, its electorate, and a technician who uses a working territory visited by tourists [VIO 99].

The brochures of tourist offices present a space of local or regional dimension insofar as the member service providers and the main tourist places favor a flexibility of the limits of the geographical perimeter since "the role of the territorial authorities is first of all to coordinate all tourist activities in a given geographical area" [BAR 05, p. 24]. So, to the question "Are printed tourist brochures still useful in the 21st century?", Kathleen L. Andereck responds in a 2005 study of American tourists that they still have a significant influence on travel decisions[3], although prior perceptions of the destination remain stronger, particularly as regards the itinerary to get there, but plays a role in terms of activities and time spent there [AND 05]. We carried out a documentary reading of the call brochures of tourist offices in the destination "châteaux de la Loire". In spring 2009, we ordered the main brochures from six tourist offices, dating from 2005 to 2009. We have selected tourist offices of main cities: Saumur, Blois, Nantes, Amboise, Tours and Angers. The method of analyzing tourism communication has already been published [GRI 07, BRO 07]. Rather than focusing on physical and cultural characteristics whose interpretation remains subjective and difficult to compare, we will choose to focus our attention on the environment of the place (in the sense of how the place is situated in relation to others) as well as on the various excursions or tours proposed from the places prescribed by the brochures.

---

3 The intention to carry out excursions or tours in the region is 33% mentioned and to stay longer (15%).

In this analysis of tourist brochures, we noted that tourist offices use relative proximity to places to locate themselves and encourage tourists to visit their territory and affirm a central position. According to the brochures of the tourist offices, all the places would be crossroads through which tourists would have to pass during their stay. The tourist offices present their territory as central in a regional tourist destination. For example, the Angers tourist office states in its brochure that "the motorway takes you to the ocean, to the highest tourist sites in the West and in 2 hours and 30 minutes you will reach the capital"[4]. We also find the two forms of proximity mentioned for the prescription of places in our analysis of tourist guides. As a reminder, the first one corresponds to geographical proximity, as shown by the indications in the brochures of the Nantes Tourist Office with the six excursions proposed according to a specific mileage for a round trip. The second corresponds to a "proximity of attraction", so some tourist places constitute poles, for example "Blois Pays de Chambord" or "Au pays d'Amboise et de Chenonceaux".

In relay of these prescriptions by the tourist offices, marked itineraries allow tourists to travel through identified places within a coherent whole. Tourist routes promote diffusion within the spaces, thus homogeneity is achieved by the materialization of identical signs along the routes, providing guidance to ensure the itinerancy of individuals, mentioning tourist routes in particular. In the 1950s, in a context of democratization of the automobile, tourism professionals proposed real tourist discovery routes. Mobility is becoming a concern of tourism policies and the rise of the individual car encourages tourist information offices to develop tours [MAN 17]. The tourist information offices announce thematic tours, by coach accompanied by hostesses. The tours start from a central point, usually a large urban center. For example, in Tours, a tour in foreign languages was proposed from the railway station to "highlighted" castles to break with a certain fatigue of traditional castle visits. In 1952, the Automobile Club and the Touring Club of Switzerland offered their members a "tourist and gastronomic" itinerary to the beaches of Brittany by the Route des Châteaux [BER 07]. It is then that a large number of networks will be built in order to make the roads to be covered (historical roads, scenic roads, etc.) legible. Distances vary, but the important places mention "obligatory passage".

---

4 "Angers, pour ici et maintenant", Tourism office of Angers Loire Tourism (2009), page 1.

In addition, in the development of these tours, the development of group travel is taken into account, requiring greater accommodation capacity and a developed tourist offer [MAN 17]. Finally, the development of tourist routes will accentuate regional cultures [BER 99]. However, these tourist routes make it possible to link and federate service providers and to affirm or reaffirm an identity [VIT 98]. The tourist route can thus materialize when it is developed by a territorial authority responsible for road signage and maintenance. It can also be more virtual when it comes to networking professionals. However, there is a divergence of objectives. Some have a desire to make traffic more fluid (e.g. government services), while others aim to link equipment and road maintenance (e.g. local authorities) and are looking to channel flows (e.g. tourism professionals). However, some itineraries work and respond to tourist practices (e.g. *La Loire à Vélo*, see Chapter 6).

7.3. The prescription for a regional experience

Many actors are involved in prescribing, but some even influence other prescribers such as tourist institutions, namely tour operators. These establish a link between tourist demand and operational activities in the field with local actors. As such, "they play the role of intermediaries [...] and information literacy is the basis of their activity" [STO 03, p. 177]. Tour operators order routes within the destination from their incoming agencies. Tourism institutions such as the departmental tourism committee or the tourist office are sensitive to the choices of tour operators, which are then led by an incoming agency, since the integration of their territory into the circuit marketed to tourists depends on it. Agencies prescribing the conditions of a tour to other tourism professionals (tourist offices, accommodation providers and restaurateurs) impose their selection of places and activities. Local actors must therefore respond to sponsors in order to be guaranteed to be included in the service. In the event of a change (e.g. the development of access to a site), the relationship is considerably threatened. This is the case of Mont-Saint-Michel as part of the work to restore the maritime character of the site (see Figure 7.3).

We will now study the cases of two international tour operators who offer tours from Paris, including Mont-Saint-Michel and the Loire castles. Globus is an American tour operator that offers an eight-day coach tour entitled

"Normandy, Brittany, and Châteaux Country"[5], while Ctrip.com International Ltd is a Chinese tour operator that offers a six-day coach tour entitled "Loire Valley + Mont-Saint-Michel + Bordeaux"[6].

Figure 7.3. *Mont-Saint-Michel (France) (source: J. Piriou, July 2016)*

COMMENT ON FIGURE 7.3.– *On April 28, 2012, 4,000 parking spaces were inaugurated on the outskirts, allowing access to the Mont via a shuttle bus in order to "manage mass tourism. We no longer want parking at the foot of the rock so that the landscape looks like a real postcard", says François-Xavier de Beaulaincourt, project manager. Several tour operators and incoming agencies are faced with difficulties in organizing their schedules, since the time required to travel 900 meters between the car park and the shuttles is too long, disrupting daily travel from Paris, for example.*

---

5 Globus Journey international website, available at: https://www.globusjourneys.com/tour/normandy-brittany-chateaux-country/rc/, accessed June 1, 2018.

6 Ctrip.com website http://vacations.ctrip.com/grouptravel/p5377639s2.html?kwd=%E6%B3%95%E5%9B%BD, accessed June 1, 2018.

Daily schedule	"Normandy, Brittany, Land of Castles" by Globus Journey		"Loire Valley + Mont-Saint-Michel + Bordeaux" by Ctrip	
	Places visited	Hosting cities	Places visited	Hosting cities
Day 1	Arrival in Paris Paris Meals at the Eiffel Tower	Paris	Arrival in Paris Paris-Saint-Malo trip Saint-Malo	Saint-Malo
Day 2	Castle and garden of Versailles Tour in Paris (Arc de Triomphe, Opera, Madeleine, Louvre, Champs-Élysées) Notre-Dame de Paris Montmartre Cruise on the Seine	Paris	Saint-Malo Mont-Saint-Michel	Rennes
Day 3	Rouen: cathedral Rue de la Grosse Horloge Cider road, Beuvron-en-Auge Caen Memorial	Caen	Chinon Chenonceau Chaumont Chenonceau (visit)	Tours
Day 4	D-Day landing beaches Arromanches American Cemetery Abbey of Mont-Saint-Michel	Près du Mont-Saint-Michel	Bordeaux: place des Quinconces	Bordeaux
Day 5	Châteaubriant Pictures of the castle of Angers Loire Valley	Angers	Saint-Émilion	Bordeaux
Day 6	Visit of Chambord Castle and Chenonceau Castle Civray Cellar	Tours	Department from Bordeaux	
Day 7	Chartres: visit of the cathedral Paris: cabaret	Paris		
Day 8	Departure from Paris			

Table 7.1. *Places integrated into the visiting tours of two tour operators (design: J. Piriou based on Globus Journey's websites and Ctrip)*

COMMENT ON TABLE 7.1.– *It can be seen on these two tours that Chambord Castle is the subject of a time devoted to a visit. The American tour operator also offers a visit to the Château de Chenonceau, but the other castles are only contemplated by road and only photos are taken. On the other hand, the choice of other places associated with these castles constitutes a proposal to tourists for the purchase of the service. The Chinese tour operator here favors a discovery of Bordeaux and its vineyards, in particular the village of Saint-Émilion. The tour operator also participates in the prescription of places that contribute to making places known to tourists.*

The inhabitants also participate in the prescription of addresses of establishments and tourist sites. These "participative" or associative approaches propose "discoveries of the territory where the inhabitants are at the 'outposts', as guides, prescribers, initiators, etc." [SIM 17a, p. 107]. Greeters is a concept born in the city, first in the United States and then everywhere else in the major cities, which qualifies residents, often volunteers, who welcome and accompany tourists wishing to meet places and inhabitants [SIM 17a]. In France, within the Loire Valley, a greeter association, created in 2012, first developed in the city of Tours and then spread to other places: Chinon, Loches, Sainte-Maure-de-Touraine, and Amboise. The web platform called "Greeters Loire Valley".

Finally, tourists can themselves be prescribers of places of interest. Social networks are a prescription tool, since tourists bring testimonies of a local experience. Tourists report on their stay in the form of a travel diary, on specialized sites such as Magali during her individual weekend by car in Blois and Chambord at the end of April 2006 on the website "vacanceo.fr.":

> "A short getaway to the castles of the Loire Valley for the weekend of May 1st. This allows you to get some fresh air, discover our beautiful country of France, and escape at a lower price! In short, 2 hours from Paris it is a very nice destination that changes weekends in Normandy (even if Normandy is very nice too!). On the schedule, departure on Saturday to avoid traffic jams, lunch break in Orléans, which is also a pretty town in which you should not miss the rather impressive cathedral (it is about the size of Notre-Dame de Paris) and the Place du

Martroi with in the middle the statue of Joan of Arc which delivered Orléans from the English in the 15th century. We also have pretty little cobbled pedestrian streets. Arrival in the afternoon in Blois. We had booked at the Hôtel de France et de Guise (2-star hotel recommended by the Guide du Routard, price of the double room 46 euros) located just in front of the castle. The room was clean and comfortable. The city of Blois is very pleasant, especially under the sun! A ride in a horse-drawn carriage allows you to fully appreciate the old town. You should also not miss the visit of the castle which was built over three eras [...]"[7].

TripAdvisor is the most widely known digital tool by millions of tourists influencing the reputation of restaurants, hotels, and various tourist facilities (museums, beaches, theme parks, etc.) contributing to prescriptions through 125 million reviews and 57 million members.

Figure 7.4. *Chinese tourists taking pictures of the Pudong district from the Bund promenade in Shanghai (China) (source: J. Piriou, December 2015)*

7 Extract from the website www.vacanceo.fr, available at: http://www.vacanceo.com/travel_members/travel_file_910.php, accessed June 19, 2012.

COMMENT ON FIGURE 7.4.– *In Shanghai, on the Bund, a large pedestrian boulevard along the Huangpu River, separating it from the city's modern district, the Oriental pearl tower, is the focus of particular attention by tourists who stroll around, especially at night because this tower, like many others, lights up and changes the perception of the place. Photography is one of the activities carried out by tourists. Some merchants also offer to immortalize the moment by selling a photo shooting service. However, by owning mobile phones, tourists are encouraged to take pictures of themselves in the form of selfies in order to share their experiences on social networks and to testify to their presence in this symbolic place of modern China.*

Tourists after their trip can post a comment and give a score from 1 to 5 for the place they visit. The note classifies by categories and helps in the choice of places to visit. A study published in 2014 by Gaël Chareyron, Saskia Cousin, Jérôme Da-Rugna and Sébastien Jacquot identified connections made by Internet users between tourist attractions, accommodations and restaurants. Depending on the number of comments per municipality, they draw up a map of France of relations between tourist services, "in the background are several types of relations between spaces within the same regional or local destination: between spaces of greed and spaces of tourist relegation". This map identifies tourist areas such as the Loire Valley, the Alpine massifs of the Tarentaise Valley, the Languedoc coast, the Vendée coast or the Côte d'Azur, as well as tourist areas such as the Arcachon basin, the Gulf of Morbihan, the Basque Country, the Camargue, the Lubéron or the Guérande peninsula [CHA 13].

In addition, the distribution of digital photographs by instant messaging or posting on social networks contributes to the reputation of the site. Digital photography is becoming a practice in its own right and contributes as a medium to the appropriation of places [STO 17a]. A study on tourist itineraries using the traces of the photo-sharing site "Flickr" shows that tourists follow the Loire and its tributaries where the main castles are located, and that the cultural sites located to the north and south of the Centre-Val de Loire region are much less part of the tourist visitation area [CHA 13].

7.4. Conclusion

Prescribing is essential for tourism professionals to direct tourists to specific places. Tourist practices therefore often correspond to the tourist information provided by tourism professionals. Moreover, as we have been able to mention, the evolution of tourism diffusion during the 20th Century has led tourist guides to adapt their content. Tourism professionals must adapt their offers according to the practices of tourists. The use of stereotypes, high places, constitutes a reservoir of images for professionals exploited in tourist brochures and guides in order to capture tourist flows. Then, the prescribers suggest other tourist places to visit, of a more or less important notoriety, but allowing them to design a tourist region wanted by these professional actors of tourism. The destination would therefore not refer to anything material since its signified can receive several possible acceptances depending on the intention of the actors.

Reading the Tourist Region Using Networks of Places Analysis

Introduction to Part 3

Knowing the spatial practices of tourists makes it possible to identify the types of places frequented and the types of mobilities used to carry out their recreational plans. The collection of spatialized stories has allowed us to discern networks of tourist places built by tourist mobilities. These networks make it possible to understand the intertwining of scales from the local to the continental or even to the global and the regional level. Regional geography is based on the flows and links between places forming networks [NON 04]. This is how we view the tourist region. In our opinion, it would be a set of tourist places networked by tourist mobilities and whose other public and private professional actors act to mobilize multiple places within these networks. We consider the tourist region as a co-construction of the tourism stakeholders.

DEFINITION.– Tourism region: dynamic territorial co-construction of tourism stakeholders, forming multi-level networks of places practiced by tourist mobilities.

By "dynamic territorial co-construction of tourism stakeholders", we refer to the previous part concerning the stakeholders logics who practice a territory, the tourist destination with a regional dimension. Indeed, they inscribe their spatial practices in a tourist destination, which is established in a regional dimension according to four identified logics: prescribers, investors, developers and tourists. As we have seen, there are many actors in tourism, who are public and private actors, local populations, as well as tourists. The tourist destination (local or regional) is the subject of a co-construction of actors, including the tourist in its development [VIO 11]. This co-construction is dynamic insofar as the places mobilized can evolve over time, and as we have seen, the choice of places is subject to the intentions of the various actors (passing trends, political strategies, etc.).

But the formation of multi-level networks of places practiced by tourist mobilities means that it is tourists who build the tourist region. In other words, they transform a tourist destination of regional dimension into a tourist region by integrating the tourist places that they consider relevant. The stakeholder logics mentioned above only create the tourist destination with a regional dimension. The actors can suggest, impose or invest in places, but if they are not covered by tourist mobilities linking these same places, this territory cannot be considered as a tourist region. This promoted and perceived territory will remain in the state of a "tourist destination" more linked to symbols or images than to a knowledge of the place and a practical experience by tourists.

To decipher this tourist region, we will start from the tourist mobilities that shape the networks of places. We will then translate the spatialized accounts of these tourist mobilities into matrices and graphs. We will measure neighborhood relationships to determine multiple levels of networks into which places are inserted. Through these multi-level regional networks of tourist places according to the identified tourist mobilities, we will be able to characterize several types of tourist regions (see Chapter 8). Then, we will try to understand why some places are practiced rather than others. In our opinion, tourists in theirs mobilities choose places that have recreational functions that justify being practiced. We will therefore evaluate the regional tourism function of the places. But we will see that the actors can act by changing the quality of the place and therefore the regional tourist function (see Chapter 9). Then, we will try to explain the regional distribution of tourist places in networks. By assessing the connectedness and connectivity of networks, we will explain the insertion of places in these networks according to tourist mobilities. We will observe that professional actors can intervene by positioning places in order to be integrated into the networks (see Chapter 10). Finally, we will see that some places are more networked than others. The evaluation of the nodal function of networked places will facilitate the understanding of the practice of these places according to tourist mobilities flows. Here again, the actors can act by suggesting a networking of tourist places, which could change the nodal function of the places networked by tourist mobilities (see Chapter 11).

8

Regional Tourism Distribution
in Networks of Places

Movement tracking of tourists during their stay is a relevant means of understanding the regional dimension of the territory practiced by them, which in our opinion shapes the tourist region. However, this tourist region is multiple and is spread on several geographical scales. We will analyze the networks of places designed by tourists according to their mobilities. The creation of graphs representing each itinerary carried out by the tourists interviewed will allow us to better understand the different forms, as well as the types of mobilities used in combination with the elementary tourist places. We will examine the relationship established between the places by the tourist mobilities, in particular the characteristics of the relationship and the recurrence of links. We wish to exploit the fact that tourists perceive a space in a reticular way by identifying the connections and contiguity of places [STO 17a]. Studying a network means "explaining the relationships between places, that is, taking into account in a concrete way the fact that observation units are not independent elements" [PUM 97, p. 90]. The network is complex, and moreover a tourist network reflects multiple spatial practices of actors, since it is "a networking of places by routes, reflecting itinerant practices more or less influenced by voluntary actions" [ÉQU 05, p. 341]. The network applied to tourism can therefore be approached in several ways. It can be a set of places, as well as tourist flows or cooperation networks between tourism professionals. We have therefore chosen to focus on tourist flows, which, through their mobility, shape the vertex and edges of the networks of tourist places. The network, made up of links between points forming lines independent of each other, thus leads to a multiplication of junctions and hierarchization of progress, and thus to its complexity. First, based on spatialized life stories, we will translate the movements and practices of places into matrices and graphs to better define the distance between places. Then, we will look at neighborhood relationships between places, in order to understand (according to the types of mobilities) how tourists combine places in their itineraries. Finally, we will propose a model for multi-level regional networks of tourist places.

8.1. Translating tourist mobilities, according to stories, into graphs and matrices

Based on schematic maps that interpret the spatialized narratives of the tourists interviewed at tourist places, it is now relevant to understand the relationship between places in networks. We therefore developed a matrix (see Table 8.1) to describe the networks, including the distance between places to reflect the spatial dimension of the networks [PUM 97].

DEFINITION.– Relationship matrix between places: the square matrix contains the same list of places in an order, either in line or in column. At the intersection of a row and a column, the value 1 is given if and only if two corresponding places are connected (d_{ij} (gaps)).

d_{ij} (gaps)	Chillon	Geneva	Gruyères	Gstaad	Aquaparc	Les Gets	Martigny	Montreux	Morzine	Vevey
Chillon	0	2	2	0	2	2	0	1	1	2
Geneva	2	0	2	2	2	0	2	1	0	2
Gruyères	2	2	0	0	2	0	0	1	0	0
Gstaad	0	2	0	0	0	0	2	1	0	0
Aquaparc	2	2	2	0	0	0	0	1	0	0
Les Gets	2	0	0	0	0	0	0	2	1	0
Martigny	0	2	0	2	0	0	0	1	0	0
Montreux	1	1	1	1	1	2	1	0	1	1
Morzine	1	0	0	0	0	1	0	1	0	0
Vevey	2	2	0	0	0	0	0	1	0	0

Table 8.1. *Example of a matrix of the places linked by the tourists interviewed in Montreux (Switzerland) [PIR 11b]*

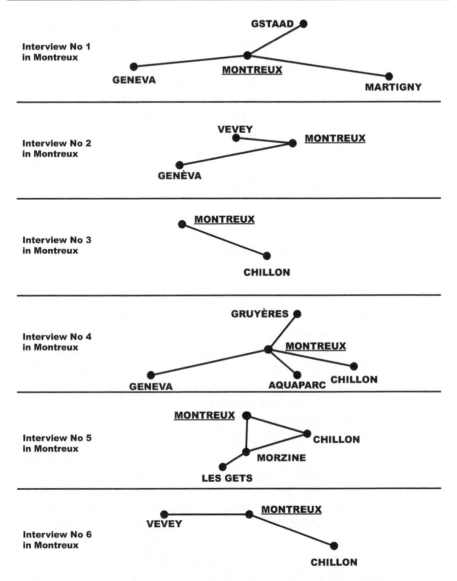

Figure 8.1. *Graphs made from tourist movements interviewed in Montreux (Switzerland)[PIR 11b]. For a color version of this figure, see www.iste.co.uk/piriou/tourism.zip*

We consider a link between all the stories collected within the interview place. On the other hand, we are not interested here in the recurrence of the relationship. For example, according to the matrix of the relationship between places practiced by the tourists interviewed in Montreux, we can see that tourists directly connect Montreux to other places (Château de Chillon, Geneva, Gruyères, etc.). Only Les Gets is separated from Montreux by a place (Morzine). Then, we made the route graphs for each interview place, as in the Montreux case (see Figure 8.1). The graph is a geometric figure that allows us to model and compare networks from a matrix [MOR 76]. The graph consists of a set of vertices or nodes and edges providing the link(s) to the vertex/vertices. The network is therefore represented in the form of a graph, which makes it possible to read the neighborhood relationships by the notion of a path linking several hubs [GIL 00].

8.2. Neighborhood relationships to analyze the regional dimension of networks

However, the production of schematic maps of itineraries according to mobility is not enough to explain the networks of tourist places and, in particular, their structures. Indeed, tourists combine several places in the same trip. Thus, tracing the itineraries practices by tourists during their stay allows us to combine both the types of mobilities and the places practiced that constitute a network. However, we must now justify neighborhood relationships. We can define the neighborhood as the whole of what is close, what is close and contiguous[1]. To analyze a network, a neighborhood analysis is done by measuring topological relationships to express adjacencies between places that are neighboring, due to a relationship by a line. Also, the neighborhood refers by its topological measurement to the notions of distance and proximity. However, the notion of distance corresponds to what separates, i.e. the distance between two places [GIL 00]. The question must be about adjacency, which corresponds to an immediate vicinity of the places. Proximity reflects what brings two places closer together. The ambiguity arises when geographical proximity is above all a "matter of distance" [TOR 09, p. 65] as it relates to the morphological criteria of space, the availability of transport infrastructures and the financial conditions of individuals who travel. In a second step, the graph and the matrix will allow us to measure the neighborhood relationships of directed graphs, i.e. the edges of the graphs become an oriented path which indicates a direction to the flow between two places.

---

1 Pumain D., "Voisinage," Hypergéo, available at: http://www.hypergeo.eu/spip.php? Article 90 accessed March 27, 2003.

8.2.1. *Neighborhood relationships of valued graphs as a measure of the gap between places within the same network*

After a first reading of the individual tourist itineraries during their stay, we presented the different possible network configurations of places according to the graphs. Now, we are trying to understand the perception of space by tourists according to theirs mobilities and to better understand the order of succession of places or the selection of a place in travel. Based on information on tourist itineraries for each interview place, we took into account the distance between the places according to the graphs and calculated, for each interview place, the average of the gaps between the places. We will speak of a neighborhood relationship of valued graphs, making it possible to know the order of the places practiced, whether by mobility or continuous mobility. The gap between the places were estimated at 1–12, with 1 corresponding to a place that is directly related to another and 12 meaning that one place is separated from another place by 11 intermediate places. We presented the results of the neighborhood relationships of valued graphs by point processes according to each interview place. Point processes on a map represent a set of locations, resulting from a process that has generated each of the points, in this case, the route of a place by tourists on their itineraries. By creating schematic maps, we will present the elementary tourist places in the form of points (see Figures 8.2 and 8.3). By this means, and using a square matrix, we try to represent the networks of places built from the routes traveled by tourists on a map by point processes [PUM 97]. The point processes allow us to better visualize the neighborhood relationships of the valued graph, i.e. to take into account the gap between two places by counting the intermediate places.

We identified three categories based on gaps and geographical distance between places. In an order of gaps from lowest to highest, we differentiated relationships with small gaps and geographical short distances; relationships with small gaps and variable geographical distances; and relationships with variable gaps and variable geographical distances (see Box 8.1).

Neighborhood relationships of valued graphs with small gaps and short geographical distances

We note this type of neighborhood relationships of valued graphs mainly for tourist resorts. Indeed, the tourists interviewed in the resorts stay in the same place and visit nearby places spatially within a geographical perimeter limited to a return to the accommodation at the end of the day. Concerning Moléson-sur-Gruyères (a small mountain resort in Switzerland), we can see no difference compared with the other places. Tourists directly connect Moléson-sur-Gruyères to Bulle or Gruyères in their travels, as evidenced by the account of a couple interviewed near the Moléson tourist office: "On Monday morning, we went shopping in Bulle and in the afternoon we went for a walk near Lac de la Gruyère".

However, there are places located in the mountains in the Prealps, as well as places located on the shores of Lake Geneva. The small gap between two places provides us with more information on tourist itineraries since tourists travel there either for accommodation or for visits, but diffusion mobility is preferred.

Neighborhood relationships of valued graphs at small deviation and variable geographical distance

The places are practiced by tourists who carry out diffusion mobility, but these can be supplemented by continuous mobility. The variable geographical distance is therefore explained between a time dedicated to visiting nearby places and a time devoted to a long journey with a visit to distant places. The tourists interviewed in front of the entrance to Chillon Castle, near Montreux, present these characteristics of the relationship between the places. It should be noted that the largest gaps correspond to the most geographically distant places. For example, there are on average six intermediate places between Chillon Castle and Basel. On the other hand, there is only a small gap between the Château de Chillon and the places located all around Lake Geneva such as Divonne-les-Bains or Villeneuve. Finally, we observe a periphery that is located south of Lake Geneva (Boëge, Sion), in Switzerland (Estavayer, La Chaux-de-Fonds, Interlaken, Brienz, Berne) or in Paris and the Loire Valley (Paris, Chambord, Chenonceaux) with larger gaps.

Neighborhood relationships of valued graphs with variable gaps and variable geographical distances

The distance between places is not necessarily correlated with geographical distance. We find this configuration for cities. That is, they are practiced by tourists from a variety of backgrounds and all types of mobilities. We find this configuration in Geneva and Lausanne. Several nearby places (located on the shores of Lake Geneva) have close neighborly relationships (e.g. Geneva or Lausanne). However, we also observe that other places much further away (located in several European countries) neighborhood relationships of valued graphs at such a small gap. We can give the example of Brussels, which is not separated from Geneva by any intermediate place. The comments collected on the Mont Blanc bridge in Geneva from a Japanese tourist on a group trip to Europe show that, in her itinerary, the city of Geneva is integrated into very distant places: "We arrived in Amsterdam, then we went to Antwerp, Brussels, and Bruges, then we went to Paris, Reims to visit the Champagne cellars, Chambord, and Geneva. Then we will go to Chamonix to see Mont Blanc, we will have a visit and especially shopping in Turin, Milan, Venice, Rome and we will take the plane back to Rome".

Box 8.1. *Results of the analysis of neighborhood relationships of valued graphs within the networks of places according mobilities of the tourists interviewed in the Lake Geneva region*

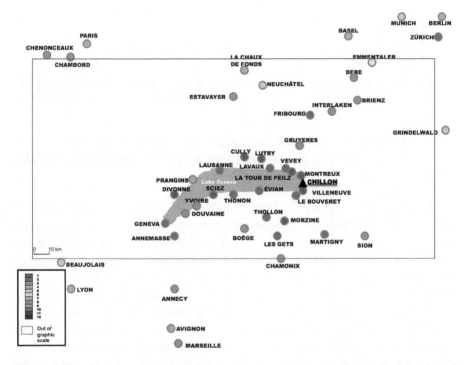

Figure 8.2. *Schematic map of point processes with gaps according to the interviewed tourists who visited Chillon Castle in Veytaux during their stay [PIR 12]*

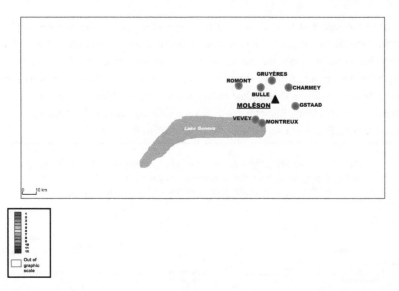

Figure 8.3. *Schematic map of point processes with gaps according to the interviewed tourists who practiced the resort of Moléson-sur-Gruyères during their stay [PIR 12]*

8.2.2. *Neighborhood relationships of directed graphs as a measure of the way in which places are connected within the same network*

Through the neighborhood relationships of directed graphs, we will deepen the neighborhood relationships between the places by taking note this time of the direction of the link(s) established between two places as well as its degree of intensity. It is the flow of people moving, and therefore the direction of the itinerary between two places, that allows us to be informed of the neighborhood relationships of directed graphs. First, the matrices allow us to read the direction of the link between two vertices (see Tables 8.2 and 8.3). In a second step, for the realization of the graphs, we replaced the edges by arcs, which we represented by directed paths (see Figures 8.4 and 8.5). However, in order to verify the occurrence of neighborhood relationships of directed graphs, we have taken into account, for the representation of graphs, only iterative flows between two places, which we have considered as a proven relationship when at least two links are established between two places, regardless of the direction of the flow. Between the diffusion mobility and continuation mobility, we have distinguished three types of neighborhood relationships of directed graphs: unilateral, bilateral and plurilateral relationships (see Box 8.2).

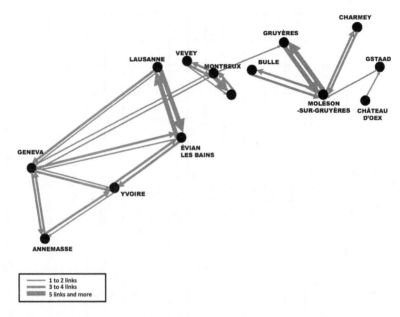

Figure 8.4. *Schematic map of directed graphs according to mobilities in terms of the diffusion mobility of the tourists interviewed in the Lake Geneva region [PIR 12]*

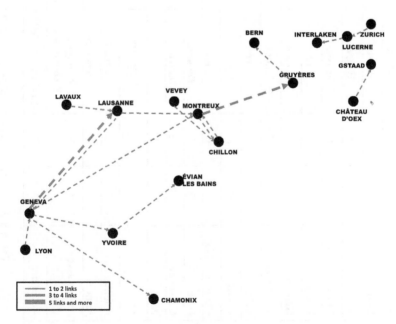

Figure 8.5. *Schematic map of directed graphs according to the continuous mobility of the tourists interviewed in the Lake Geneva region [PIR 12]*

Flow/places	Entrance	Exit	Flow/places	Entra	Exit	Flow/places	Entranc	Exit
Moléson	17	15	Bern	1	1	Lavaux	1	1
Beaujolais	1	0	Brigue	1	1	Les Diablerets	1	1
Boëge	2	1	Bruges	1	1	Les Gets	1	1
Chenonceaux	1	0	Brussels	1	1	Martigny	2	2
Evian	20	0	Bulle	4	4	Montbovon	1	1
Geneva	22	21	Chambord	2	2	Morat	3	3
Montreux	18	17	Chamonix	1	1	Morzine	2	2
Reims	1	0	Charmey	4	4	Neuchâtel	4	4
Yvoire	12	11	Chillon	9	9	Romont	1	1
Château d'Œx	5	6	Cully	5	5	Rougemont	1	1
Lyon	0	1	Divonne	3	3	Rumilly	1	1
Lausanne	10	12	Douvaine	1	1	Saas-Grund	1	1
Paris	1	3	Gex	1	1	Sciez	4	4
Thonon	1	5	Gruyères	13	13	St-Julien-en-Genevois	3	3
Abondance	2	2	Gstaad	5	5	Thollon	1	1
Annecy	4	4	Hermance	1	1	Vevey	6	6
Annemasse	8	8	La Chapelle-d'Abondance	2	2	Vitam Parc	1	1
Aquaparc	3	3	La-Tour-de-Peilz	4	4			

Table 8.2. Example of a matrix of neighborhood relationships of directed graphs according to the diffusion mobility of the tourists interviewed in the Lake Geneva region

Flow/places	Entrance	Exit	Flow/places	Entrance	Exit	Flow/places	Entrance	Exit
Geneva	7	12	Gruyères	6	5	Gstaad	1	1
Basel	1	3	Jura	1	0	Interlaken	5	5
Zurich	2	4	Marseille	1	0	La Chaux-de-Fonds	1	1
Amsterdam	0	1	Nice	1	0	Lavaux	3	3
Dover	0	1	Perpignan	1	0	Lucerne	2	2
Estavayer	1	2	Provence	1	0	Martigny	2	2
Lausanne	9	10	Sion	2	1	Maurienne	1	1
Le Bouveret	0	1	Zermatt	1	0	Milan	1	1
Lyon	2	3	Montreux	7	5	Munich	1	1
Paris	2	3	Rome	2	0	Neuchâtel	2	2
Puy de Sancy	0	1	Aigle	1	1	Prangins	1	1
Rumilly	0	1	Anvers	1	1	Rougemont	1	1
Thonon	1	2	Avignon	1	1	Saas-Grund	1	1
Vercors	0	1	Beaufortin	1	1	St-Gingolph	1	1
Bern	3	2	Berlin	1	1	Tarentaise	1	1
Chamonix	3	2	Brienz	1	1	Turin	1	1
Châtel	1	0	Brussels	1	1	Vanoise	1	1
Crans-Montana	1	0	Château d'Œx	1	1	Venice	1	1
Cully	1	0	Chillon	4	4	Vevey	1	1
Emmentaler	1	0	Col des Mosses	1	1	Villeneuve	1	1
Evian	1	0	Dole	1	1	Yvoire	1	1
Grindelwald	1	0	Fribourg	1	1			

Table 8.3. Example of a matrix of neighborhood relationships of directed graphs according to the continuous mobility of the tourists interviewed in the Lake Geneva region

Unilateral neighborhood relationships of directed graphs

They are characterized by the reception of flows from a single other place. The places concerned by neighborhood relationships of directed graphs are terminuses. They are a final step before returning home as part of a tourist continuous mobility. We can mention Chamonix and Lyon, which are in this configuration among all the stories of interviewees. We also note that these places are located on the outskirts of the Lake Geneva region. Then, we note discontinuities in mobility flows. Some places have a difference between incoming and outgoing flows. On the other hand, some places can be considered as gateways when the stay begins with continuous mobility.

Bilateral neighborhood relationships of directed graphs

They reflect the situation of places that receive a single incoming flow and a single outgoing flow whether they come from or move towards one or more places. Some places are characterized by this type of neighborhood relationships of directed graphs towards diffusion mobility (Bulle, Charmey, Annemasse), while others are characterized by this type of neighborhood relationships in the framework of continuous mobility (Interlaken, Lucerne). Once again, we note a geographical distance from the places practiced via continuous mobility. However, other places have the same characteristics of neighborhood relationships in terms of diffusion mobility and continuous mobility, for example Yvoire. In this case, these places are intermediate on a itinerary including several places of continuous mobility. This is also the case for diffusion mobility, as it may be the main place of residence. In addition, there is a role as a "transformer" of certain places. For example, Gstaad is affected by unilateral oriented graph neighborhood relationships in the context of continuous mobility and bilateral neighborhood relationships of directed graphs in the context of diffusion mobility. In the case of Geneva, the city has bilateral neighborhood relationships of directed graphs according to diffusion mobility, but plurilateral in continuous mobility. Finally, Gruyères benefits plurilateral neighborhood relationships of directed graphs on diffusion mobility, but bilateral in terms of continuous mobility. This role of "transformer" characterizes the place as a stopover place, marking a break in the sequencing of the itinerary.

Plurilateral neighborhood relationships of directed graphs

These are the places impacted by several incoming flows and outgoing flows, whether they come from or go to different places. In terms of diffusion mobility, the Moléson-sur-Gruyères resort is exclusively concerned by this type of neighborhood relationships of directed graphs. In fact, these places are the object or focus of excursions. It is therefore logical that this mountain resort should be found in this configuration, as it welcomes tourists on holidays and offers activities (sports, panoramas, etc.) for day visitors. The cities of Lausanne and Montreux are affected by this type of neighborhood relationship, regardless of mobility. This confirms the role of cities hosting tourists from multiple origins and with multiple routes and itineraries.

Box 8.2. *Results of neighborhood relationships of directed graphs (places networks) according to mobilities of tourist interviewed within the Lake Geneva region*

8.3. Multi-level regional networks of tourist places according to mobilities

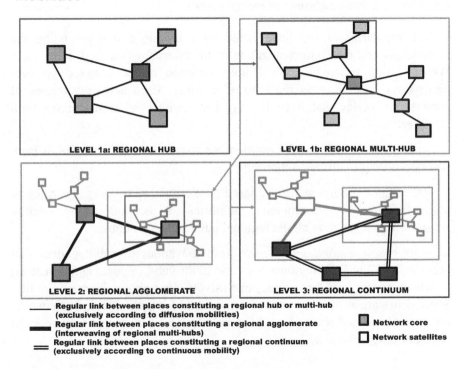

Figure 8.6. *Models of multi-level regional networks of tourist places [PIR 12]*

From the graphs that represent the neighborhood relationships of directed graphs, we can propose models of multi-level regional networks of tourist places. We have identified, according to the tourist mobilities of a regional network of tourist places, a supra-regional network of tourist places. These models allow us to delimit the tourist region that is practiced by tourists, as well as to better understand how the networking of elementary places that constitute it works. We have taken over the neighborhood relationships of directed graphs, according to the types of mobilities, in order to define the regularity of links between places. As a reminder, we consider as a regular link at least two flows of tourist mobilities that connect two tourist places. The flows established by the tourist mobilities during their stay therefore indicate the regularity of the links between the nodes, as a reminder of the tourist places in our purpose, constituting a network, as well as the interweaving of the networks creating sub-networks. We have defined *multi-level regional networks of tourist places*.

The regularity of the links is evolutionary since it depends on the respondents and the contextualization of the interview (location, time, etc.). We note that the regularity of links between nodes is based on four dimensions depending on the type of mobility. Each network consists of core(s), i.e. nodes that have the greatest number of regular links with satellites:

– the *regional hub* and the *regional multi-hub* are exclusively built from cores according to diffusion mobility;

– the *regional agglomerate* is based on a regularity of links according to both diffusion and continuous mobilities. It is built from satellite sub-networks formed by all the regional hubs and multi-hubs;

– the *regional continuum* forms from the nodes of sub-networks that become "satellites" (of regional hubs and multi-hubs, regional agglomerates) to which other places are added, exclusively through continuous mobility. Some nodes are also, in the case of the regional continuum, pivots. Networks are intertwined, and some places become interfaces between two networks of different geographical scales.

8.3.1. *The regional hub and the regional multi-hub: nodes linked from the core(s)*

The *regional hub* is the largest geographical scale of regional networks of tourist places. It is a network structured by regularity of the links between a node and several other nodes (see Figure 8.7), with these nodes being tourist places. The regularity of the links is exclusively established according to the diffusion mobility, which is limited to a daily trip. According to the accounts of the tourists interviewed, we have identified five main regional hubs within the Lake Geneva region (see Box 8.3).

We have identified five main regional hubs: Evian-les-Bains, Lausanne, Geneva, Moléson-sur-Gruyères and Montreux. Only the regional hub of Évian-Lausanne consists of a single regular link between Lausanne and Évian-les-Bains. This situation can be explained by the presence of a shuttle boat that provides a link between these two places located on either side of Lake Geneva. The other regional hubs are structured around a "core". For example, Moléson-sur-Gruyères is articulated with several "satellites": Bulle, Gruyères, Charmey or Gstaad.

Box 8.3. *Regional hubs identified within the Lake Geneva region according to the practices of the tourists interviewed*

Then, we found that some nodes, whether cores or satellites, are found in several regional hubs. Thus, according to the links established by the tourist mobilities constituting a network, the regional hubs, through these interfaces, are intertwined and create a new network of a new geographical scale: the *regional multi-hub*. Within the Lake Geneva region, several regional hubs are intertwined to form a regional hub (see Box 8.4). We find the core places of Geneva and Evian-les-Bains (see Figure 8.8)

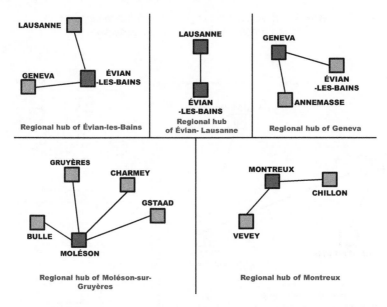

Figure 8.7. *Main regional hubs within the Lake Geneva region [PIR 12]*

Geneva, Evian-les-Bains and Lausanne appear several times within the regional hubs. These places are therefore part of a network of geographical scale that is the multi-hub. We also note that all the "core" regional hubs justify their place within the networks of places according to their diffusion mobility, since they are mainly accommodation places.

We observe that only two nodes are interfaces, structuring the regional multi-hub of Lake Geneva, namely Geneva and Evian-les-Bains. These two "core" nodes of the regional hubs structure the multi-hub through a regular link between Geneva and Evian-les-Bains with the regional hubs of Evian-les-Bains and Geneva, as well as through a regular link between Evian-les-Bains and Lausanne in the regional hubs of Lausanne and Evian-les-Bains. We note that there are only a few nodes that are interfaces between the regional and multi-polar regional hubs of Lake Geneva. This gives it a smaller geographical dimension. This weak entanglement of regional hubs can be explained by its integration into short networks, which are rather the subject of direct mobility to nodes without intermediate locations. In addition, the "core" of this network is shared between Geneva and Evian-les-Bains, which makes it more localized around Lake Geneva. Finally, tourists spread more widely within isolated regional hubs than within a more complex group (the multi-hub).

Box 8.4. *Lake Geneva regional multi-hub according to the practices of the tourists interviewed*

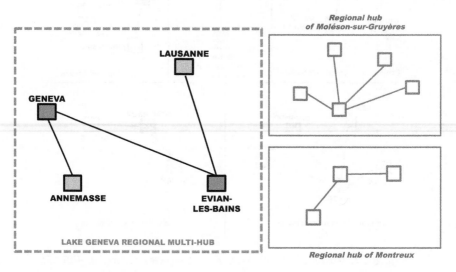

Figure 8.8. *Regional multi-hub of Lake Geneva regional multi-hub [PIR 12]*

8.3.2. *The regional agglomerate based on diffusion and continuous mobilities*

The *regional agglomerate* is built from nodes that can be located in a regional hub or multi-hub[2], as well as other isolated places. It creates interfaces where mobility crossing the regional agglomerate practiced, and a network of larger geographical scale such as the regional hub or multi-hub. The "core" corresponds to the node with the greatest number of regular links within the agglomerate, and satellites are the other nodes integrated by this same network. The nodes of the sub-networks also correspond to "satellites" for the regional agglomerate. It should therefore be noted that the regional agglomerate corresponds to a network of tourist places with tourist mobilities on a smaller geographical scale than the regional multi-hub, as well as lower than the regional hub. This sometimes even extends to a national or continental dimension. Within the Lake Geneva region, we have noted a regional agglomerate organized around eight pivotal nodes (see Box 8.5). Montreux is, however, the central core of the regional agglomerate of the Lake Geneva region (see Figure 8.9).

The regional agglomerate has eight hub nodes with other sub-networks, and Montreux is the central core. Among these interfaces, five are part of regional hubs (Geneva, Lausanne, Evian-les-Bains, Montreux and Gruyères). The village of Gruyères becomes an interface node; however, it was not the core of the regional hub to which it belongs (i.e. Moléson-sur-Gruyères). We can justify this by the continuous mobility, which explains the role of Gruyères as an interface between the regional hub of Moléson-sur-Gruyères and the regional agglomerate of the Lake Geneva region. Then, we observe that the village of Yvoire is integrated into the regional agglomerate, whereas this node was not integrated into any regional hub. On the other hand, all the nodes belonging to the Montreux regional hub (including Montreux, Vevey and Chillon Castle) are integrated into the regional agglomerate; however, they do not contribute to forming the multi-hub. In this specific case, we can justify that continuous mobility makes it possible to connect the regional hubs and share the regular links made by diffusion mobility. However, taken independently, diffusion mobility does not cover the same networks from place to place in regional hubs, with the exception of Geneva and Evian-les-Bains. Finally, we identify another regional agglomerate to the east of the Lake Geneva regional agglomerate, the Pays d'en haut-Saanenland, including the nodes of Gstaad and Château d'Œx. It is interesting to note that this regional agglomerate is linked

---

2 These places can also be cores or satellites within their regional or multi-regional hubs.

to a sub-network called the Moléson-sur-Gruyères regional hub, as is the regional agglomerate of the Lake Geneva region.

Box 8.5. *Lake Geneva regional agglomerate according to the practices of the tourists interviewed*

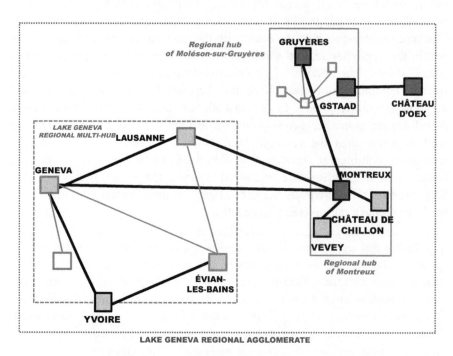

Figure 8.9. *Lake Geneva regional agglomerate [PIR 12]*

8.3.3. *The regional continuum structured by continuous mobilities*

The regional continuum is the smallest-scale network. This would be a sub-network of global regional basins (see Chapter 2), since it would be part of "international tourist territories" of rank A or rank B according to the model proposed by Olivier Dehoorne [DEH 03].

As a result, this network may have a national or continental dimension. The regional continuum is discerned according to the regular links established by exclusively continuous mobilities. The latter is structured from a few nodes already belonging to sub-networks (such as regional hubs and multi-hubs, as well as regional agglomerates), and also from other isolated places. The nodes in the regional continuum are "satellites". Only a few nodes with the most regular links to "core(s)" can be interfaces, if they belong to a sub-network. As for the other nodes, they integrate "sub-networks"; they are also satellites, but secondary.

We observed a regional continuum within the Lake Geneva region (see Box 8.6). Geneva and Gruyères are the two hub nodes to other regional sub-networks (see Figure 8.10).

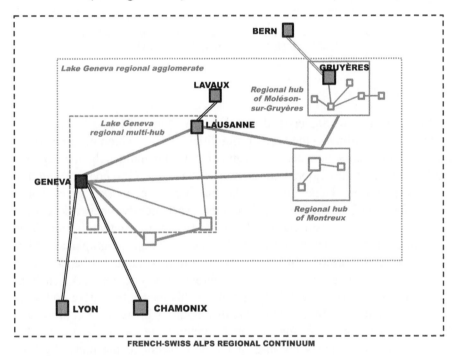

Figure 8.10. *French-Swiss Alps regional continuum [PIR 12]*

We have identified two pivotal nodes to sub-networks, namely Gruyères and Geneva. The regional continuum links Bern to Gruyères. The village of Gruyères is also an interface node with the sub-networks of the regional agglomerate of the Lake Geneva region and the regional hub of Moléson-sur-Gruyères. These two nodes have a large number of regular links with the other nodes, which informs a triple interface of the Gruyères node between the regional hub of Moléson-sur-Gruyères, the regional agglomerate of the Lake Geneva region and the French-Swiss Alps regional continuum.

Geneva is even a quadruple interface, since this node is also part of the regional multi-hub of Lake Geneva.

Moreover, with the largest number of regular links, Geneva is the core of the French-Swiss Alps regional continuum, which ultimately only completes the regional agglomerate of the Lake Geneva region, in the sense that Geneva is an interface node. Lausanne is also an interface node since, on the one hand, it links Lavaux to the regional continuum and, on the other hand, it integrates the regional hubs of Evian-les-Bains, Evian-les-Bains-Lausanne, the Lake Geneva regional multi-hub and the Lake Geneva regional agglomerate.

Box 8.6. *French-Swiss Alps regional continuum according to the practices of the tourists interviewed*

8.4. Conclusion

In conclusion, we understand that the networking of nodes by tourists is established according to the type of mobilities. Places, which become nodes, are often interfaces between the regional hub and multi-hub, the regional agglomerate and the regional continuum. Geneva and Gruyères are found in this configuration. Depending on the number of networks for which it creates the interface, the node will be a dual (between two networks), triple (between three networks) and quadruple (between four networks) interface. In addition, these nodes become interfaces at different geographical scales. For example, Montreux only becomes an interface node in the case of a regional agglomerate. Other nodes integrate only one network, such as Moléson-sur-Gruyères for the regional hub. This means that these nodes are traversed exclusively by a single type of mobility (diffusion or continuous). However, we note that the regional agglomerate is the network that federates the most nodes because of the networking of the nodes by both types of mobilities. Also, the regional agglomerate extends the network of the multi-hub. The regional continuum network is based on sub-networks and is developing. These have interface nodes, which are also cores, which makes them "gateways" to sub-networks, as is the case in Geneva. Finally, the presence of peripheral regional continuums gives us an indication of the national or continental dimension of the tourist region according to continuous mobilities.

9

Definition of Regional Tourist Functions of Places

In their tourist mobilities, tourists make choices of places. If tourists practice these places, they find them interesting. Sometimes they choose tourist places by opportunity, such as a place of accommodation ideally located on a long itinerary in order to reduce the travel time in two separate trips. Also, in our approach to the regional dimension of tourism practices, we need to better understand how and why places are differentiated from each other. To use Denis Retaillé's expression, "geography means recognizing and naming the difference between places" [RET 97, p. 77], but we must also highlight the tourist quality of places in a regional perspective. We define the quality of place as the set of conditions of place, which, in the light of the values and norms in force in a society, can be distinguished from other places in a hierarchical and relative way [MOR 08].

As we have presented, places are first of all differentiated according to elementary forms (see Chapter 1). Then, there are various recreational functions, first applied to the city, such as accommodation, food and drink, entertainment, shopping and attractions [ASH 00]. However, this list does not justify the choice of places. The interviews conducted with tourists around Lake Geneva enabled us, through their accounts, to identify the reasons for the practice of tourist places, particularly justifying their travel (see Chapter 4).

We have identified the main activities that we believe correspond to three main recreational functions. Then, we calculated the regional tourist functions according to a specialization in recreational functions. We will see that there is a differentiation of tourist places according to various regional tourist functions, also justifying tourist mobilities and explaining the networking of places.

Finally, we will see how professional actors, especially investors, are working to develop the regional tourism function of the places and encourage tourists to include places in their tourist mobility itineraries.

9.1. The recreational functions of places according to tourist practices

The exploitation of the stories proposed by tourists during our investigation around Lake Geneva can be deepened by seeking to understand the relationship between the place practiceed and the motives of the tourists that led them to go to one place rather than another. We question the quality of the places according to an approach of tourist practices and mobilities with a regional dimension. In order to measure the activities deployed by tourists in the places and thus characterize them in a context of practices with a regional dimension, we repeated our interviews with tourists in various places in the Lake Geneva region and listed the reasons for visiting certain places (see Box 9.1).

Excerpt from the life story of a tourist interviewed on the Mont Blanc bridge in central Geneva (Switzerland)

Florian is a German tourist who is participating a group tour with the city of Geneva as the arrival point from Germany. It is also the starting point for the return home. He tells us about his stay:

"We arrived in Geneva on Monday, we had a fondue in a restaurant in downtown. On Tuesday, we visited downtown Geneva with a guide and we visited CERN in the afternoon with engineers, we had a conference on CERN projects, we were very interested. This morning, we went to the Swiss National Museum (Prangins) and had lunch in Lausanne in Ouchy. This afternoon we visited the Olympic Museum and tonight we have a theatre evening. Tomorrow, we will go to Lutry to discover the wine of Lavaux and then we will go to the castle of Chillon. We sleep in Villeneuve. On Friday, we will go to the Gianadda Foundation (Martigny) and Sion. Then we will return by bus to Geneva to return to Berlin".

Analysis of recreational activities by places cited

In this account, we distinguish several places that are associated with recreational activities:

– Geneva: traditional local meal, company visit;

– Prangins: museum visit;

– Lausanne: lunch, theater, museum visit;

– Lutry: wine tasting;

– Chillon castle: visit of the castle;

– Villeneuve: accommodation;

– Martigny: visit of a museum;

– Sion: visit of the city.

Box 9.1. *Example of reading the tourist story and analysis of recreational activities*

Recreational activities can be grouped to characterize *recreational functions* of the tourist place.

DEFINITION.– Recreational functions of a tourist place: all the recreational activities that justify the practice of a place by tourists. Through these recreational functions, the place responds to the recreational project of tourists and informs them of the complementarity or specificity of this place within a regional group of tourist places.

Based on these results from field reports, we have grouped recreational activities into three categories of recreational functions according to their dominance within tourist places (see Table 9.1):

– the *service function* that participates in the practical organization of the stay, in particular activities identical to those carried out in the daily life of a place;

– the *contemplation function* that corresponds to everything that the tourist can see and understand through observation, like a simple landscape viewing;

– the *exploration function* corresponds to an in-depth visiting of the territory through a media or human accompaniment.

According to the accounts collected from interviews with tourists, we have provided a table by tourist places cited that describes the different activities that we have classified by recreational functions (see the example of Geneva given in Table 9.2).

Contemplation function (A)	Exploration function (B)	Service function (C)
– Panoramic view – Strolling, walking, hiking, etc. – Golf, cycling, beach, skiing (outdoor panoramic activity, etc.) – View of gardens, wharves, ports, castles, etc.	– Visit and tasting (local products, etc.) – Guided or thematic visit of a port, a fort, a museum, etc. – Local market, shopping, flea market, art gallery – Thalassotherapy, bath, cure – Company visits	– Restaurant (except thematic and local) – Classic hosting – Purchase, food shopping – Rental of a vehicle – Transportation – Cinema, bowling

Table 9.1. *Recreational function categories by tourism activities*

Functions	Activities described	Number of citations per activity	Number of citations per function
Contemplation function	Stroll	5	7
	View of the gardens	1	
	View of the water stream	1	
Exploration function	Visit of the city	9	20
	Visit of the museum	6	
	Shopping	5	
Service function	Accommodation	11	19
	Transport	7	
	Meal	1	

Table 9.2. *Description of activities and ranking by recreational functions in Geneva*

COMMENT ON TABLE 9.2.– *Of the 57 tourists interviewed in Annemasse, Château de Chillon, Divonne-les-Bains, Évian-les-Bains, Geneva, Gruyères, Lausanne, Moléson-sur-Gruyères, Montreux, Thonon-les-Bains and Yvoire, 34 went to Geneva, including 9 interviewed in that place. Based on the stories (see Box 9.1), we identified three activities related to the contemplative function (stroll, view of the gardens, view of the water jet), three activities related to the exploration function (practice of the city and museum, shopping) and finally three activities related to the service function (accommodation, transport, meals). Despite a visit recurrence of the city for accommodation, it can be seen that the city is practiced in a slightly dominant way for an exploration function. However, the service function is important. However, these results only correspond to an interpretation of the stories of the tourists interviewed at some point in the autumn of 2009.*

9.2. The regional tourism function of places according to recreational functions

Based on these categories of recreational functions, we define the *regional tourism function* of the places according to recreational activities, characterizing dominant recreational functions.

DEFINITION.– Regional tourism function of a place: contribution of a place to a regional group of tourist places according to recreational functions identified by tourist practices.

We have identified six regional tourism functions (see Table 9.3).

9.2.1. *Types of regional tourism functions*

First, we identify three regional tourism functions that are characterized by the exclusive practice of a recreational function:

– the *observation place* is used exclusively for a contemplation function;

– the *practiced place* is exclusively for an exploration function;

– the *service place* is used exclusively for a service function.

Other places can be used for several recreational functions:

– the *transit place* is visited both for a function of contemplation and a function of exploration;

– the *excursion place* is used for an exploration function and a service function;

– the *break place* is practiced for a contemplative function and a service function;

– the *stopover place* is the most complex place in terms of tourism practices since it is used for all functions, observation, exploration and services.

Regional tourism functions	Recreational functions		
	Contemplative function	Exploration function	Service function
Observation place	✓		
Visited place		✓	
Service place			✓
Transit place	✓	✓	
Excursion place		✓	✓
Break place	✓		✓
Stopover place	✓	✓	✓

Table 9.3. *Characterized regional tourism functions by dominant recreational functions*

9.2.2. Calculation of the specialization index to measure the regional tourism function of places

In order to measure the regional tourism function of the places, we used the specialization index. We use this calculation method commonly used in transport geography to determine the specialization of port terminals in freight transshipment [ROD 09]. The specialization index is interesting to manipulate to determine the specialization of a place in one or more recreational functions in order to define its regional tourism function.

DEFINITION.– Specialization index: either a square matrix of the total number of activities related to a recreational function performed in a place i(f)i, or the square of the total number of activities performed related to all recreational functions in a place:

$$"SI = \sum_i t_i^2 / (\sum_i t_i)^{2"}$$

The closer the specialization index is to 1, the more specialized the place is in a particular recreational function. Conversely, if the index is 0 or close to 0, it means that the place benefits from diversified functions. A place that will have a very strong specialization with an index equal to 1 in a function will be either an observation place, a visited place or a service place. Some places can also be the subject of several specializations (transit place, excursion place, break place and stopover place).

9.2.3. *Some results of the regional tourism function of the Lake Geneva region places*

In the Lake Geneva region, the accounts collected from the tourists we met did not allow us to identify any observation places. On the other hand, we have characterized the other places by the other regional tourist functions: exploration places, service places, transit places, excursion places, break places and stopover places. We will now illustrate each of them with the recreational functions.

Example of a visited place

Among the visited places, which are therefore exclusively characterized by an exploration function, we noted the Swiss city of Martigny located in the Valais. Four tourists interviewed at our various survey places stated that they had visited the Gianadda Foundation's museographic space. Also, according to our study, the city of Martigny provides an exploration function to the regional networks of tourist places according to the practices of the tourists interviewed.

Examples of service places

We found several service places performing service functions, mainly for hosting. This is the case in the French city of Annemasse, located on the Swiss border in the urban area of Geneva, where four tourists interviewed go to stay. The city of Zurich in northern Switzerland is also a service place, where tourists travel to catch a plane via the international airport.

Examples of transit places

Several crossing points were highlighted, however, with a dominance of recreational exploration functions. Thus, the castle of Chillon is mentioned four times for the visit of the place and three times for the view of the place on Lake Geneva. The same is true for the French village of Yvoire, which was mentioned six times for visits and once for a "stroll". The Swiss resort of Gstaad was mentioned once for a visit and once for a walk.

Examples of excursion places

Excursion places have also emerged with a difference in dominant recreational functions. Thus, the French city of Lyon is used more for service functions, four times cited for accommodation and exploration functions and three times cited for visits. In contrast, the city of Basel in northwestern Switzerland is mentioned three times for a visit to the museum of contemporary art, once for a visit to the city and once for finding a means of transport.

Examples of stopover places

Most of the places cited by the tourists interviewed are stopovers since they fulfill several recreational functions. However, there are dominant recreational functions depending on the location. Thus, the village of Gruyères and the city of Vevey are mentioned for exploration functions. On the other hand, Evian-les-Bains, Montreux and Lausanne are cited more for service functions.

Box 9.2. *Results of the regional tourism functions of Lake Geneva region places the Lake Geneva region according to the calculation of the specialization index*

Figure 9.1. *Medieval village of Yvoire (France) (source: J. Piriou, July 2012). For a color version of this figure, see www.iste.co.uk/piriou/tourism.zip*

COMMENT ON FIGURE 9.1.– *The medieval village of Yvoire is the subject of many recreational activities according to tourist practices. Tourists enjoy both observing the village on the shores of Lake Geneva and exploring the area by visiting the remarkable garden.*

In this study, we note that according to practice, we find places with multiple functions. We will try to explain it. First of all, we note that the "stopover places" correspond to the main cities around the lake: Geneva, Evian-les-Bains, Lausanne, Vevey and Montreux. On the periphery of the lake, we can see two other "stopover places", Bulle, Gruyères in the Prealps and in northern Switzerland, or in the Mittelland in Basel or Bern. Second, "transit places" are places of major tourist use such as Yvoire (600,000 visitors in 2006) and the Château de Chillon (270,000 visitors in 2006)[1]. We can make the same observation for the visited places (Martigny, Charmey and Neuchâtel) or for the service places (Annemasse, Thonon-les-Bains, Zurich), which are located slightly on the periphery of the stopover places.

Figure 9.2. *Entrance to Chillon Castle (Switzerland) (source: J. Piriou, June 2009)*

1 Figures provided by the management of the Yvoire tourist office and the management of the Château de Chillon, both interviewed in 2007 as part of our doctoral work.

COMMENT ON FIGURE 9.2.– *Chillon Castle is one of Switzerland's most popular tourist destinations. This castle located on Lake Geneva allows visitors to discover the history of the place and to enjoy a landscape of fortress castle and views of Lake Geneva.*

9.3. Evolution of a place to develop the regional tourist function

Tourists, through their mobilities, assign regional tourist functions to places in order to organize their stay and define the tourist region adapted to their recreational plans. However, the professionals can intervene if they wish to develop the regional tourist function of the places. In our opinion, investors contribute to the change quality of the place. At each *moment place*, the MIT team defines the moments that correspond to the ruptures or accelerations marked in the evolution of a place. It is a transition from one state to another, defined as the moment when, in a given place, tourism, and according to our comments on spatial practices of regional dimension, is constituted as a significant factor in the organization of the place [ÉQU 05].

The *ex nihilo* creation of equipment can contribute to the development of tourism in a given place, or even to the integration of circuits or tourist routes. As we have seen previously, the creation of theme parks makes it possible to attract tourists to rural areas where they would not have come, for example, in the case of Center Parcs (see Chapter 4). But the creation of new equipment does not necessarily mean a total conversion to tourism for the territory. For example, the Louvre Museum, which relocated part of its museum space to Lens in the Pas-de-Calais region at the end of 2012, is struggling to attract an international tourist clientele. Indeed, at the end of 2017, during the five years of the site's opening, despite a traffic of approximately 450,000 visitors per year, only 17% of them come from abroad and mainly from the countries bordering the Benelux[2]. These are therefore local residents who are making a daily excursion. Lens has become a little more touristy than before, but tourists are fully involved in a touristic region that includes other places such as Lille.

---

2 According to Agence France-Presse, relayed by Le Point.fr, *"Cinq ans du Louvre-Lens: un beti culturel réussi, un impact limité pour le bassin minier"*, available at: http://www.lepoint.fr/culture/cinq-ans-du-louvre-lens-un-pari-culturel-reussi-un-impact-limite-pour-le-bassin-minier-01-12-2017-2176541_3.php, online since December 1, 2017, accessed June 1, 2018.

Existing places can also evolve, impacting the moment of the place. In Brighton, Britain's worldly seaside resort has become a city with urban activities such as sightseeing, shopping or various events, while keeping some seaside activities. In addition, the strengthening of this urban identity is marked by a policy of building heritage enhancement and, in particular, the architectural traces of tourism. Mathis Stock noted that "buildings dating from the Regency, the Royal Pavilion, and the rehabilitation of the West Pierdument marked for tourists are indicators of this" [STO 01, p. 130]. According to him, the decrease in seasonality in Brighton and Hove has changed the tourism practices that are spread out all year round and whose resort, now a city, has had to adapt. The same phenomenon can be found in French tourist places. For example, the French resort of Dinard located in Brittany has classified more than 400 villas as a protected area and has benefited from the Ministry of Culture's status as a city of art and history since 2003. Tours with tour guides are available on the history of seaside tourism in the resort.

A final case shows an evolution desired by investors in order to change the moment of the place. Ekaterina Andreeva-Jourdain demonstrated how the Russian resort of Sochi has changed since the early 2000s by diversifying the availability and proposing various activities for various tourist profiles. The Sochi region is committed to all-season tourism, since in summer tourists enjoy the Black Sea coast, and in winter they practice winter sports in the Caucasus resorts. In a desire to deseasonalize tourism, the Russian government has involved public and private actors (including Gazprom, Interros and Umaco) to develop tourist facilities (luxury hotels, marinas, golf). There is also a development along the coast from Sochi to Adler [AND 16]. It should be noted that the Winter Olympic Games held in Sochi in 2014 led to the creation of several resorts in the Caucasus mountains, such as *Krosnaïa Poliana*.

9.4. Conclusion

The regional tourism function of places allows us to better understand the spatial practices of tourists. Indeed, the practice of places is justified and involves tourist mobilities. Tourists are found to assess the places according to their recreational functions, and their practices reflect the regional tourism function. As a result, professional actors can become involved by changing the moment of the place. An investment, for example the creation of new equipment, or the enhancement of heritage, helps to change the moment of the place. However, tourists must have an interest in them, and through their mobilities, they should integrate these places into their multi-level regional networks of tourist places.

10

Place Positions in the Tourist Region

Tourists practice places that must fulfill their recreation plan. As we have seen from their practices, they assign a regional tourist function to them in order to justify a trip to a particular place by means of a tourist diffusion mobility or a tourist continuous mobility. Through their spatial practices of regional dimension, tourists establish networks of tourist places, which are intertwined and take different forms.

We will first analyze the integration of places into the networks created by tourist practices. To do this, we will measure the network connectedness index. In addition, some places are within circuits, whether they are networks of places composed according to diffusion mobility or continuous mobility. We will then identify these locations by the connectivity index. Finally, we will see how professional actors act (especially developers) to try to change the position of places in networks.

10.1. The inclusion of places in the networks of tourist places according to mobilities

Tourists, via their mobilities, develop networks of places, which can be understood on several scales. We have defined regional networks of multi-level tourist places (see Chapter 8) that now ask us to consider the conditions for integrating places into these networks. We used the matrices and directed graphs developed from the stories provided by the tourists interviewed during their stay[1]. Then we measured the inclusion of the places

---

1 See Chapter 8 on this subject, with the example of neighborhood relationships of directed graphs and matrix based on the tourist interviewed in Montreux.

into the networks using two indices: the *connectedness index* and the *connectivity index*.

10.1.1. *The connectedness index to better understand the inclusion of places according to the complexity of the networks*

Connectedness refers to the ability of a network to connect nodes to the outskirts of an area [PUM 97]. A graph is related if one or more of the subparts are not related to the others. Connectedness communicates (if it is possible) from any node, in this case according to our purpose of tourist places, to be linked to other nodes (other tourist places).

The *connectedness index* provides information on the fragmentation of a graph into related components that are separated from each other. We have taken up the matrices and directed graphs that schematize the routes described by the tourists we interviewed (see Chapter 8). In order to measure the connectedness, we consider a graph with N nodes and L edges.

DEFINITION.– Connectedness index: the connectedness index β is calculated by relating the number of edges (L) to the number of vertices (N), or β = L/N.

The maximum connectedness of the graph is reached when each of the number of vertices, N, is directly linked by an edge to each of the other N-1 vertices. In this case, the maximum number of edges is 3 (N-2). On the other hand, when edges are missing, not all vertices are directly linked to each other.

The larger the index, the stronger the connectedness, i.e. the place is within a complex graph, i.e. a long and extended route for continuous mobilities or multiple and polarized itineraries around places for diffusion mobility.

The place will be considered to be located in a network with low connectedness when $\beta < 0.80$, medium connectedness when $0.81 < \beta < 0.90$, high connectedness when $0.91 < \beta < 1$ and, finally, very high connectedness when $\beta > 1$.

10.1.2. *Some results of network connectedness and place integration in the Lake Geneva region*

Geographical distance and types of mobilities (continuous or diffusion) contribute to determining the network connectedness and the places integrated. There is also a distinction according to the types of places, whether they are large European cities, small- or medium-sized cities, or resorts.

Remote places geographically embedded in highly connectedness networks

We note that the degree of network connectedness changes with geographical distance. For example, the castles of the Loire (Chenonceau and Chambord), cited by the tourists interviewed on tourist places in the Lake Geneva region, are part of networks with a connectedness index greater than 1. These places are part of networks of long-distance spatial practices and are in fact steps at the beginning or end of an itinerary.

Large European cities in highly connectedness networks

We have noted above that many places situated far away from the Lake Geneva region are located in highly connectedness networks. We also note that several large European cities have an index close to 1, such as Brussels and Lyon (1), Paris (0.93), and Milan (0.92). These cities are part of long continuous mobilities networks. We have identified in this same configuration for some alpine tourist resorts, such as Flaine, Morzine and Les Gets (1), Interlaken (0.95), and Chamonix (0.86). On the other hand, these places are located in networks according to diffusion mobility, but these networks have many arcs, or even loops.

Places included in networks with medium connectedness

Most of the places cited by tourists are, according to their practices, located in networks with medium connectedness. There are also European cities such as Berlin, Munich, Rome and Venice, but also the cities and resorts in the Lake Geneva region, such as Fribourg (0.9), Bern, Evian-les-Bains (0.87), Divonne-les-Bains (0.85) and Moléson-sur-Gruyères (0.82). We note that these places, which are part of networks of medium connectedness, are present in much shorter networks, i.e. with fewer vertices according to the continuous mobilities and with fewer arcs or less complexity of the network according to the diffusion mobility.

Places included in low connectedness networks

Several places in the Lake Geneva region cited by tourists in their spatial practices are identified in low connectedness networks. We find, in particular, the places practiced according to highly specialized regional tourist functions. For example, the cities of Annemasse in France or Bulle in Switzerland are cited for recreational service functions (shopping, accommodation). Tourists come from or travel to these places by short distances per kilometer as part of diffusion mobility. The example of the city of Geneva, which is located in low connectedness networks (0.76), is also an interesting case. In fact, the city of Geneva is practiced within the framework of diffusion mobility, but with few vertices, then it is there that a switch to continuous mobility takes place. It can be deduced from this that the city of Geneva is a gateway to the Lake Geneva region.

Box 10.1. *Results of network complexity and places inclusion within the Lake Geneva region according to the calculation of the connectedness index*

In the end, we learn that cities are located in networks with rather strong connectedness. This result can be explained by the change in mobility that takes place in these cities, from continuous mobility to diffusion mobility. The high accommodation capacity and multimodal connections (air, rail, road) available in major European cities partly explain this possibility of changing the type of mobility. In other places, a switch from one mobility to another is not necessarily established, but they can be integrated into networks with strong connectedness. However, we note that the places that are part of highly connectedness networks are rather far from the interview places. Places in networks with lower connectedness not only reflect a spatial practice of shorter kilometer distances by tourists, but also, as we have seen in the case of Geneva, a shift in the type of mobility.

10.1.3. *The connectivity index to better understand the connection density of places in networks*

The connectivity of a network makes it possible to evaluate the possibilities of linking different nodes [PUM 97]. It describes the connection density within a network by alternative routes between two nodes. Still from the matrices and graphs of directed graph neighborhood relations, previously mentioned, we can calculate the connectivity index.

DEFINITION.– Connectivity index: The connectivity index α is calculated by identifying the sub-sets of vertices (S) connected by edges (L) and is calculated by the number of existing circuits (C) that is related to the maximum number of possible circuits (2S-L), i.e. $\alpha = C/(2S-L)$.

The connectivity index takes into account values between 0 (minimum connectivity) and 1 (maximum connectivity). We qualify the results as we consider $\alpha < 0.1$ as a low connectivity network, $0.1 < \alpha < 0.1999$ as a medium connectivity network, $0.2 < \alpha < 0.3$ as a high connectivity network and $\alpha > 0.3$ as a very high connectivity network. Note that not all graphs have a circuit.

10.1.4. *Some results of the network connectivity and the inclusion of places within the Lake Geneva region*

The connectivity index makes it possible to determine the architecture or topology of the networks within which the nodes (tourist places) are included according to tourist mobilities. We distinguish the tree network where a place is included at the head of a network (a point) and then linked to other places (arcs), from the "circuit" network where the places (points) are all linked to each other (arcs).

Cities in networks with low connectivity

We note that cities are located in low connectivity networks, such as Lausanne (0.06) and Geneva (0.05). As these cities are traveled through according to continuous mobility, we can explain this result.

Resorts in medium connectivity networks

The resorts are included into medium connectivity networks. We can mention Thonon-les-Bains (0.12), Evian-les-Bains (0.10) and Divonne-les-Bains (0.11). This average network connectivity can be explained by the diversity of spatial practices between diffusion and continuous mobilities. The resorts provide accommodation in a way that allows tourists to diffuse into places in the surrounding area. However, they are also visited in the context of continuous mobility over longer distances.

Box 10.2. *Results of network density and places inclusion within the Lake Geneva region according to the calculation of the connectivity index*

Finally, we find that few locations are in networks with high connectivity. The few circuits identified include places on the shores of Lake Geneva. But the majority of the places mentioned by the tourists interviewed at this time in autumn 2009 do not integrate into "circuit" networks, but rather into "tree" networks. That is, it is the development of related networks whose number of links is equal to the number of nodes.

10.2. Developers are involved in positioning the place to be integrated into tourists' spatial practices

Tourism professionals want their locations to be integrated into tourist itineraries. Moreover, they often even want tourists to stay as long as possible in their places, avoiding roaming to other tourist places. Some professionals have also wished to strengthen the enhancement of their territories, in particular by mobilizing the actors. We will present two strategies identified by developers: one within the Lake Geneva region, and the other in Brittany.

10.2.1. *The case of Franco-Swiss cross-border cooperation to promote the practice of tourist places around Lake Geneva*

As mentioned previously, tourists travel around Lake Geneva, on both sides of the national border between France and Switzerland. We have even found that tourist places around the lake can be part of national or continental spatial networks. However, professional actors, particularly official institutions for the promotion of tourism, worked until the end of the 20th Century in a dissociated or even competing manner. This is explained by very distinct tourist positions on both shores.

On the Swiss side, there are cities such as Geneva and Lausanne that have gained international recognition since the 18th Century for their living environment, whether scientific or climate-related [TIS 07, HUM 07]. On the French side, only two small resort spas attract tourism, of which only Evian-les-Bains barely reaches 10% of all overnight stays in Lausanne [DUR 09]. However, in 1995, the idea of creating *"Léman sans frontière"* [Lake Geneva without borders] , an association promoting Franco-Swiss tourism, was born at the initiative of actors from two territories: the prealpine resort of Moléson-sur-Gruyères and the lakeside commune of Le Bouveret, represented by its development company [PIR 18b]. For the small resort of Gruyère, the aim was to capture summer tourist flows for winter sports activities. For the small lake municipality, the aim was to convince vacationers who go to the mountains in winter to enjoy the lakeshores in summer. This principle of making tourists circulate interested other actors, such as the Evian mineral water bottling company. In 2018, the association has 35 members, including 23 places in Switzerland and 12 places in France.

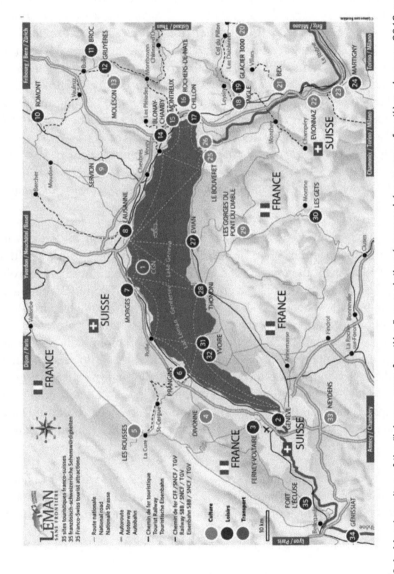

Figure 10.1. *Member sites of the "Léman sans frontière" association (source: Léman sans frontière, January 2018, with the kind permission of the General Secretariat). For a color version of the figures in this chapter, see www.iste.co.uk/piriou/tourism.zip*

COMMENT ON FIGURE 10.1.– *The "Léman sans frontière" association brings together various tourist attractions (transport, museums, castles, amusement parks, manufacturing plant tours, etc.), which are divided into three categories indicated in green, blue and red: culture, loisirs (hobbies) and transport. They are spread over France and Switzerland (Suisse) around Lake Geneva. The main tourist attractions of the Lake Geneva region[2] are Chillon Castle (367,500 visitors in 2016) and the Olympic Museum of Lausanne (304,800 visitors in 2016), as well as more modest sites in terms of the number of visits are the Jardin des Cinq Sens in Yvoire (36,869 visitors in 2016) and the Château de Ripaille in Thonon-les-Bains (24,080 visitors in 2016). According to the association's statutes, in accordance with Article 60 of the Swiss Civil Code, the association's objective is clear: "...to bring together tourist attraction sites with a high potential of visitors and offering a diversification of the offerings in order to boost promotional forces to better satisfy the public and offer them a variety of quality excursions"[3].*

Among the members of the association, there are local investors with tourist attractions (foundations, museums, gardens, thermal baths, ski lifts, etc.), as well as institutional actors in tourism who have a development role, or even a prescription role. These are mainly French (Yvoire, Divonne-les-Bains, Monts-Jura, Thonon-les-Bains, etc.) and Swiss (Romont, Gruyères) tourist offices. All these French and Swiss actors are involved in this Franco-Swiss development project with the aim of promoting the movement of tourists within their territories and tourist places. Also, to reach tourists during their preparation for their stay or on their routes and movements during the stay, several actions are carried out. First, a directory guide has been prepared and 320,000 copies are distributed each year on all member sites and in the various promotional information points (accommodation, catering, tourist offices, etc.).

In 2011, to further encourage cross-border travel, and with the financial support of a European program, the association created 80 tourist packages in the form of excursions or stays. Then, in 2015, in order to fully support

---

2 According to the figures provided by the directorates of tourist offices and tourist places during our field interviews, as part of the doctoral work in 2009.

3 According to article II of the statutes of the association "Léman sans frontière".

tourists in their journeys between tourist places, the "Mobi-Léman" project proposes 18 thematic itineraries on other sides of the lakeshores, with a geolocation and animation service via a smartphone application. This project uses different modes of transport (car, bicycle, boat, pedestrian) and links member sites by identifying at least 15 points of interest on routes in the French departments and Swiss cantons. There is therefore a tourism development initiative, participating in the decision-making process of tourists in the construction of their tourist mobilities, designing networks of tourist places, and therefore the tourist region.

10.2.2. The case of a redistribution of regional tourist destinations to adapt to the practices of tourist places in Brittany

In the west of France, the Brittany region has four administrative departments. However, the regional tourism plan adopted by the Regional Council of Brittany in June 2012 mentions a redrawing of the administrative territories in order to rethink the organization and ensure development and promotion of tourism on the basis of the number of visitors and the reputation of the places. Also, as a follow-up to a "MORGOAT" data collection study, conducted by the Brittany Tourism Observatory between 2005 and 2008, 11 tourist destinations were identified, redrawing the administrative boundaries of the departments and regions. Three of them particularly demonstrate this:

– "Bretagne – Loire-Océan" located in the south of Brittany, which partially integrates the Loire-Atlantique department, although administratively located in the Pays de la Loire region;

– "Cœur de Bretagne – Kalon Breizh", which includes several municipal and intermunicipal territories located in the departments of Côtes-d'Armor, Finistère and Morbihan;

– "Saint-Malo – Baie du Mont-Saint-Michel" located in the northeast of the region, straddling the departments of Côtes-d'Armor, Ille-et-Vilaine and as far as Normandy, mentioning the name of Mont-Saint-Michel whose bay is shared between the two administrative regions.

For tourism developers in Brittany, this approach reflects a desire to offer territories that are more in line with visitors' expectations and practices. The Regional Council of Brittany, through its Regional Tourism Committee, has developed destinations by local consensus concerning the delimitation perimeter, the name and the determination of the local facilitating structure for implementation, as mentioned in the diagram "the development of destinations is based on the vitality of the tourist entities that compose them for which they constitute the scale of coherence adapted for the attractiveness and the development of tourism"[4].

Already in 2006, the Regional Tourism Observatory of Brittany had developed a laboratory to measure tourist hyperfrequentation within the destination "Saint-Malo Baie du Mont Saint-Michel"[5]. The tourism analysis institution refers to "hyperfrequentation" since the population present in this territory has a capacity to be multiplied by 2.24 compared to 1.50 on average in Brittany. The center of this territory is the city of Saint-Malo and 17 municipalities in the surrounding area between Cap Fréhel and Mont-Saint-Michel from the northwest to the northeast and as far as Dinan and Combourg in the southwest and southeast. As early as the 1960s, authors had identified the presence of a tourist conurbation [MEY 69, LAR 82] (see Chapter 1). The measurement of practices within this area shows that tourism is concentrated on the coast and is less widespread in the hinterland. This study was updated in 2011 with a similar finding concerning a concentration of accommodation supply, with 68% of tourist accommodation on the Côte d'Émeraude and its hinterland grouped in three places: Cancale, Dinard and Saint-Malo. In addition, vehicle traffic counters have been installed on-site in car parks. The density observed was also remarkable in 2011, with 900 people per day per square kilometer at Cap Fréhel, 3,000 people per day per square kilometer at Pointe du Grouin and finally 5,000 people per day per square kilometer at Mont-Saint-Michel.

---

4 Extract from Act II of the regional tourism plan of Brittany 2012-2014, "Making Brittany an exceptional tourist destination", Regional Council of Brittany, Rennes, 2012, p. 71.

5 Regional Observatory of Tourism of Brittany, "Côte d'Émeraude and its hinterland. Space watch. Laboratory for measuring tourist density and its effects 2006-2010", Regional Council of Brittany, Rennes, 2011.

Figure 10.2. *Concentration of tourists and inhabitants on the ramparts of the intramural city of Saint-Malo (France), day of the "Tide of the century". (source: J. Piriou, March 2015)*

COMMENT ON FIGURE 10.2.– *March 21, 2015 was a day of astronomical conjunction by the alignment of the Earth, Moon and Sun at a time when the distance between the stars was minimal. The consequence was a spring tide in new moon (or syzygy) with large coefficients. Thus, residents and tourists gathered massively on the ramparts of the intramural city of Saint-Malo waiting for the high seas at 8:27 p.m. with a coefficient of 118, in order to attend a show of high waves that burst on the breakwaters or at the foot of the ramparts, and whose scum watered the passers-by. Such a winter concentration in Saint-Malo, although exceptional, nevertheless reveals the appropriation of tourists of this place as central within a coast that offers multiple headlands (Bay of Mont-Saint-Michel, Pointe du Décollé, Cap Fréhel, etc.). The tourist policy of the city of Saint-Malo is to try to deseasonalize tourism, which is more concentrated in the spring and summer seasons, by proposing a discovery of the natural environment through these phenomena of high tides, particularly spectacular during stormy winter seasons.*

Finally, this proposal to track the tourist area has the merit of reporting on tourist practices and identifying the places frequented in the area. However, it does not take sufficient account of the tourist profiles or the types of mobilities that would explain, on the one hand, the reasons for the practice of a particular place and, on the other hand, the time devoted to their practice. Recently, the law on the new territorial organization of the French Republic known as NOTRe[6] of August 7, 2015, specified that tourism had become a mandatory competence of intermunicipal authorities, with the exception of a few tourist resorts. Inter-municipalities must acquire a minimum threshold of 15,000 inhabitants. Several intermunicipal mergers also took place at the beginning of 2017, impacting the tourism development perimeter. Thus, within the perimeter of the Côte d'Émeraude and its hinterland, on July 1, 2017, six tourist offices (Dinan, Fréhel, Plancoët, Matignon, Plévenon and Saint-Cast-le-Guildo) and the tourist country of Dinan merged to create the Dinan Cap Fréhel Community Tourism Office. It should be noted that the name chosen identifies both the city-center and also the tourist highlight place of the territory. The same phenomenon can be found in the eastern part of the territory with the merger of local tourist institutions to create the Saint-Malo Baie du Mont-Saint-Michel community tourism office. Here too, the name refers to both a central city, Saint-Malo, and a major tourist destination, Mont-Saint-Michel. We can therefore see an evolution in the development of tourism in the territories, adapting to the perceptions of the territories practiced by tourists.

10.3. Conclusion

The study of tourists' mobilities teaches us how to integrate places into their networks of spatial practices. We have observed a rational organization of tourists in the practice of the places according to their itineraries. The geographical distance and the typology of the place play a role in networking. Indeed, we have observed a strong connectedness between the networks in which places are located, even though they are located at a great distance from the interview places. This degree of connectedness is first and foremost an indicator of the importance of the place; in this case, it may be a high place since it is part of many networks. The degree of network connectedness is also high for continuous mobility, as well as for diffusion mobility, with many arcs. On the other hand, tourist resorts, where tourists can stay for a longer period of time, are part of much shorter networks. It is therefore understandable that tourism professionals structure an offer of a multitude of tourist sites in order to allow tourists to reach a restricted area.

---

6 Act No. 2015-991 of August 7, 2015, on the new territorial organization of the Republic.

In this case, tourists limit themselves to the day to get around before returning to their accommodation in the resort. The network connectedness in which cities are located is also important, but connectivity is weaker. In the city, there is indeed a diversity of spatial practices between diffusion and continuous. Also, the evolution of destinations with cities as gateways associated with a high place seems interesting since tourists visualize the relationship between the two places and the mobility networks that can be established there. In a city, you can find a tourist who travels on a national or continental scale, as well as a tourist on a day trip on a local scale. In addition, in cities, there is a shift in the type of mobilities from continuous to diffusion. The city is conducive to multimodality between airplane/train and car/coach, for example. Here too, we understand the observation of the attendance density at tourist places in order to adapt the means of transport as best as possible.

11

Connection of Tourist Places in Networks via Tourist Mobilities

Tourist mobilities inform us of the networks in which tourist places are located. We have noted that tourists make choices to network places according to their elementary types and according to a regional tourist function assigned by tourists. The connectedness and connectivity of the networks to which the places belong, which are built via tourist mobilities, provide information on their spatial dimensions and their complexity. In the analysis of the neighborhood relationships of directed graphs, we have identified nodes that correspond to the crossing of lines towards graph vertices. As a reminder, these nodes, according to our statements, correspond to tourist places. Now the study of the nodality degree will provide us with information on the nodal function of places in networks. The node is characterized by the number of branches, i.e. in graph theory, the number of incident arcs reflecting the degree of a vertex. The concept of nodality therefore makes it possible to provide information on the characteristics of a node according to the relationships maintained with the other nodes of the network [DUP 85]. First, we will present the tool used to measure the nodality degree. Then, from the graphs and the matrix presenting the neighborhood relationships of directed graphs (see Chapter 8), we will define the nodal function of the places in the networks. Finally, we will see how the professional actors intervene, in particular through their prescriptions. They contribute to the evolution of the nodal function of tourist places in networks with a regional dimension and therefore suggest linking them together. They encourage a connection between places that is made through the spatial practices of tourists, the secondary tourist mobilities, whether in terms of diffusion or continuous.

11.1. Measurement of the nodality degree of tourist places in networks

To understand the function of nodes in the network, we borrowed a law of physics related to electricity networks; it is Kirchhoff's law which expresses the conversion of flows at a node [BON 05].

DEFINITION.– Kirchhoff's law: it is the algebraic sum of the intensity of the flows that access through a node that is equal to the algebraic sum of the intensities of the flows that leave it. Let $\sum$ be the algebraic sum, taking into account the direction of the flow (I):

$$"\sum I_n = 0"$$

The converging direction, i.e. from the exterior to the node, will be declared positive and the diverging direction, i.e. from the node to the exterior, negative. Jean-Jacques Bavoux, based on his work in nodal physiology, distinguishes six functions that the place can have in the network [BAV 05].

First, three functions correspond to the circulatory continuity of a flow upstream and downstream of the node:

– the *connection function* gives the place an interface role, between one or more network lines, or even between one or more networks;

– the *shelter function* allows a break in a longer route;

– the *relay function* ensures continuity between the starting point and the end point.

In a second step, three functions of the node create a discontinuity:

– the *load-break function* consists of loading or unloading the frequency of a flow in the passage of the node[1];

– the *mode change function* consists of a change of the flow type[2];

– the *spatiotemporal range* change function allows networks that operate at different levels to be connected, according to a folding-splitting system

---

1 This may involve the transshipment of goods or passengers.
2 In transport geography, this change consists of a modal shift from pedestrian travel to public transport travel.

(for microarray) by organizing the interface with a continuity of the flow over a longer distance (macroarray).

According to our study of flows based on diffusion or continuous mobilities, we will analyze the differential between incoming and outgoing flows (all mobilities combined) in order to define the nodal function of the places. We will consider that:

– if $\sum_{I_n} = 0$, we will have a *relay node*;

– if $\sum_{I_n} \neq 0$, it will be a *diffusing node* in the case of a large number of outgoing flows than incoming flows and a *polarizing node* in the case of a small number of outgoing flows than incoming flows.

11.2. Some results of the nodal function of the tourist places within the Lake Geneva region

In the Lake Geneva region, we have noted that the typology of the places and the distance from the area studied contribute to determining the nodal function of tourist places in regional networks.

Resorts with polarizing nodal function according to diffusion mobility

The resort of Évian-les-Bains on the French shore of Lake Geneva receives 20 flows of mobility and distributes 19 of them. The Montreux resort is also in the same configuration with 18 flows received and 17 flows distributed. We note that the polarizing nodal function is weak, since only one received flux makes it a polarizing node. These are almost like relay nodes. Among the relay nodes exclusively concerned with diffusion mobility, there are cities near Lake Geneva and in the area studied, such as Annecy, Bulle and Annemasse. In our study, the city of Annemasse, located on the eastern outskirts of Geneva, receives eight flows of mobilities and diffuses seven flows.

Relay nodes with places of high tourist intensity

Tourist villages or tourist sites are involved. Chillon Castle is a relay node according to diffusion mobility as well as continuous mobility. This can be explained by the fact that it is a site, with no accommodation or real activity to stay there, so tourists continue their itineraries. Other places with high tourist intensity also have a nodal function as relays according to differentiated mobility. Gruyères has a nodal function as a relay according to diffusion mobility, since the Swiss city receives and diffuses 13 flows. Moreover, we can see, with regard to continuous mobility, that it is a weak polarizing nodal function with six received flows for five diffused flows (it is almost a relay node with a diffusing flow close). Yvoire is in an inverse configuration with a nodal relay function according to continuous mobility and a weak polarizing nodal function for diffusion mobility (but again, it is almost a nodal function of flow relays receiving nearby). The low polarizing nodal function, almost reaching the nodal relay function, is again explained by a low accommodation capacity in these two villages. Globalization can be achieved through a low service capacity. Although in the regional tourism function, Gruyères seems to offer more recreational functions. However, we note in the case of Yvoire and Chillon Castle that these are places of passage according to the regional tourist function previously measured, i.e. tourists do not use these places to find recreational service functions (see Chapter 9).

Cities near the lake with a diffusing nodal function according to diffusion and continuous mobilities

Several cities located on the shores of Lake Geneva have a diffusing nodal function, such as Geneva and Lausanne. For example, Lausanne receives nine mobility flows to diffuse 12 of them. Its nodal function is also diffusing with regard to diffusion mobility. This means that these places are centers for excursions to other tourist places. On the other hand, depending on continuous mobility, the case of Geneva is different since its nodal function is polarizing, even almost a relay with 22 mobility flows received for 21 diffused flows. This nodal function means that, in Geneva, tourists arrive at their destination, stay in the city or continue on the same type of continuous mobility. Concerning diffusion mobility, this confirms that the diffusing nodal function expresses the irrigation of flows to the surrounding areas. According to several types of mobilities and the nodal functions they attribute, the visit of these cities is also explained by the measured regional tourism function. Indeed, these cities are places where tourists seek multiple recreational functions, which they offer because of their size, as they are stopovers.

Cities far from the lake with a diffusing nodal function according to continuous mobility

Several cities far from the interview places have a diffusing nodal function. These include the cities of Paris, Lyon, Basel and Zurich, as well as Geneva which we have just presented. We can explain this by the presence of transport infrastructure and the possibility of multimodality. These cities are also frequented for their services as a recreational function.

Box 11.1. *Results of the nodal functions of the Lake Geneva region places according to Kirchhoff's law*

Moreover, from the matrix of neighborhood relationships of directed graphs, we were able to determine within the Lake Geneva region the role of nodes as interfaces in networks of tourist places.

11.3. Suggesting the connection of tourist places and changing nodality

For each place, the nodal function is evolving according to the period or duration of the tourist interview. Our results do not reflect a determinism but provide an interpretation of a tourism situation at a given time. Professional actors can also contribute to the evolution of the nodal function of these places.

The work of Forer and Pearce (1984) in New Zealand had already identified the fact that the cities of Christchurch and Auckland are well integrated in the routes' networks, but benefit from only a few nights' accommodation compared to the small city of Te Anau [FOR 84]. Indeed, this small town has a tourist organization that receives and disseminates flows (see Chapter 4). But other cases have also caught our attention.

Jean-Christophe Gay observed, through a study in New Caledonia on the area visits of international tourists in 2007, differences according to the nationality of tourists [GAY 12]. Indeed, while Australians and New Zealanders stay mainly in Nouméa with some related stays on Ile des Pins, the Japanese also travel to Nouméa and Ile des Pins on the Loyalty Islands. The metropolitan French, on the other hand, have much more varied practices both towards the islands mentioned and in the northern and southern provinces. Other cases have caught our attention.

First, the organization of tourism in archipelagic territories testifies to the intervention of different professional actors in the nodal function of the places, contributing to a specific diffusion of tourist flows in a regional dimension.

In French Polynesia, Caroline Blondy identifies a capital island that has service infrastructures, including an airport that connects people to continents. In addition to this capital island, there are peripheral islands towards which tourism is spreading. In French Polynesia, Tahiti is the main pole, as this island hosts the international airport. Then other archipelagos are secondary poles, but whose hotel concentration is mainly on Bora-Bora and Moorea. Other islands are less well equipped and therefore less frequented [BLO 17].

On Mauritius, Hélène Désiré-Pébarthe observes that the resorts present since the 1950s have developed towards other islands in the region such as the Seychelles and the Maldives. The Constance Resorts group, present in Mauritius, has chosen to open an establishment in Praslin in the Seychelles, rather than on the capital island of Mahé. The same strategy was applied in an isolated archipelago in the Maldives [BLO 17]. We can see here that this hotel group has chosen to develop the nodal functions of archipelagic places by redistributing flows to more isolated places.

In the Seychelles , this desire can be likened to making Mahé Island, which has the international airport, a flow relay node that would continue towards Praslin Island. Jean-Christophe Gay has identified three models of tourism diffusion in tropical archipelagos [GAY 13]:

– a close diffusion from the capital island;

– a diffusion from one capital island to another and then from a remote secondary island involved in tourism, taking into account its hierarchical position, in particular accessibility, or its reputation;

– a diffusion from two islands connected directly to the outside.

Then, in China, Benjamin Taunay and Philippe Violier also report on different Chinese practices between Chinese and Westerners. They point out that the Silk Road is not a tourist route for the Chinese. Similarly, on the local level, as in Beijing, the Hutong, districts of traditional settlements, are only of interest to Western tourists, according to the authors:

> "Tourism is essentially a Western practice. Chinese society first rejected this degraded old habitat, preferring the modernity of towers and bars, before tourists invented this space for tourists" [TAU 15, p. 108].

On the other hand, they note that regional tourist places are visited by the Chinese, but not visited by Westerners. Therefore, the island of Hainan is frequented mainly by Chinese people. This island is perceived as a luxury destination, and Chinese tourism professionals wish to make it an international reference on the comparative basis of the American island of Hawaii.

Hence, the role of prescribers is to make the places known and ensure consistency of their practice in tourist projects. In the case of the French city of Lyon, Pierre-Yves Saunier studied tourist guides between 1800 and 1914, and notes that the status of area has evolved from picturesque, historical and emotional characteristics to practical characteristics that allow people to find their way around and identify what to see and move from one monument to another [SAU 93]. In the case of Paris, Laurie Lepan and Philippe Duhamel analyzed the evolution of the suggestion of tourist places to visit in the *Guides Joanne* and the Blue Guides between 1863 and 2010. They note suggested place changes and explain it both through the urban transformation of the city and for the evolution of the taste and expectations of tourists. This adaptation is necessary to ensure the durability of these structures and to be consulted by tourists [LEP 12].

Figure 11.1. *Tourist welcome guide and suggestions for itineraries on the square from Amsterdam Central Station (Netherlands) (source: J. Piriou, August 2015). For a color version of the figures in this chapter, see www.iste.co.uk/piriou/tourism.zip*

COMMENT FIGURE 11.1.– *In the square in front of the Amsterdam Central train station, a welcome guide is available to complete the signage information. The city of Amsterdam is very cosmopolitan and a major tourist place in Europe. Spatial practices of individual tourists are oriented by a city strongly marked by a tourist imagination (sex, drugs, alcohol) to which the city tries to change by deploying a territorial marketing of the city that is mainly oriented towards culture and events [CHA 12].*

Moreover, today, social networks facilitate simultaneity in the search for or suggestions of information and the spatial visit of places (see Chapter 8). The techniques used by digital marketing show an increase in the search for simultaneity, as in the case of mobile-to-store, which consists of broadcasting mobile advertising according to spatially targeted customers to encourage them to go to a particular point of sale. Also, tourism professionals already use different social networks to suggest and advise people to go to a particular place. The village of Gruyères, in Switzerland, is the main tourist place in the Gruyère destination (see Figure 11.2); however, professional actors are seeking to direct flows to other places. We followed the Facebook page of the tourist office of the Gruyère[3] region for eight days and we noted the suggestions (see Box 11.2).

June 8, 2018: "It has been 20 years since the incredible artist H. R. Giger opened his museum in the heart of the medieval village of Gruyères. Join us on June 23 to celebrate the creation of this fantastic place".

June 9, 2018: "The Brevet des Armaillis – Summer will begin tomorrow between Les Paccots and Moléson and the weather looks good! To your walking and mountain bike shoes".

June 11, 2018: "In Broc, you were all waiting for it, the news has finally arrived... The gorges of the Jogne are once again accessible".

June 12, 2018: "This weekend there is a celebration on the Vounetse mountain in Charmey".

June 14, 2018: "The music festival in Bulle is this Sunday".

Box 11.2. *Messages posted on Facebook by La Gruyère tourist office*

---

3 Official page of the Gruyère Tourisme, tourist office of the Gruyère district, available at: https://www.facebook.com/RegionLaGruyere/, accessed on June 14, 2018.

We note that different places and activities are suggested (museum in a medieval city, hiking between two mountain resorts, a natural site, events). *Ultimately*, the objective is to disseminate the flows throughout the territory. Also, by these suggestions, tourists can perceive an interest, by specific recreational functions, qualifying the place as a regional tourist function and justifying a trip by diffusion mobility or continuous mobility and making all the flows.

Figure 11.2. *Village center of Gruyères (Switzerland) (source: J. Piriou, May 2017)*

COMMENT ON FIGURE 11.2.– *By the name "Gruyères", the image of the famous Swiss cheese factory immediately comes to the forefront of any visitor. The tourist ritual is thus a set of processes by which people appropriate the virtues of the area they travel. The visit duration is also an important process for marking the place. Gruyères is the example of a city where the visitor will only be passing through, nevertheless it shows a certain cult of the place, it is the essential tourist place of Switzerland.*

11.4. Conclusion

The linking of places through tourist mobilities creates regional networks. However, not all places that constitute nodes in networks have the same function. This is explained not only by the types of mobilities used (whether they are continuous or diffusion) but also by the quality of the place which, in our opinion, has a regional tourist function. Moreover, defining the nodal function of tourist places has allowed us to understand their roles in networks built according to tourist mobilities. We have identified diffusion, polarizing and relay nodal functions that are justified based on the integration of the place into regional multi-level networks. Professional actors can take advantage of this nodal function to make it evolve, either through infrastructure investments or by prescribing places to direct flows.

Conclusion

The exercise of appropriating one of the most polysemic, or even the vaguest, concepts of geography can be a challenge. However, some initial analysis from field observations have allowed us to better understand the subject. First of all, we found that the destination promoted by tourism professionals is of variable scale. This can be a resort, a city and an agglomeration, as well as a department, a region, or a tourist route. However, for tourism professionals, it is difficult to know precisely the tourists' plan and the spatial scale practiced during their stays. Statistical studies exist concerning attendance, but they remain relatively vague and imprecise as to the identification of individuals between excursionists, tourists or inhabitants. Most of these studies are based on the definition of the World Tourism Organization which, as a reminder, considers a tourist as anyone who travels outside their usual environment for leisure or business purposes, provided that they are not remunerated. But a tourist is not just any visitor, he/she has a plan that is different from other individuals. His or her recreational plan is carried out by a temporary distance from their daily environment and they devote a dedicated amount of time to it, but this time remains limited. Through their stay, they seek relaxation, discovery, a healing that they would not have had in their usual environment, nor as part of a daily excursion.

Starting from the typology of elementary places has helped to provide a framework for our research. Indeed, we understand that places can be complementary, and tourists who visit a set of places would find there the necessary services and activities to best accomplish the recreational plan. However, a difficulty remains in the spatial delimitation of a territory that integrates these places and that would constitute a region. A deterministic reading based on various and varied geographical objects (rivers, mountains, valleys, etc.) cannot definitively characterize a tourist region. As we have seen, land use planning with the creation of *ex nihilo* resorts contributes to putting into tourism a space that previously did not have any interest for a tourist. A phenomenological reading based on the identification of places and practices within a given territory also contributes to perfecting the knowledge of regional tourist areas. However, this approach does not take into account the mobilities of individuals exercised during a tourist stay. As for regional geography, it has favored the analysis of territories characterized by a presence of tourism. On the other hand, it does not take sufficient account of the relationships between places or the plans of individuals. The center–periphery model was used to explain a certain hierarchy of places. Also, the consideration of attractions and travel facilitated the distinction of several regional forms of tourist destinations. Work on tourist mobilities was then developed, including models of regional spatial practice models. However, this work does not explain the role of the various actors in the development of these "regional groups", nor the reasons why tourists visit certain places rather than others. We will therefore summarize our comments using an explanatory diagram of the tourist region (see Figure C.1).

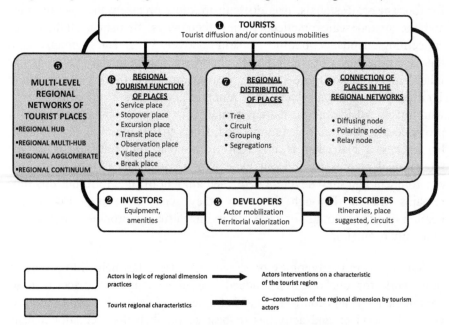

Figure C.1. *Model of the co-construction of the tourist region (source: J. Piriou)*

The tourist destination is both a territory promoted by professionals and perceived by tourists. We have also identified several stakeholders' logics that lead them to practice a regional dimension. First of all, tourists design multi-level regional networks of tourist places according to tourist mobilities, whether they are continuous or diffusion (1). Investors (2) equip the space with infrastructure. The creation of tourist resorts, sites and resort complexes structures in the area provides communication routes that allow travel on a regional scale to multiple tourist places. Developers (3) act, for their part, to promote a regional tourist destination operating a territorial homogenization, to enhance the value of their territories. They sometimes operate as a network, according to various organizations, such as partnerships, associations or cooperations. Prescribers (4) seek to direct tourists to this or that place, sometimes even recommend itineraries.

The understanding of the spatial practices of the actors in a regional dimension has enabled us to define the tourist region. In our opinion, it would be a dynamic territorial construction of tourism stakeholders, forming multi-level networks of places practiced by tourist mobilities. To understand the functioning of these networks, we have also analyzed, according to several indicators, the relationship between tourist places operated by tourist mobilities and we have specified how professional actors can intervene to change the situation of a tourist place within these regional networks.

We started from the spatial practices of tourists. Based on the collected life stories, we determined multi-level regional networks of tourist places based on tourist mobilities (5). We have identified several levels of networks. First of all, the regional hub is organized around a core and one or more satellites, to the node with the greatest number of links and becomes the core of the multi-hub. At a higher level, still based on diffusion mobility, the regional multi-hub is a grouping of regional hubs whose cores are transformed into satellites, to the benefit of the node with the greatest number of links and becomes the core of the multi-pole. The last network that is structured not only by diffusion mobility but also by continuous mobility is the regional agglomerate. This is the case of sharing satellites from the multi-poles. The node with the most links is the nucleus and the other nodes are satellites. Finally, in a supra-regional dimension, the regional continuum is established on the basis of continuous mobility. It establishes a location between several networks, through certain nodes.

Tourists act on the structuring of multi-level regional networks of tourist places because it is according to the mobilities utilized that the places become network nodes, which can become interface nodes between several network levels. The choice of places is made according to a regional tourist function assigned to them (6). We were able to define seven regional tourism functions. Some sites specialize in a single recreational function (visited places, service places, observation places). Others are practiced for various recreational functions (break places, transit places, excursion places). Finally, other sites include all recreational functions (stopover places). Thus, a place that, for tourists, has no interest in being used for recreational functions other than services (accommodation, food, transportation), should be combined with other places offering other recreational functions (observation, exploration). We have noted that resorts and cities are more likely to be stopovers, while places are more likely to be visit or excursion places. However, the regional tourism function of the places is evolving, as investors can contribute to a change in the moment of the place. The creation of new equipment, such as an accommodation complex, a theme park or the development of a new communication route, can lead tourists to make new choices of place combinations using various forms of mobilities.

Then, we analyzed the regional distribution of tourist places in the networks (7). Network connectedness is strong when cities are present. The high hosting capacity and multimodal connections available in these places explain the degree of connectedness. These are mainly places located on long routes that are crossed by continuous mobility. On the one hand, the degree of connectedness of the networks in which the sites and resorts are located is less important due to the practice of diffusion mobility. On the other hand, there is a distinction according to the connectivity of the networks between "circuit" and "tree" forms. Indeed, diffusion and continuous mobilities make it possible to create these two forms of networks of places. However, we note that the poor connectivity of networks applies to places where there is more continuous mobility, particularly large cities. Medium connectivity networks are subject to a diversity of types of mobilities and include resorts and small towns. Developers also participate in the positioning of the places, so that they are integrated into the networks. The cooperation of tourist sites or the redistribution of tourist destinations contributes to the presentation of relevant tourist places to tourists.

Furthermore, to determine the connection of tourist places in networks, we have defined the nodal function of these places (8). We have identified three main node functions in networks. Relay nodes are places that allow a continuity of tourist flows without interruption. On the other hand, there is discontinuity in flows, through a positive change in the number of links for diffusion nodes, and a negative change in the number of links for polarizing nodes. We have noted that in the context of continuous mobility, polarizing nodes are either far from the interview places or located in the hub of the spaces studied. These places are interfaces that fit into several multi-level networks. Moreover, they become relay nodes in the context of diffusion mobility. Prescribers can suggest combinations of places, ensuring an intensity of flow diffusing from places. However, we note that the actors are trying to keep tourists within their places, acting for polarizing flows.

Finally, during our measurement and analysis of the tourist region, we observed that the characteristics inherent in tourist places justify their networking through tourist mobilities. In our research, we took into account the elementary places as a whole. However, we believe that the whole of a place does not fully meet the expectations of tourists. Moreover, the recreational functions that make it possible to qualify the regional tourism function of the places show that there can be a specialization of places according to tourist practices. In some cases, only certain sites or neighborhoods are of interest to tourists in the realization of their recreational plans. It is therefore questionable whether tourists who visit a tourist region exclusively visit certain neighborhoods or places identified within elementary places. Therefore, it would be relevant to focus on the sub-area (i.e. the facilities, sites and neighborhoods) that would justify integration into multi-level regional networks of tourist places.

References

[ABA 00] ABALAIN H., *Histoire de la langue bretonne*, Éditions Gisserot, Paris, 2000.

[AGU 06] AGUILERA A., PROULHAC L., "Le polycentrisme en Île-de-France: quels impacts sur la mobilité?", *Territoire en Mouvement*, no. 2, pp. 15–25, 2006.

[AMÉ 07] AMÉLIE-EMMANUELLE M., Les territoires du tourisme en ville. La pratique des acteurs du tourisme dans les villes d'Amboise, de Blois et de Tours, PhD thesis, Université d'Angers, 2007.

[AND 51] ANDRIEUX J., "Dinard: évolution d'une station balnéaire", *Annales de Bretagne*, vol. 58, no. 1, pp. 180–183, 1951.

[AND 05] ANDERECK K.L., VALENTINE K.M., KNOPF R.C., *et al.*, "Residents' perceptions of community tourism impacts", *Annals of Tourism Research*, vol. 32, no. 4, pp. 1056–1076, 2005.

[AND 16] ANDREEVA-JOURDAIN E., "Le pari de la durabilité à Sotchi sur le littoral russe de la mer Noire", *Mondes du tourisme*, special edition, 2016, available at: http://journals.openedition.org/tourisme/1176, accessed July 1, 2018.

[ARV 99] ARVIN-BEROD P., BOUILLÉ P.-Y., *Megève, du village à la station*, Édimontagne, Servoz, 1999.

[ASH 00] ASHWORTH G.J., TUNBRIDGE J.E., *The Touristic-Historic City: Retrospect and Prospect of Managing the Heritage City*, Pergamon, Oxford, 2000.

[AUG 15] AUGIER P., "Postface. Deauville ou comment une station historique du bord de la Manche devient un lieu du monde", in P. DUHAMEL, M. TALANDIER, B. TOULIER (eds), *Le balnéaire, de la Manche au monde*, Presses universitaires de Rennes, Rennes, 2015.

[BAC 95] BACHIMON P., "La fréquentation touristique des gorges de l'Ardèche", *Montagnes méditerranéennes*, no. 2, pp. 117–120, 1995.

[BAI 95] BAILLY A., "Les représentations en géographie", in A. BAILLY, R. FERRAS, T. SAINT-JULIEN (eds), *Encyclopédie de la géographie*, Économica, Paris, 1995.

[BAL 94] BALLADUR J., La Grande-Motte. L'architecture en fête ou la naissance d'une ville, Espace Sud, Montpellier, 1994.

[BAR 70] BARBAZA Y., "Trois types d'intervention du tourisme dans l'organisation de l'espace littoral", *Annales de géographie*, vol. 79, no. 434, pp. 446–469, 1970.

[BAR 87] BARBEY G., "La persistance du mythe montreusien", *Arch. & Comport./Arch. Behay*, vol. 3, no. 4, pp. 327–340, 1987.

[BAR 96] BARON-YELLÈS N., "La Pointe du Raz, de l'image à l'aménagement d'un site phare", in G. LE BOUÉDEC, F. CHAPPE (eds), *Actes de la table ronde. Les usages des littoraux XVe-XXe siècles*, pp. 92–102, 1996.

[BAR 99] BARON-YELLÉS N., *Le tourisme en France: territoires et stratégies*, Armand Colin, Paris, 1999.

[BAR 05] BARTHÈS C., "Méthodes et outils pour bâtir une stratégie touristique de territoire", *Guide d'ingénierie territoriale*, La lettre du cadre territorial, Paris, 2005.

[BAR 09] BARTHEL P.-A., "Faire la preuve de l'urbanisme durable: les enjeux de la régénération de l'île de Nantes", *VertigO*, vol. 9, 2009, available at: http://vertigo.revues.org/8699, accessed September 12, 2016.

[BAV 05] BAVOUX J.-J., "La nodalité: un concept fondamental de l'organisation de l'espace", *Cahiers scientifiques du transport*, no. 48, pp. 5–14, 2005.

[BEA 71] BEAUJEU-GARNIER J., *La géographie: méthodes et perspectives*, Masson, Paris, 1971.

[BEA 96] BEAUDET G., "Un bref regard sur l'architecture de la villégiature et du tourisme", *Téoros*, vol. 15, no. 1, pp. 39–42, 1996.

[BEL 75] BELOT C., "Livreurs de vin et bouilleurs de cru du Pays de Cognac?", *Norois*, no. 86, pp. 243–257, 1975.

[BEL 14] BELLE E., "Aix-les-Bains, carrefour de villégiatures: thermalisme, climatisme, sports d'hiver et bords de lac", *In Situ*, no. 24, 2014, available at: http://journals.openedition.org/insitu/11132, accessed June 1, 2018.

[BEN 06] BENKO G., "Les villes dans l'économie globale: les stations de ski vues par le marketing", in D.-G. TREMBLAY, R. TREMBLAY (eds), *La compétitivité urbaine à l'ère de la nouvelle économie, enjeux et défis*, Presses de l'Université de Québec, Quebec, 2006.

[BER 80] BERTHO-LAVENIR C., "L'invention de la Bretagne. Genèse sociale d'un stéréotype", *Actes de la recherche en sciences sociales*, vol. 35, no. 35, pp. 45–62, 1980.

[BER 96a] BERNARD G., "La crise du cognac des années 1990", *Norois*, no. 172, pp. 767–774, 1996.

[BER 96b] BERTHO-LAVENIR C., "La fragmentation de l'espace national en paysages régionaux, 1800–1900", in F. CHENET (ed.), *Le paysage et ses grilles. Actes du colloque de Cerisy-la-Salle "Paysages? Paysage?"*, L'Harmattan, Paris, 1996.

[BER 99] BERTHO-LAVENIR C., *La roue et le stylo. Comment nous sommes devenus touristes*, Odile Jacob, Paris, 1999.

[BER 00] BERQUE A., *Écoumène. Introduction à l'étude des milieux humains*, Belin, Paris, 2000.

[BER 03] BERQUE A., "Lieu", in J. LÉVY, J. LUSSAULT (eds), *Dictionnaire de la géographie et de l'espace des sociétés*, Belin, Paris, 2003.

[BER 05] BERTAUX D., *L'enquête et ses méthodes: le récit de vie*, Armand Colin, Paris, 2005.

[BER 07] BERTHO-LAVENIR C., "La visite du château", in V. PERLÈS (ed.), *Made in Chambord*, Éditions du patrimoine, Paris, 2007.

[BER 17] BERROIR S., DELAGE M., FLEURY A. *et al.*, "Mobilités au quotidien et ancrage local dans les espaces périurbains", *Annales de géographie*, no. 713, pp. 31–55, 2017.

[BLA 06] BLANCHARD R., *La Flandre, étude géographique de la plaine flamande en France, Belgique et Hollande*, Danel, Lille, 1906.

[BLO 17] BLONDY C., GAY J.-C., PÉBARTHE-DÉSIRÉ H., "Îles tropicales et tourisme: entre périphéricité instrumentalisée et conquête de centralité. Regards croisés sur trois territoires: Maurice, Nouvelle-Calédonie et Polynésie française", in N. BERNARD, C. BLONDY, P. DUHAMEL (eds), *Tourisme et périphéries. La centralité des lieux en question*, Presses universitaires de Rennes, Rennes, 2017.

[BOI 03] BOIZET F., "Les limites temporelles de l'urbain: vers un urbain sans limites? L'exemple de Paris et sa région", *Travaux de l'Institut de Géographie de Reims*, nos 113–114, pp. 19–43, 2003.

[BON 05] BONNARD P., PAVARD M., TESTUD G., *Réseaux d'inconnexion et de transport: fonctionnement*, Techniques de l'ingénieur, Paris, 2005.

[BOT 13] BOTTI L., PEYPOCH N., SOLONANDRASANA B., *Économie du tourisme*, Dunod, Paris, 2013.

[BOU 80] BOURDIEU P., *Le Sens pratique*, Éditions de Minuit, Paris, 1980.

[BOU 98] BOUCHÉ N., "Tourisme et patrimoine urbain: les grandes interrogations", in G. CAZES, F. POTIER (eds), *Le tourisme et la ville: expériences européennes*, L'Harmattan, Paris, 1998.

[BOU 04] BOURREAU C., *Avoriaz, l'aventure fantastique*, La Fontaine de Siloé, Chambéry, 2004.

[BOY 72] BOYER M., *Le tourisme*, Le Seuil, Paris, 1972.

[BOY 02] BOYER M., *L'invention de la Côte d'Azur. L'hiver dans le midi*, Éditions de l'Aube, La Tour d'Aigues, 2002.

[BOY 05] BOYER M., *Histoire générale du tourisme du XVIe au XXIe siècle*, L'Harmattan, Paris, 2005.

[BRI 61] BRIÈRE R., "Les cadres d'une géographie touristique du Québec", *Cahiers de géographie du Québec*, vol. 6, no. 1, pp. 39–64, 1961.

[BRO 07] BROWAEYS X., TABEAUD M., "L'imagerie stéréotypée des brochures des offices de tourisme", *Cahiers Espaces*, no. 246, pp. 31–35, 2007.

[BRU 67] BRUNET R., *Les phénomènes de discontinuités en géographie*, Éditions du CNRS, Paris, 1967.

[BRU 72] BRUNET R., "Pour une théorie de la géographie régionale", *Travaux de l'Institut de Géographie de Reims*, no. 11, pp. 3–14, 1972.

[BRU 90] BRUNET R., DOLLFUS O., *Mondes nouveaux*, Hachette/Reclus, Paris/Montpellier, 1990.

[BRU 93] BRUNET R., FERRAS R., THÉRY H., *Les mots de la géographie. Dictionnaire critique*, Reclus/La Documentation française, Montpellier/Paris, 1993.

[BRU 97] BRUSTON M., DEPREST F., DUHAMEL P. *et al*, "Une approche géographique du tourisme", *L'Espace géographique*, vol. 27, no. 4, pp. 194–203, 1997.

[BUL 05] BULÉON P., DI MÉO G., *L'espace social. Lecture géographique des sociétés*, Armand Colin, Paris, 2005.

[BUR 63] BURNET L., *Villégiature et tourisme sur les côtes de France*, Hachette, Paris, 1963.

[BUR 91] BURTENSHAW D., BATERMAN M., ASHWORTH G.J., *The European City: A Western perspective*, David Fulton, London, 1991.

[CAL 77] CALS J., JULI E., TEIXIDOR C., "Les processus d'urbanisation touristique", *Revue géographique des Pyrénées et du Sud-Ouest*, vol. 48, no. 2, pp. 199–208, 1977.

[CAM 67] CAMPBELL C.K., "An approach to research in recreational geography", *B.C. Occasional Papers*, no. 7, pp. 85–90, 1967.

[CAR 71] CARTER M.-R., "A method of analyzing patterns of tourist activity in a large rural area. The Highlands and Islands of Scotland", *Regional Studies*, no. 5, pp. 29–37, 1971.

[CAS 67] CASSOU J., "Du voyage au tourisme", *Communications*, no. 10, pp. 25–34, 1967.

[CAS 77] CASSOU-MOUNAT M., La vie humaine sur le littoral des Landes de Gascogne, Thesis, Université de Bordeaux II, 1977.

[CAZ 72] CAZES G., "Réflexions sur l'aménagement touristique du littoral du Languedoc-Roussillon", *L'Espace géographique*, vol. 1, no. 3, pp. 193–210, 1972.

[CAZ 73] CAZES G., "Géographie du tourisme", *Travaux de l'Institut de Géographie de Reims*, nos 13–14, pp. 13–14, 1973.

[CAZ 86] CAZES G., *Le tourisme en France*, Presses universitaires de France, Paris, 1986.

[CAZ 88] CAZES G., "Les grands parcs de loisirs en France. Réflexions sur un nouveau champ de recherches", *Travaux de l'Institut de Géographie de Reims*, nos 73–74, pp. 57–89, 1988.

[CAZ 92] CAZES G., Fondements pour une géographie du tourisme et des loisirs, Bréal, Paris, 1992.

[CAZ 99] CAZELAIS N., NADEAU R., BEAUDET G., *L'espace touristique*, Presses de l'Université du Québec, Quebec, 1999.

[CER 80] CERTEAU M. (ed.), *L'invention du quotidien, tome 1: Arts de faire*, Union Générale d'Éditions, Paris, 1980.

[CÉR 08] CÉRIANI G., GAY J.-C., KNAFOU R. et al., "Conditions géographiques de l'individu contemporain", *Espacetemps*, 2008, available at: http://espacestemps.net/document4573.html, accessed September 21, 2008.

[CHA 50] CHARTIER M., "En vue de l'étude de l'habitat rural", *L'Information géographique*, vol. 14, no. 3, pp. 111–114, 1950.

[CHA 88] CHADEFAUD M., Aux origines du tourisme dans les Pays de l'Adour. Du mythe à l'espace: un essai de géographie historique, PhD thesis, Université de Pau, 1988.

[CHA 93] CHAPUIS R., LANNEAUX M.-A., "Les parcs régionaux français", *Annales de géographie*, vol. 102, no. 573, pp. 519–533, 1993.

[CHA 00] CHALAS Y., *L'invention de la ville*, Anthropos, Paris, 2000.

[CHA 12] CHAPUIS A., Performances touristiques et production des identités spatiales individuelles à Amsterdam, PhD thesis, Université de Paris Panthéon-Sorbonne, 2012.

[CHA 13] CHAREYRON G., DA RUGNA J., BRANCHET B., "Mining tourist routes using Flick traces", in J. ROKNE, C. FALOUTSOS (eds), *Proceedings of the 2013 IEEE/ACM International Conference on Advances in Social Networks Analysis and Mining*, ACM, New York, 2013.

[CHR 55] CHRISTALLER W., "Beiträge zu einer Geographie des Fremdenverkehrs", *Erdkunde*, vol. 9, no. 1, pp. 1–19, 1955.

[CHR 68] CHRISTALLER W., Die zentralen Orte in Süddeutschland. Eine ökonomisch-geographische Untersuchung über die Gesetzmäßigkeit der Verbreitung und Entwicklung der Siedlungen mit städtischen Funktionen, Wissenschaftliche Buchgesellschaft, Darmstadt, 1968.

[CIA 07] CIATTONI A., VEYRET Y., *Les fondamentaux de la géographie*, Armand Colin, Paris, 2007.

[CLA 77] CLARY D., *La façade littorale de Paris. Le tourisme sur la côte normande, étude géographique*, Ophrys, Paris, 1977.

[CLA 93] CLARY D., *Le tourisme dans l'espace français*, Masson, Paris, 1993.

[CLA 06] CLAVAL P., *Géographie régionale, de la région au territoire*, Armand Colin, Paris, 2006.

[COË 06] COËFFÉ V., "Les marqueurs spatiaux comme enjeux de la mise en tourisme de Waikiki", in J. RIEUCAU, J. LAGEISTE (eds), *L'empreinte du tourisme. Contribution à l'identité du fait touristique*, L'Harmattan, Paris, 2006.

[COË 08] COËFFÉ V., VIOLIER P., "Les lieux du tourisme: de quel(s) paradis parle-t-on? Variations sur le thème de l'urbanité touristique", *Articulo*, no. 4, 2008, available at: http//journals.openedition.org/articulo/158, accessed June 1, 2018.

[COË 10] COËFFÉ V., "La plage, fabrique d'une touristicité idéale", *L'information géographique*, no. 3, pp. 51–68, 2010.

[COË 17] COËFFÉ V. (ed.), *Le tourisme. De nouvelles manières d'habiter le Monde*, Ellipses, Paris, 2017.

[COH 85] COHEN E., "The tourist guide: the origins, structure and dynamics of a role", *Annals of Tourism Research*, no. 12, pp. 5–29, 1985.

[COO 81] COOPER C.P., "Spatial and temporal patterns of tourist behavior", *Regional Studies*, vol. 15, no. 5, pp. 359–371, 1981.

[COR 68] CORNA PELLEGRINI G., *Studi e ricerche sulla regione turistica. I Lidi ferraresi*, Vita e Pensiero, Milan, 1968.

[COR 88] CORBIN A., *Le territoire du vide. L'Occident et le désir du rivage, 1750–1840*, Flammarion, Paris, 1988.

[COU 06] COUSIN S., "De l'Unesco aux villages de Touraine: les enjeux politiques institutionnels et identitaires du tourisme culturel", *Autrepart*, vol. 4, no. 40, pp. 15–30, 2006.

[COU 11] COUSIN S., *Les miroirs du tourisme. Ethnographie de la Touraine du Sud*, Descartes & Cie, Paris, 2011.

[COU 15] COUPY P., PINSON N., "La Loire à Vélo: une success story à la française !", *Annales des Mines, Réalités industrielles*, no. 3, pp. 34–37, 2015.

[COU 14] COUSIN S., CHAREYRON G., DA RUGNA J. *et al.*, "Étudier TripAdvisor. Ou comment Trip-patouiller les cartes de nos vacances", *Espacestemps.net*, 2014, available at: http//www.espacestemps.net/articles/etudier-tripadvisor/, accessed June 1, 2018.

[CRE 04] CRÉVOISIER O., KAUFMANN V., ROSSEL P. *et al.*, "Mobilité et motilité, de l'intention à l'action", *Cahier du LaSUR*, no. 4, 2004.

[CRE 06] CRESSWELL T., *On the Move. Mobility in the Modern Western World*, Routledge, London, 2006.

[CRI 65] CRIBIER F., "Les estivants au Touquet", *Annales de géographie*, vol. 74, no. 40, pp. 38–49, 1965.

[DAU 86] DAUDÉ G., "Tourisme et nature: à travers l'exemple des gorges de l'Ardèche", *Revue de Géographie de Lyon*, no. 4, pp. 409–440, 1986.

[DEB 87] DEBARBIEUX B., GUMUCHIAN H., "Représentations spatiales et dénomi-nations des territoires: l'inscription toponymique des aménagements touristiques récents dans les Alpes du Nord (Savoie)", *Revue de géographie alpine*, vol. 75, no. 2, pp. 171–182, 1987.

[DEB 95] DEBARBIEUX B., *Tourisme et montagne*, Économica, Paris, 1995.

[DEC 05] DECROP A., SNELDERS D., "A grounded typology of vacation decision-making", *Tourism Management*, no. 26, pp. 121–132, 2005.

[DEH 97] DEHOORNE O., "Le tourisme, un nouvel atout pour le développement aveyronnais?", *Revue du Rouergue*, no. 52, pp. 530–548, 1997.

[DEH 98] DEHOORNE O., "Le Futuroscope et les politiques touristiques du département de la Vienne", *Norois*, no. 45, pp. 531–542, 1998.

[DEH 99] DEHOORNE O., "Le tourisme rural en Aveyron: l'affirmation d'une nouvelle activité économique", in P. VIOLIER (ed.), *L'espace local et les acteurs du tourisme*, Presses universitaires de Rennes, Rennes, 1999.

[DEH 03] DEHOORNE O., "Le monde du tourisme", in M. STOCK (ed.), *Le tourisme. Acteurs, lieux et enjeux*, Belin, Paris, 2006.

[DEL 56] DELOUCHE D., "L'activité touristique de la région malouine", *Norois*, no. 112, pp. 439–451, 1956.

[DEL 01] DELPRAT F., "Quand nature et culture sont indissociables", in C. GIUDICELLI (ed.), *Le paysage I*, Presses de la Sorbonne Nouvelle, Paris, 2006.

[DEM 05] DEMANGEON A., La Picardie et les régions voisines, Artois, Cambrésis, Beauvaisis, Armand Colin, Paris, 1905.

[DEV 09] DEVANTHÉRY A., "Encyclopédies du voyage et Cartoville. Pourquoi deux guides Gallimard consacrés à Lausanne?", *Articulo, Journal of Urban Research*, special edition 2, 2009, available at: http://articulo.revues.org/1117, accessed October 10, 2011.

[DEV 16] DEVINÉ M., *Marketing B to B. Principes et outils, de la stratégie à la vente*, Vuibert, Paris, 2016.

[DEW 84] DEWAILLY J.-M., Tourisme et loisirs dans le Nord-Pas-de-Calais. Approche géographique de la récréation dans une région urbaine et industrielle de l'Europe du Nord-Ouest, Thesis, Université de Paris IV, 1984.

[DEW 00] DEWAILLY J.-M., FLAMENT E., *Le tourisme*, SEDES, Paris, 2000.

[DIM 91] DI MÉO G., *L'homme, la société, l'espace*, Économica, Paris, 1991.

[DIM 98] DI MÉO G., *Géographie sociale et territoires*, Nathan, Paris, 1998.

[DIM 02] DI MÉO G., VEYRET Y., "Problématiques, enjeux théoriques et épisté-mologiques pour la géographie", in L. CARROUÉ, P. CLAVAL, G. DI MÉO, et al. (eds), *Limites et discontinuités en géographie*, SEDES, Paris, 2002.

[DIM 03] DI MÉO G., "Région", in J. LÉVY and J. LUSSAULT (eds), *Dictionnaire de la géographie et de l'espace des sociétés*, Belin, Paris, 2003.

[DON 07] DONDERO M.-G., "Les pratiques photographiques du touriste entre construction d'identités et documentation", *Communication et Langages*, no. 151, pp. 21–37, 2007.

[DRE 99] DREDGE D., "Destination place planning and design", *Annals of Tourism Research*, no. 4, pp. 772–791, 1999.

[DUB 98] DUBOIS V. (ed.), *Politiques locales et enjeux culturels*, La Documentation française, Paris, 1998.

[DUH 99] DUHAMEL P., SACAREAU I., *Le tourisme dans le monde*, Armand Colin, Paris, 1999.

[DUH 06] DUHAMEL P., "Les lieux touristiques", in M. STOCK (ed.), *Le tourisme. Acteurs, lieux et enjeux*, Belin, Paris, 2006.

[DUH 07] DUHAMEL P., KNAFOU R., "Le tourisme dans la centralité parisienne", in T. SAINT-JULIEN, R. LE GOIX (eds), *La métropole parisienne, centralités, inégalités, proximités*, Belin, Paris, 2007.

[DUH 08] DUHAMEL P., "Les communautés vacancières", *Norois*, no. 206, pp. 21–36, 2008.

[DUH 09] DUHAMEL P., VIOLIER P., *Tourisme et littoral, un enjeu du monde*, Belin, Paris, 2009.

[DUH 13] DUHAMEL P., "Des mobilités et du tourisme", in P. VIOLIER (ed.), *Le tourisme, un phénomène économique*, La Documentation française, Paris, 2013.

[DUH 18] DUHAMEL P., *Géographie du tourisme et des loisirs. Dynamiques, acteurs, territoires*, Armand Colin, Paris, 2018.

[DUM 72] DUMAZEDIER J., *Vers une civilisation du loisir?*, Le Seuil, Paris, 1972.

[DUP 85] DUPUY G., *Systèmes, réseaux et territoires: principes de réseautique territoriale*, Presses de l'École nationale des ponts et chaussées, Paris, 1985.

[DUR 09] DURAND G., FEREROL M.-E., "Le tourisme, positionnement stratégique au sein d'une métropole: le choix d'Évian vis-à-vis de la métropole transfrontalière franco-valdo-genevoise", *L'Information géographique*, no. 3, pp. 23–45, 2009.

[DUV 06] DUVAL M., "Les gorges de l'Ardèche: ressources touristiques et enjeux territoriaux", *Actes du colloque Transport et tourisme*, Université de Savoie, Chambéry, 2006.

[ELI 76] ELIAS N., "Sport et violence", *Actes de la recherche en sciences sociales*, vol. 2, no. 6, pp. 2–21, 1976.

[ELI 94] ELIAS N., DUNNING E., *Sport et civilisation: la violence maîtrisée*, Fayard, Paris, 1994.

[ENZ 12] ENZENSBERGER H.M., *Culture ou mise en condition?*, Les Belles Lettres, Paris, 2012.

[ÉQU 02] ÉQUIPE MIT, *Tourisme 1. Lieux communs*, Belin, Paris, 2002.

[ÉQU 05] ÉQUIPE MIT, *Tourisme 2. Moments de lieux*, Belin, Paris, 2005.

[ÉQU 11] ÉQUIPE MIT, *Tourisme 3. La révolution durable*, Belin, Paris, 2011.

[FAB 13] FABRY N., "Cluster de tourisme et ancrage territorial. L'expérience du cluster tourisme du Val d'Europe", *Mondes du tourisme*, no. 6, pp. 41–54, 2013.

[FAB 15] FABRY N., ZEGHNI S., "Peut-on clustériser l'économie touristique? Le cas de Deauville", in P. DUHAMEL, M. TALANDIER, B. TOULIER (eds), *Le balnéaire. De la Manche au monde*, Presses universitaires de Rennes, Rennes, 2015.

[FLA 75] FLAMENT E., "Quelques remarques sur l'espace touristique", *Norois*, no. 88, pp. 609–621, 1975.

[FLO 05] FLOGNFELDT T., "The tourist route system – Models of travelling patterns", *Belgeo*, no. 1/2, pp. 35–58, 2005.

[FOR 84] FORER P.C., PEARCE D.G., "Spatial patterns of package tourism in New Zealand", *New Zealand Geographer*, no. 40, pp. 34–42, 1984.

[FOU 04] FOUGER F., "L'importance des sociétés de chemin de fer dans le déve-loppement de la première station de ski française ; le Mont-Revard", *In Situ*, no. 4, 2004, available at: http://journals.openedition.org/insitu/1906, accessed June 1, 2018.

[FOU 17] FOURNIER C., "Le tourisme dans la métropole parisienne", in G. WACKERMANN (ed.), *Les espaces du tourisme et des loisirs*, Ellipses, Paris, 2017.

[FRA 01] FRANCON M., *Le Guide Vert Michelin: l'invention du tourisme culturel populaire*, Économica, Paris, 2001.

[FRE 99] FRÉMONT A., *La région, espace vécu*, Flammarion, Paris, 1999.

[GAI 02] GAIDO L., "Du concept de station au concept de district", *Revue de géographie alpine*, vol. 90, no. 4, pp. 109–112, 2002.

[GAM 06] GAMBLIN S., "Thomas Cook en Égypte et à Louxor: l'invention du tourisme moderne au XIXe siècle", *Téoros*, vol. 25, no. 2, pp. 19–25, 2006.

[GAU 93] GAUDIN J.-P., *Le milieu du monde*, Reclus, Montpellier, 1993.

[GAU 00] GAUGUE A., "Espaces touristiques et territoires identitaires en Bretagne", *Norois*, vol. 3, no. 187, pp. 303–316, 2000.

[GAU 09] GAUCHON C., "Les gorges de l'Ardèche et la grotte Chauvet. Redéfinition d'une région touristique", *Téoros*, vol. 28, no. 1, pp. 80–92, 2009.

[GAY 95] GAY J.-C., *Les discontinuités spatiales*, Économica, Paris, 1995.

[GAY 10] GAY J.-C., VIOLIER P., "Tous touristes ! Le monde comme espace touristique", in D. RETAILLÉ (ed.), *La mondialisation*, Nathan, Paris, 2010.

[GAY 12] GAY J.-C., "Le tourisme", in J. BONVALLOT, J.-C. GAY, E. HABERT (eds), *Atlas de la Nouvelle-Calédonie*, IRD-Congrès de la Nouvelle-Calédonie, Marseille/Nouméa, 2012.

[GAY 13] GAY J.-C., "Les îles du Pacifique dans le monde du tourisme", *Hermès-Lavoisier*, no. 65, pp. 84–88, 2013.

[GAY 16] GAY J.-C., *L'homme et les limites*, Économica/Anthropos, Paris, 2016.

[GAY 17a] GAY J.-C., "Monde touristique: aperçu et ressorts d'une diffusion planétaire", in V. COËFFÉ (ed.), *Le tourisme. De nouvelles manières d'habiter le monde*, Ellipses, Paris, 2017.

[GAY 17b] GAY J.-C., MONDOU V., *Tourisme et transport. Deux siècles d'interactions*, Bréal, Paris, 2017.

[GEN 86] GENTRY M., DELBRU R., "Regards sur le tourisme en Périgord au milieu des années 1980", *Revue géographique des Pyrénées et du Sud-Ouest*, vol. 57, no. 4, pp. 541–558, 1986.

[GEO 06] GEORGE P., VERGER F., *Dictionnaire de la géographie*, Presses universitaires de France, Paris, 2006.

[GET 97] GETZ D., *Event management and event tourism*, Cognizant Communication Corporation, New York, 1997.

[GIL 00] GILLY J.-P., TORRE A. (eds), *Dynamiques de proximité*, L'Harmattan, Paris, 2000.

[GIL 05] GILLI F., "Le Bassin parisien. Une région métropolitaine", *Cybergeo*, 2005, available at: http://cybergeo.revues.org/3257, accessed August 19, 2011.

[GIN 63] GINIER J., "Les buts de voyage des touristes étrangers en France (1949–1961)", *Annales de Géographie*, vol. 72, no. 394, pp. 728–731, 1963.

[GIN 72] GINIER J., "Le tourisme finistérien", *Norois*, no. 173, pp. 103–114, 1972.

[GIR 09] GIRAUD-LABALTE C., MORICE J.-R., VIOLIER P., *Le patrimoine est-il fréquentable? Accès, gestion, interprétation*, Presses de l'Université d'Angers, Angers, 2009.

[GOU 74] GOULD P., WHITE R., *Mental Maps*, Penguin Books, Harmondsworth, 1974.

[GRA 00] GRANDPRÉ F. (ed.), "Le découpage des régions touristiques du Québec – Éléments d'analyse et pistes de recherches", *Téoros*, vol. 19, no. 3, pp. 40–43, 2000.

[GRA 08] GRANDPRÉ F. (ed.), "Les contributions de la culture à la mise en tourisme régionale et les retombées sur la construction identitaire", in J.-C. NÉMÉRY, M. RAUTENBERG, F. THURIOT (eds), *Stratégies identitaires de conservation et de valorisation du patrimoine*, L'Harmattan, Paris, 2008.

[GRA 10a] GRANDET M., PAJOT S., SAGOT-DUVOUROUX D. *et al.*, *Nantes, la Belle éveillée: le pari de la culture*, Éditions de l'Attribut, Toulouse, 2010.

[GRA 10b] GRAVARI-BARBAS M., JACQUOT S., "Introduction et problématique de la journée", in A.-C. MERMET (ed.), *Villes françaises du patrimoine mondial et tourisme. Protection, gestion, valorisation*, Study day proceedings, Unesco, Université Paris 1 Panthéon-Sorbonne, Paris, 2010.

[GRI 07] GRIFFOND-BOITIER A., "L'image des villes à travers la communication touristique", *Images de Franche-Comté*, no. 36, pp. 20–24, 2007.

[GUE 12] GUEX D., ROY J., SAUTHIER G., La trajectoire historique du développement touristique de Montreux entre 1850 et 2010, Working document no. 2, IUKB Kurth Bösch, Sion, 2012.

[GUN 65] GUNN C.A., *A Concept for the Design of a Tourism-recreation Region*, BJ Press, Mason, 1965.

[GUN 88] GUNN C.A., *Vacationscape, Designing Tourist Regions*, Van Nostrand Reinhold, New York, 1988.

[HAG 65] HAGGETT P., *Locational Analysis in Human Geography*, Edward Arnold Ltd, London, 1965.

[HAL 09] HALL C.M., "Changement climatique, authenticité et marketing des régions nordiques", *Téoros*, vol. 28, no. 1, pp. 70–79, 2009.

[HÉB 05] HÉBERT D., "Deauville: création et développement urbain", *In Situ*, no. 6, 2012, available at: http://journals.openedition.org/insitu/8569, accessed June 1, 2018.

[HEI 58] HEIDEGGER M., *Essais et conférences*, Gallimard, Paris, 1958.

[HEL 04] HELLE C., "Le Lubéron, refuge d'artistes", *Mappemonde*, no. 73, 2004, available at: http://mappemonde.mgm.fr/num1/articles/art04101.html, accessed October 13, 2012.

[HER 07] HERVOUËT V., "La mobilité du quotidien dans les espaces périurbains, une grande diversité de modèles de déplacements", *Norois*, no. 205, 2007, available at: http://norois.revues.org/2073, consulté le September 30, 2016.

[HER 16] HERPIN E., *La Côte d'Émeraude: Saint-Malo, ses souvenirs*, Hachette, Bibliothèque nationale de France, Paris, 2016.

[HEY 92] HEYRAUD E., "Archéologie spatiale de la Côte d'Azur", *Mappemonde*, no. 92, pp. 41–43, 1992.

[HOE 08] HOERNER J.-M., *Géopolitique du tourisme*, Armand Colin, Paris, 2008.

[HOU 96] HOUÉE P., *Les politiques du développement rural. Des années de croissance au temps d'incertitude*, Économica, Paris, 1996.

[HUM 07] HUMAIR C., "Ville, tourisme et transport: la compagnie du chemin de fer Lausanne-Ouchy (1869–1914)", *Entreprises et histoire*, vol. 2, no. 47, pp. 11–25, 2007.

[HUM 14] HUMAIR C., GIGASE M., LAPOINTE-GUIGOZ J. *et al.*, *Système touristique et culture technique dans l'Arc lémanique. Analyse d'une success story et de ses effets sur l'économie régionale (1852–1914)*, Presses universitaires de Suisse, Neuchâtel, 2014.

[HUY 08] HUYGHUES-DESPOINTES F., Des barrages au patrimoine mondial: La Loire comme objet d'action publique, PhD thesis, Université François-Rabelais, Tours, 2008.

[JAC 17] JACQUOT S., "Tourisme et métropolisation: les métropoles comme destinations touristiques?", in FAGNONI E. (ed.), *Les espaces du tourisme et des loisirs*, Armand Colin, Paris, 2017.

[JAF 88] JAFARI J., "Le système du touriste: modèles socio-culturels en vue d'applications théoriques et pratiques", *Loisir et Société*, vol. 11, no. 1, pp. 59–80, 1988.

[JAN 98] JANSEN-VERBEKE M., "Le tourisme culturel des villes historiques. Revitalisation urbaine et capacité de charge: le cas de Bruges", in G. CAZES, F. POTIER (eds), *Le tourisme et la ville: expériences européennes*, L'Harmattan, Paris, 1998.

[JOA 07] JOANNE A., *Les châteaux de la Loire pour visiter rapidement et économiquement en chemin de fer, en automobile ou en bicyclette*, Hachette, Paris, 1907.

[JOL 07] JOLIET F., MARTIN T., "Les représentations du paysage et l'attractivité touristique: le cas "Tremblant" dans les Laurentides", *Téoros*, vol. 26, no. 2, pp. 53–58, 2007.

[KEL 09] KELLER K.L., KOTLER P., *Marketing Management*, Pearson Education, Paris, 2009.

[KNA 78] KNAFOU R., *Les stations intégrées de sports d'hiver des Alpes françaises. L'aménagement de la montagne à la "française"*, Masson, Paris, 1978.

[KNA 87] KNAFOU R., "L'évolution récente de l'économie des sports d'hiver et de l'aménagement touristique de la montagne en France", *Revue de géographie alpine*, vol. 75, no. 2, pp. 101–114, 1987.

[KNA 91] KNAFOU R., "L'invention du lieu touristique: la passation d'un contrat et le surgissement simultané d'un nouveau territoire", *Revue de géographie alpine*, vol. 4, pp. 11–19, 1991.

[KNA 92] KNAFOU R., "L'invention du tourisme", in A. BAILLY, R. FERRAS, D. PUMAIN (eds), *Encyclopédie de la géographie*, Économica, Paris, 1992.

[KNA 95] KNAFOU R., "Incertitudes, paradoxes et ambiguïtés du tourisme diffus", in JAMOT C., VITTE P. (eds), *Le tourisme diffus*, Ceramac, Clermont-Ferrand, 1995.

[KNA 97a] KNAFOU R., *Tourisme et loisirs. Atlas de France*, vol. 7, La Documentation française, Paris, 1997.

[KNA 97b] KNAFOU R., BRUSTON M., DEPREST F. *et al.*, "Une approche géographique du tourisme", *L'Espace géographique*, vol. 26, no. 3, pp. 193–204, 1997.

[KNA 00a] KNAFOU R., "Les mobilités touristiques et de loisirs et le système global des mobilités", in M. BONNET, D. DESJEUX (eds), *Les territoires de la mobilité*, Presses universitaires de France, Paris, 2000.

[KNA 00b] KNAFOU R., "Une introduction aux espaces régionaux, espaces touristiques", in G. CHABAUD, E. COHEN, N. COQUERY *et al.* (eds), *Les guides imprimés du XVIe siècle au XXe siècle. Villes, paysages, voyages*, Belin, Paris, 2000.

[KNA 03] KNAFOU R., "Loisirs", in J. LÉVY, J. LUSSAULT (eds), *Dictionnaire de la géographie et de l'espace des sociétés*, Belin, Paris, 2003.

[KNA 09] KNAFOU R., "Les villes touristiques à patrimoine en Europe", *Actes du colloque Tourisme urbain patrimoine et qualité urbaine en Europe*, Rennes, France, 26 and 27 March 2009.

[LAC 86] LACOSTE Y., *Géopolitiques des régions françaises*, Fayard, Paris, 1986.

[LAR 82] LARIVIÈRE J.-P., "Saint-Malo et ses problèmes économiques", *Norois*, vol. 115, pp. 451–454, 1982.

[LAZ 95] LAZZAROTTI O., *Les loisirs à la conquête des espaces périurbains*, L'Harmattan, Paris, 1995.

[LAZ 11] LAZZAROTTI O., *Patrimoine et tourisme. Histoires, lieux, acteurs, enjeux*, Belin, Paris, 2011.

[LEC 98] LE COADIC R., *L'identité bretonne*, Presses universitaires de Rennes, Rennes, 1998.

[LEC 07] LE CARO Y., *Les loisirs en espace agricole, l'expérience d'un espace partagé*, Presses universitaires de Rennes, Rennes, 2007.

[LEF 13] LE FUR Y., La patrimonialisation des grands sites: exemple des promontoires littoraux emblématiques bretons: évolution des doctrines et transformation des espaces, PhD thesis, Université de Rennes 2, 2013.

[LEI 79] LEIPER N., "The framework of tourism: towards a definition of tourism, tourist and the tourist industry", *Annals of Tourism Research*, vol. 6, no. 4, pp. 390–406, 1979.

[LEI 90] LEIPER N., "Tourism attraction systems", *Annals of Tourism Research*, vol. 17, pp. 367–384, 1990.

[LEI 08] LEICESTER T., "Conflits et enjeux identitaires dans le tourisme rural à Yanghuo, Chine", *Civilisations*, vol. 57, pp. 223–241, 2008.

[LEP 12] LEPAN L., DUHAMEL P., "Un discours mis en image: Paris à travers les Guides Joanne – Guides Bleus (1863 à 2010). Une approche exploratoire et diachronique de l'espace touristique", *Mondes du tourisme*, vol. 6, pp. 6–22, 2012.

[LEP 13] LEPAN L., L'espace touristique de la grande ville: une approche par les pratiques et les mobilités touristiques. Le cas de la destination Paris, PhD thesis, Université d'Angers, 2013.

[LER 00] LEROY S., "Sémantiques de la métropolisation", *L'Espace géographique*, vol. 1, pp. 78–86, 2000.

[LER 07] LEROUX S., "Les temporalités des touristes itinérants dans le Sud marocain ou la quête de liberté", *Espace populations sociétés*, vol. 2/3, pp. 273–284, 2007.

[LÉV 94] LÉVY J., *L'espace légitime. Sur la dimension géographique de la fonction politique*, Presses de la Fondation nationale des sciences politiques, Paris, 1994.

[LÉV 00] LÉVY J., "Les nouveaux espaces de la mobilité", in M. BONNET, D. DESJEUX (eds), *Les territoires de la mobilité*, Presses universitaires de France, Paris, 2000.

[LÉV 03a] LÉVY J., "Distance", in J. LÉVY, J. LUSSAULT (eds), *Dictionnaire de la géographie et de l'espace des sociétés*, Belin, Paris, 2003.

[LÉV 03b] LÉVY J., "Centre/périphérie", in J. LÉVY, J. LUSSAULT (eds), *Dictionnaire de la géographie et de l'espace des sociétés*, Belin, Paris, 2003.

[LÉV 03c] LÉVY J., LUSSAULT J., "Habiter", in J. LÉVY, J. LUSSAULT (eds), *Dictionnaire de la géographie et de l'espace des sociétés*, Belin, Paris, 2003.

[LÉV 08] LÉVY J., *Échelles de l'habiter*, PUCA, Paris, 2008.

[LEW 87] LEW A.A., "A framework of tourist attraction research", *Annals of tourism research*, vol. 14, pp. 553–575, 1987.

[LI 12] LI L., Les pratiques touristiques des touristes français en Chine, PhD thesis, Université d'Angers, 2012.

[LÖS 43] LÖSCH A., *Die räumliche Ordnung der Wirtschaft*, Fischer G., Jena, 1943.

[LOY 01] LOYER F., TOULIER B. (eds), *Le régionalisme, architecture et identité*, Éditions du patrimoine, Paris, 2001.

[[LOZ 85] LOZATO-GIOTART J.-P., *Géographie du tourisme: de l'espace consommé à l'espace maîtrisé*, Masson, Paris, 1985.

LOZ 08] LOZATO-GIOTART J.-P., *Géographie du tourisme: de l'espace consommé à l'espace maîtrisé*, Pearson, Paris, 2008.

[LUM 00] LUMSDON L., *Tourism marketing*, International Thomson Business Press, Londres, 2000.

[LUN 84] LUNDGREN J.O.J., "Geographic concepts and the development of tourism research in Canada", *GeoJournal*, vol. 9, no. 1, pp. 17–25, 1984.

[LUS 03] LUSSAULT M., STOCK M., "Mobilité", in J. LÉVY, J. LUSSAULT (eds), *Dictionnaire de la géographie et de l'espace des sociétés*, Belin, Paris, 2003.

[LUS 13] LUSSAULT M., *L'avènement du monde*, Le Seuil, Paris, 2013.

[LYO 05] LYONS G., URRY J., "Travel time use in the information age", *Transportation Research*, vol. 39, no. 2/3, pp. 257–276, 2005.

[MAC 76] MACCANNELL D., *The Tourist: A New Theory of the Leisure Class*, Schocken Books, New York, 1976.

[MAN 07] MANCEAU J.-J., "Avoriaz en piste pour le haut de gamme", *L'Expansion.fr*, 2007, available at: https://lexpansion.lexpress.fr/actualite-economique/avoriaz-en-piste-pour-le-haut-de-gamme_1434700.html, accessed June 1, 2018.

[MAN 17] MANFREDINI J., *Les syndicats d'initiative. Naissance de l'identité touristique de la France*, Presses universitaires François-Rabelais, Tours, 2017.

[MAO 05] MAO P., CORNELOUP J., "Approche géo-historique des formes de développement d'un territoire touristique et sportif de nature. La construction du haut-lieu "gorges de l'Ardèche" durant le XXe siècle", *Loisir et Société/Society and Leisure*, vol. 28, no. 1, pp. 117–140, 2005.

[MAR 02] MARTONNE E. (ed.), *La Valachie, essai de monographie géographique*, Armand Colin, Paris, 1902.

[MAR 12] MARCELPOIL E., FRANÇOIS H., "Vallée de la Tarentaise: de l'invention du Plan neige à la constitution d'un milieu innovateur dans le domaine du tourisme d'hiver", *Histoire des Alpes*, no. 17, pp. 227–242, 2012.

[MAR 69] MARIOT P., "Priestorové aspekty cestovnélio rechu a okázky gravitaného zázemia návstevnych miest", *Geografick'y Casopis*, vol. 21, no. 4, pp. 287–312, 1969.

[MAU 07] MAUNIER C., "Une approche triadique du marketing des destinations", *Market Management*, vol. 2, no. 7, pp. 41–64, 2007.

[MCK 12] MCKERCHER B., SHOVAL B., NG E., *et al.*, "Using GPS Data to compare first-time and repeat visitors in Hong Kong", *Tourism Geographies*, vol. 14, pp. 147–161, 2012.

[MER 03] MERENNE-SCHOUMAKER B., *Géographie des services et des commerces*, Presses universitaires de Rennes, Rennes, 2003.

[MER 08] MERLIN P., *Tourisme et aménagement touristique*, La Documentation française, Paris, 2008.

[MES 15] MESPLIER A., *Le tourisme en France, étude régionale*, Bréal, Paris, 2015.

[MEY 69] MEYNIER A., "Une enquête britannique sur la région malouine", *Norois*, vol. 2, no. 1, pp. 279–280, 1969.

[MEY 12] MEYRONIN B., *Marketing territorial. Enjeux et pratiques*, Vuibert, Paris, 2012.

[MIC 83] MICHAUD J.-L., *Le tourisme face à l'environnement*, Presses universitaires de France, Paris, 1983.

[MIC 97] MICHELIN, *Châteaux de la Loire*, Guide Vert Michelin, Clermont-Ferrand, 1997.

[MIÈ 33] MIÈGE J., "La vie touristique en Savoie", *Revue de géographie alpine*, vol. 22, no. 1, pp. 749–817, 1933.

[MIL 85] MILL R.C., MORRISON M., *The Tourism System: An Introductory Text*, Prentice Hall, Englewood Cliffs, 1985.

[MIO 77] MIOSSEC J.-M., "Un modèle de l'espace touristique", *L'Espace géographique*, vol. 1, pp. 41–48, 1977.

[MON 00] MONNET J., "Les dimensions symboliques de la centralité", *Cahiers de géographie*, vol. 44, no. 123, pp. 399–418, 2000.

[MON 07] MONTEILS J.-P., "Tout territoire n'a pas vocation à devenir touristique", *Source*, vol. 92, pp. 1–2, 2007.

[MON 17] MONOT A., PARIS F., *Les espaces du tourisme et des loisirs*, Éditions Bréal, Paris, 2017.

[MOR 76] MORIN D., GAUTHIER P., BERNATCHEZ M., "La théorie des graphes: le cas du réseau routier de l'université Laval", *Cahiers de géographie du Québec*, vol. 20, no. 51, pp. 551–559, 1976.

[MOR 08] MORICE J.-R., DÉSIRÉ-PÉBARTHE H., VIOLIER P., "Itinéraires de lieux touristiques du littoral atlantique", *Norois*, vol. 206, pp. 9–20, 2008.

[MOR 09] MORICE J.-R., VIOLIER P., "De l'évènementiel culturel à la destination touristique: les cas de Lille et Nantes", *Bulletin de l'Association de géographes français*, vol. 3, pp. 377–387, 2009.

[NIC 65] NICE B., "Geografia e studi turistici", *Rivista Geografica Italiana*, vol. 3, pp. 249–267, 1965.

[NKO 08] NKOGHE S., *La psychologie du tourisme*, L'Harmattan, Paris, 2008.

[NON 04] NONN H., "Régions, nations", in A. BAILLY (ed.), *Les concepts de la géographie humaine*, Armand Colin, Paris, 2004.

[OMT 10] ORGANISATION MONDIALE DU TOURISME., Recommandations interna-tionales sur les statistiques du tourisme, Madrid, 2010.

[OZO 92] OZOUF-MARIGNIER M.-V., *La formation des départements: la représentation du territoire français à la fin du XVIIIe siècle*, EHESS, Paris, 1992.

[PAE 84] PAESLER R., "Die Zentralen Orte im randalpinen Bereich Baverns – Zur Entwicklung versorgungsfunktionaler Raumstrukturen", in K. RUPPERT (ed.), *Geographische Strukturen und Prozessabläufe im Alpenraum*, Lassleben, Regensburg, 1984.

[PAG 79] PAGNINI M.P., BATTISTI G., "Considerations about the "peripheral places" of tourism", in J. MATZNETTER (ed.), *Tourism and Borders: Proceedings of the Meeting of the IGU Working Group: Geography of Tourism and Recreation*, University of Frankfurt, Frankfurt, 1979.

[PEA 93] PEARCE D., *Géographie du tourisme*, Nathan, Paris, 1993.

[PEC 96] PECQUEUR B., *Dynamiques territoriales et mutations économiques*, L'Harmattan, Paris, 1996.

[PER 08] PERLÈS V., "Petit patrimoine des touristes: les souvenirs de vacances", in L.-S. FOURNIER (ed.), *Le "petit patrimoine" des Européens: objets et valeurs du quotidien*, L'Harmattan, Paris, 2008.

[PIC 02] PICKEL S., "Représentation de la nature dans la mise en tourisme de Saint-Trojan-les-Bains", *Mappemonde*, vol. 67, no. 2002–3, pp. 28–31, 2002.

[PIC 61] PICARD A., "Les paysans et le tourisme dans le Tirol autrichien", *L'information géographique*, pp. 101–103, 1961.

[PIN 01] PINSON D., THOMANN S., *La maison en ses territoires: de la villa à la ville diffuse*, L'Harmattan, Paris, 2001.

[PIR 09] PIRIOU J., "Une approche régionale de la destination touristique", in J.-P. LEMASSON, P. VIOLIER (eds), *Destinations et territoires, vol. 1, Coprésence à l'œuvre*, Presses de l'Université du Québec, Paris, 2009.

[PIR 11a] PIRIOU J., "Le haut-lieu touristique: un cadre d'analyse de l'excellence d'une destination", *Téoros*, vol. 30, no. 1, pp. 23–30, 2011.

[PIR 11b] PIRIOU J., "Destinations et positions de lieux de l'Arc lémanique", in P. DUHAMEL, B. KADRI (eds), *Tourisme et mondialisation*, Espaces, Paris, 2011.

[PIR 12] PIRIOU J., Enquête sur la région touristique. Une recherche sur les pratiques spatiales de dimension régionale des acteurs du tourisme, PhD thesis, Université d'Angers, 2012.

[PIR 14] PIRIOU J., "Le fest-noz, patrimoine culturel immatériel classé par l'Unesco: une ressource touristique ? Exploration de la promotion des destinations touristiques locales de Bretagne", in C. CLERGEAU, J. SPINDLER (eds), *L'immatériel touristique*, L'Harmattan, Paris, 2014.

[PIR 17] PIRIOU J., "Pointe du Raz en Cap Sizun", in V. VLÈS, S. CLARIMONT (eds), Impacts des mesures de préservation des sites naturels exceptionnels: rapport final de recherche, Research Report, UMR CERTOP 5044/UMR PASSAGES 5319, Toulouse/Pau, pp. 419–469, 2017.

[PIR 18a] PIRIOU J., "The Cognac vineyard area: territorial quality as a focus for tourism development within the context of a globally consumed product", in N. BELLINI, C. CLERGEAU, O. ETCHEVERRIA (eds), *Gastronomy and Local Development: The Quality of Products, Places and Experiences*, Routledge, London, 2018.

[PIR 18b] PIRIOU J., "Partage de compétence de la promotion des destinations touristiques en France et en Suisse. Le cas de l'espace transfrontalier de l'Arc lémanique", in N. FABRY, J. SPINDLER (eds), *Le tourisme, un domaine de compétence partagé*, L'Harmattan, Paris, 2018.

[POS 01] POSCHET L., WUST S., BASSAND M., La métropole lémanique, Rapport final, contribution à la mise en réseau de compétence sur la métropolisation, pôle Rhône-Alpes-Suisse, programme Interreg IIc, Institut de recherche sur l'environnement construit, IREC, École polytechnique fédérale de Lausanne, Lausanne, 2001.

[POU 14] POULIQUEN C., Le développement du tourisme dans les espaces de nature protégés français et européens: les cas du Parc National du Lake District (Royaume-Uni), de l'Espace Naturel de Doñana (Espagne) et du Parc Naturel Régional du Verdon (France), PhD thesis, Université d'Angers, 2014.

[PRE 68] PRÉAU P., "Essai d'une typologie des stations de sports d'hiver dans les Alpes du Nord", *Revue de géographie alpine*, vol. 56, no. 1, pp. 127–140, 1968.

[PRE 82] PRÉAU P., "Tourisme et urbanisation en montagne: le cas de la Savoie", *Revue de géographie alpine*, vol. 70, nos 1–2, pp. 137–151, 1982.

[PRE 95] PRETES M., "Postmodern tourism: The Santa Claus industry", *Annals of Tourism Research*, vol. 22, no. 1, pp. 1–15, 1995.

[PRY 97] PRYER M., "The traveler as a destination pioneer", *Progress in Tourism and Hospitality Research*, no. 3, pp. 225–237, 1997.

[PUM 97] PUMAIN D., SAINT-JULIEN T., *L'analyse spatiale. Tome 1: Localisations dans l'espace*, Armand Colin, Paris, 1997.

[RAC 80] RACINE P., Mission impossible ? L'aménagement du littoral Languedoc-Roussillon, Midi-Libre, Montpellier, 1980.

[RAF 80] RAFFESTIN C., *Pour une géographie du pouvoir*, Librairies techniques, Paris, 1980.

[RAF 86] RAFFESTIN C., "Nature et culture du lieu touristique", *Méditerranée*, 3rd series, vol. 58, no. 3, pp. 11–17, 1986.

[REC 76] RECLUS E., *Nouvelle géographie universelle*, Hachette et Cie, Paris, 1876.

[REN 02] RENARD J.-P., "La frontière: limite politique majeure mais aussi aire de transition", in L. CARROUÉ, P. CLAVAL, G. DI MÉO, *et al.* (eds), *Limites et discontinuités en géographie*, SEDES, Paris, 2002.

[RET 03] RETAILLÉ D., "Topogenèse", in J. LÉVY, J. LUSSAULT (eds), *Dictionnaire de la géographie et de l'espace des sociétés*, Belin, Paris, 2003.

[RET 97] RETAILLÉ D., *Le monde du géographe*, Presses de Sciences Po, Paris, 1997.

[REV 89] REVEL J., "La région", in P. NORA (ed.), *Les lieux de mémoire*, vol. 2, Gallimard, Paris, 1989.

[REY 75] REYNAUD A., "Éléments pour une épistémologie de la géographie du tourisme ", *Travaux de l'Institut de Géographie de Reims*, nos 23–24, pp. 5–12, 1975.

[RIE 00] RIEUCAU J., "La Grande-Motte, ville permanente, ville saisonnière", *Annales de géographie*, vol. 109, no. 616, pp. 631–654, 2000.

[RIN 06] RINALDI E., "La construction des hôtels de Montreux et les italiens à la fin du XIXe siècle", *Revue historique vaudoise*, no. 114, pp. 241–252, 2006.

[ROD 09] RODRIGUE J.-P., COMTOIS C., SLACK B., *The Geography of Transport Systems*, Routledge, London, 2009.

[ROG 81] ROGNANT L., Type de regions géographiques en Italie. Essai de macrogéographie, Thesis, Université de Nice, 1981.

[ROL 04] ROLLAN F., "Les réseaux d'équipements sportifs dans les stations balnéaires: l'exemple du tennis", *In Situ*, no. 4, 2004, available at: http://journals.openedition.org/insitu/1846, accessed June 1, 2018.

[ROO 93] ROO P. (ed.), "La métropolité", in A. SALLEZ (ed.), *Les villes, lieux d'Europe*, DATAR/Éditions de l'Aube, Paris/La Tour d'Aigues, 1993.

[RUB 03] RUBY C., "Pratique", in J. LÉVY, J. LUSSAULT (ed.), *Dictionnaire de la géographie et de l'espace des sociétés*, Belin, Paris, 2003.

[SAG 01] SAGNES J., *Deux siècles de tourisme en France*, Presses universitaires de Perpignan, Perpignan, 2001.

[SAL 08] SALAZAR N.B., ""Enough stories!" Asian tourism redefining the roles of Asian tour guides", *Civilisations*, no. 57, pp. 207–222, 2008.

[SAN 18] SANJUAN T., *Atlas de la Chine. Les nouvelles échelles de la puissance*, Autrement, Paris, 2018.

[SAU 93] SAUNIER P.-Y., "Le guide touristique, un outil pour une possible histoire de l'espace: autour des guides de Lyon 1800-1914", *Géographie et cultures*, no. 13, pp. 35–54, 1993.

[SCA 97] SCARAFFIOTTI J., Avantage concurrentiel des sites touristiques d'hiver: la contribution des facteurs allocatifs et organisationnels, PhD thesis, Université de Savoie, 1997.

[SCE 74] SCEAU R., "Évian-les-Bains, station thermale et touristique", *Revue de géographie de Lyon*, vol. 49, no. 1, pp. 51–75, 1974.

[SIM 17a] SIMON A., *Les espaces du tourisme et des loisirs*, Dunod, Paris, 2017.

[SIM 17b] SIMON G., "Hybridations, conflits et politique des usagers", in M. DELAPLACE, G. SIMON (eds), *Touristes et habitants. Conflits, complémentarités et arrangements*, Infolio, Gollion, 2017.

[STA 08] STASZAK J.-F., "Danse exotique, danse érotique. Perspectives géogra-phiques sur la mise en scène du corps de l'Autre (XVIIIe-XXIe siècles)", *Annales de géographie*, nos 660–661, pp. 129–158, 2008.

[STA 70] STANSFIELD C., RICKERT J., "The recreational business district", *Journal of Leisure Research*, vol. 2, no. 4, pp. 213–225, 1970.

[STO 01] STOCK M., "Brighton and Hove: station touristique ou ville touristique ? Étude théoricoempirique", *Géocarrefour*, vol. 76, no. 2, pp. 127–131, 2001.

[STO 03] STOCK M. (ed.), *Le tourisme: acteurs, lieux et enjeux*, Belin, Paris, 2003.

[STO 06] STOCK M., Penser géographiquement, Géopoint 2006, Demain la géo-graphie, pp. 23–37, CNRS, Paris, 2006.

[STO 17a] STOCK M., COËFFÉ V., VIOLIER P., *Les enjeux contemporains du tourisme. Une approche géographique*, Presses universitaires de Rennes, Rennes, 2017.

[STO 17b] STOCK M., "Le concept de centralité à l'épreuve du tourisme. Réflexions à partir du modèle des lieux centraux", in N. BERNARD, C. BLONDY, P. DUHAMEL (eds), *Tourisme et périphéries. La centralité des lieux en question*, Presses universitaires de Rennes, Rennes, 2017.

[TAU 08] TAUNAY B., "Le développement touristique de deux sites chinois 'incontournables': Beihai et Guilin (Guangxi)", *Articulo*, no. 4, 2008, available at: http://journals.openedition.org/articulo/429, accessed April 30, 2018.

[TAU 12] TAUNAY B., VIOLIER P., "L'émergence au prisme du tourisme chinois", *EchoGéo*, no. 21, 2012, available at: http://journals.openedition.org/echogeo/13190, consulté le April 30, 2018.

[TAU 15] TAUNAY B., VIOLIER P., "Un modèle chinois des pratiques touristiques ? Analyse des spécificités et des invariants au niveau des pratiques et des lieux fréquentés par les touristes chinois et internationaux en Chine", in I. SACAREAU, B. TAUNAY, E. PEYVEL (eds), *La mondialisation du tourisme*, Presses universitaires de Rennes, Rennes, 2015.

[THI 91] THIESSE A.-M., *Écrire la France: le mouvement littéraire régionaliste de langue française entre la Belle Époque et la Libération*, Presses universitaires de France, Paris, 1991.

[TIM 98] TIMOTHY D.J., "Collecting places: geodetic lines in tourist space", *Journal of Travel & Tourism Marketing*, vol. 7, no. 4, pp. 123–129, 1998.

[TIS 00] TISSOT L., *Naissance d'une industrie touristique. Les Anglais et la Suisse au XIXᵉ siècle*, Payot, Lausanne, 2000.

[TIS 06] TISSOT L., "La quête du haut", *Revue historique vaudoise*, no. 114, pp. 195–212, 2006.

[TIS 07] TISSOT L., "Le tourisme: de l'utopie réalisée au cauchemar généralisé ?", *Entreprises et histoire*, vol. 2, no. 47, pp. 5–10, 2007.

[TOB 17] TOBELEM J.-M., "Permanence et mutations du tourisme culturel", in E. FAGNONI (ed.), *Les espaces du tourisme et des loisirs*, Armand Colin, Paris, 2017.

[TOC 99] TOCQUER G., ZINS M., *Marketing du tourisme*, G. Morin, Levallois-Perret, 1999.

[TOR 09] TORRE A., "Retour sur la notion de proximité géographique", *Géographie, Économie, Société*, vol. 11, pp. 63–75, 2009.

[TOS 57] TOSCHI U., Aspetti geografici dell'economia turistica in Italia. Atti XVII Congresso geografico italiano, II, Bari, 1957.

[TOU 00] TOULIER B., "L'influence des guides touristiques dans la représentation et la construction de l'espace balnéaire (1850-1950)", in G. CHABAUD, E. COHEN, N. COQUERY, *et al.* (eds), *Les guides imprimés du XVIᵉ au XXᵉ siècle. Villes, paysages, voyages*, Belin, Paris, 2000.

[TSA 10] TSAUR S.-H., YEN C.-H., CHEN C.-L., "Independent tourist knowledge and skills", *Annals of Tourism Research*, vol. 37, no. 4, pp. 1035–1057, 2010.

[URB 93] URBAIN J.-D., *L'idiot du voyage: histoires de touristes*, Payot, Lausanne, 1993.

[URR 90] URRY J., *The Tourist Gaze. Leisure and Travel in Contemporary Societies*, Newbury Park, Sage, London, 1990.

[URR 00] URRY J., *Sociology Beyond Societies,* Routledge, New York, 2000.

[URR 05] URRY J., *Sociologie des mobilités: une nouvelle frontière pour la sociologie ?,* Armand Colin, Paris, 2005.

[VAR 97] VARLET J., "La déréglementation du transport aérien et ses conséquences sur les réseaux et sur les aéroports", *Annales de géographie,* vol. 106, no. 593/594, pp. 205–217, 1997.

[VEB 99] VEBLEN T., *The Theory of the Leisure Class,* Macmillan Publishers, Basingstoke, 1899.

[VEY 63] VEYRET P., "Le tourisme en Tchécoslovaquie", *Revue Géographique de l'Est,* vol. 3, no. 2, pp. 131–136, 1963.

[VIA 00] VIARD J., *Court traité sur les vacances, les voyages et l'hospitalité des lieux,* Éditions de l'Aube, La Tour d'Aigues, 2000.

[VID 88] VIDAL DE LA BLACHE P., "Des divisions fondamentales du sol français", *Bulletin littéraire,* pp. 1–7 and pp. 49–57, 10 October–10 November, 1888.

[VID 03] VIDAL DE LA BLACHE P., *Tableau de la géographie de la France,* Hachette, Paris, 1903.

[VID 13] VIDAL DE LA BLACHE P., "Des caractères distinctifs de la géographie", *Annales de géographie,* no. 22, pp. 289–299, 1913.

[VID 00] VIDAL R., *Les origines de Sables-d'Or-les-Pins, le projet de Roland Brouard et des Frères Treyve dans l'histoire de l'urbanisme balnéaire,* "Étapes de recherche en paysage" seminar proceedings, no. 2, École nationale supérieure du paysage, Versailles, 2000.

[VIO 02] VIOLIER V., "La Baule, du tourisme au lieu de vie", *Mappemonde,* vol. 2, no. 66, pp. 20–24, 2002.

[VIO 07] VIOLIER V., "Tourisme et medias: regards d'un géographe", *Le Temps des médias,* no. 8, pp. 159–170, 2007.

[VIO 08] VIOLIER P., *Tourisme et développement local,* Belin, Paris, 2008.

[VIO 09] VIOLIER P., "Proposition pour un modèle d'analyse dynamique des lieux touristiques", in J.-P. LEMASSON, P. VIOLIER (eds), *Destinations et territoires, vol. 1, Coprésence à l'œuvre,* Presses de l'Université du Québec, Paris, 2009.

[VIO 11] VIOLIER V., "Les lieux du monde", *Espacestemps.net,* 2011, available at: http://espacestemps.net/document8948.html, accessed September 21, 2011.

[VIO 13] VIOLIER P., *Le tourisme, un phénomène économique,* La Documentation française, Paris, 2013.

[VIO 17] VIOLIER P., "Les régions touristiques de la France", in E. FAGNONI (ed.), *Les espaces du tourisme et des loisirs*, Armand Colin, Paris, 2017.

[VIO 98] VIOLIER P., "À la recherche du tourisme urbain: exploration nantaise", in G. CAZES, F. POTIER (eds), *Le tourisme et la ville: expériences européennes*, L'Harmattan, Paris, 1998.

[VIO 99] VIOLIER P., "Les acteurs du système touristique et leurs logiques spatiales", in P. VIOLIER (ed.), *L'espace local et les acteurs du tourisme*, Presses universitaires de Rennes, Rennes, 1999.

[VIT 98] VITTE P., "Tourime en espace rural, le territoire à l'épreuve", *Revue de géographie alpine*, vol. 86, no. 3, pp. 69–85, 1998.

[VLE 06] VLÈS V., *Politiques publiques d'aménagement touristique: objectifs, méthodes, effets*, Presses universitaires de Bordeaux, Talence, 2006.

[VLE 96] VLÈS V., *Les stations touristiques,* Économica, Paris, 1996.

[VOG 76] VOGT J.W., "Wandering youth and travel behaviour", *Annals of Tourism Research*, no. 4, pp. 25–41, 1976.

[VOU 99] VOURC'H A., "L'opération grand site de la Pointe du Raz. Une réhabili-tation exemplaire", *Cahiers Espaces*, no. 62, pp. 59–64, 1999.

[WAC 02] WACKERMANN G., *Géographie régionale*, Ellipses, Paris, 2002.

[WAN 08] WANG X., Le développement du tourisme à Pékin, PhD thesis, Université d'Angers, 2008.

[WIL 98] WILLIAMS S., *Tourism Geography*, Routledge, London, 1998.

Index

Other titles from

2017

DUGUÉ Bernard
Information and the World Stage – From Philosophy to Science, the World of Forms and Communications
(Engineering, Energy and Architecture Set – Volume 1)

GESLIN Philippe
Inside Anthropotechnology – User and Culture Centered Experience
(Social Interdisciplinarity Set – Volume 1)

2016

EL FALLAH SEGHROUCHNI Amal, ISHIKAWA Fuyuki, HÉRAULT Laurent, TOKUDA Hideyuki
Enablers for Smart Cities

2013

NAIT-SIDI-MOH Ahmed, BAKHOUYA Mohamed, GABER Jaafar, WACK Maxime
Geopositioning and Mobility

2012

HAMMADI Slim, KSOURI Mekki
Advanced Mobility and Transport Engineering